The Essential Guide to Using the Web for Research

The Essential Guide to Using the Web for Research

Nigel Ford

Los Angeles | London | New Delhi
Singapore | Washington DC

Loughborough
COLLEGE

First published 2012

SAGE Publications Ltd
I Oliver's Yard
55 City Road
London ECIY IS

SAGE Publications Inc.
2455 Teller Road
Thousand Oaks, California 91320

SAGE Publications India Pvt Ltd
B1/1 1 Mohan Cooperative Industrial Area
Mathura Road, New Delhi 110 044
India

SAGE Publications Asia-Pacific Pte Ltd
33 Pekin Street #02-01
Far East Square
Singapore 048763

Library of Congress Control Number: 2011920595

British Library Cataloguing in Publication data

A catalogue record for this book is available from the British Library

ISBN 978-0-85702-364-3
ISBN 978-0-85702-365-0

Typeset by C&M Digitals (P) Ltd, Chennai, India
Printed and bound by CPI Group (UK) Ltd, Croydon, CR0 4YY
Printed on paper from sustainable resources

Contents

About the author

Nigel Ford is Professor at the University of Sheffield's Information School. He is Director of Research, and has taught research and information seeking skills at undergraduate, postgraduate and doctoral research levels for over 30 years. He has successfully supervised numerous undergraduate, Masters and PhD projects, and has been examiner for over 40 research theses at Sheffield and a range of other universities. The University of Sheffield's Information School is unique in having come first in its field in every national Research Assessment Exercise (RAE) since the assessments began in 1986.

He is unusually well placed to author a book that brings together research, study and information skills. Working in the country's leading information school, his teaching and research focus for many years has been this very integration, and he has directed several large funded research projects in the area. Recent Arts and Humanities Research Council (AHRC) funded projects he has directed include 'Developing effective web-based information seeking for inquiry-based learning' and 'Developing deep critical information behaviour.' He has published extensively in the areas of effective teaching and learning in higher education in international refereed journals and conferences, and has published five teaching texts.

ONE
Introduction

Why read this book?

To succeed at university you need to know how to produce high-quality academic work. This requires a number of key skills, which are not always obvious, or clearly explained to students. Nor do you necessarily need to have developed or used them to be successful at school. What is required at university level – and increasingly as you progress from your first year to more advanced levels of study – can differ significantly from what you have been used to at school.

At this level, using the web to find information is a vital and integral part of academic work. But the web offers both great potential and serious problems. As a *potential* source of high-quality, relevant and up-to-date information on almost any topic the web is unparalleled. But to translate this potential into reality you need to know how to pinpoint *high-quality* information amongst the vast mass of mediocre, inaccurate and downright misleading 'information' that can so easily hijack your search.

Web search engines such as *Google* are powerful tools. But they are neither the only nor necessarily the most appropriate tools for finding the type and level of information you need for academic work. As well as knowing how to make advanced use of them, you also need to be familiar with the range of scholarly search tools specifically designed to find the type of high-quality information that is required.

Some of these study and web skills may seem obvious at first sight, but delve a little deeper and you will realise that things are not quite so straight forward. This book is designed specifically to explain what these are and help you develop them.

- The first skill you need is to know what is required of you – what your lecturers expect to see in a good piece of work at university level, and what differentiates it from a less good piece of work. (Chapter 2)
- If an essay question asks you to *describe*, *analyse* or *evaluate* a topic, you need to know exactly what these words mean and how they differ. It's no good producing a first-class *description* when your lecturer wants an *analysis* or an *evaluation*. In other words, you need to be able to accurately decode and interpret the specific instructions you are given for each piece of coursework. (Chapter 3)

- As your course progresses, you will increasingly be expected to develop and display skills in finding information for yourself – rather than relying on reading lists given to you by your lecturers. You'll be expected to know what *peer-reviewed* information is, and to be able to find it. This is not just a case of using *Google* or your university library catalogue. There is a range of sophisticated tools available to you specifically designed to find *high-quality* information. This book will introduce these to you and show you how to use them to best effect. (Chapters 4–8)
- You will then be expected to use it to build an *evidence-based* response to your essay or research question – the hallmark of a high-quality piece of work. This will entail analysing, synthesising, evaluating and selecting information. You need to be able to present your argument in an academically convincing way – to convince the person marking your work that the evidence that you are putting forward to support your arguments is valid, reliable and unbiased. You must know exactly what these terms mean, and how you can make sure that your work meets these essential quality criteria. This book will clearly explain these terms and will take you through these processes step by step. (Chapter 9)
- It will be essential to show that your work is your own. You must avoid plagiarism at all costs. Plagiarism is passing off the ideas of other people as your own and it can be done unintentionally as well as deliberately. It is a serious offence, and there are many cases of students being given severe penalties when found guilty of it. However, to produce high-quality work, you do need to draw on and use the ideas of others – writers and experts in the field. The key skill enabling you to build on other people's work whilst at the same time avoiding plagiarism is knowing how to correctly attribute your sources. This book takes you through this process, and gives many examples of how to correctly cite different types of source. (Chapter 10)
- Showing that you have made use of information that is not only suitably authoritative but also the latest available will greatly benefit your work. You need to keep up to date with what is being published on the topics you are working on in your courses. However, you do not need to constantly keep checking to see if anything new has been published. This would be a waste of your time, especially if nothing new has appeared since last time you checked. This book explains a number of techniques that will enable you to receive automatic updates straight to your computer whenever something new is published on your topics. (Chapter 11)
- You can also save time if you organise your information effectively. Your personal store of information sources will become increasingly large as you work your way through your university courses. Storing them in your own personalised online library, searchable by author, title, keyword and your own tags, can save a lot of time and effort – for example, if you are trying to link ideas and quotations in an essay or report back to where you originally found them. Reference management tools are designed to help you manage your information sources in this way. They can also enable you automatically to create and update bibliographies in your work – and to change the citation style at the click of a button. You can also share your references – and your comments and tags – with friends and fellow students over the web. (Chapter 12)

Figure 1.1 summarises the key questions this book is designed to answer.

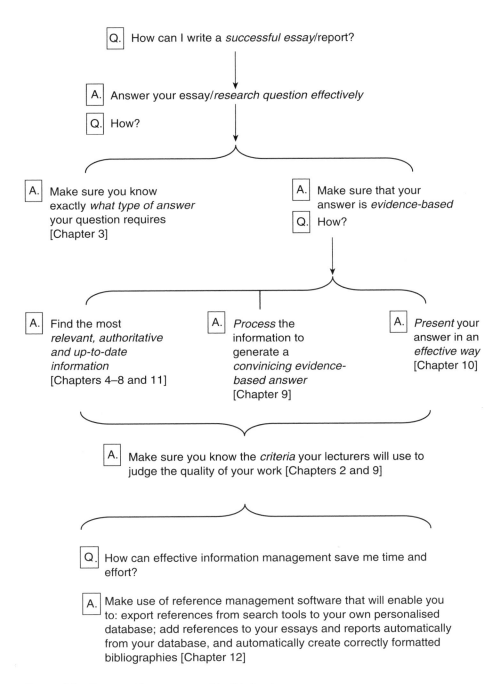

Figure 1.1 Key questions answered in this book

The book's underlying rationale

Teaching and learning place much less emphasis than hitherto on students' ability to absorb information given to them by their teachers in the form of lectures and reading lists. Such didactic teaching still has a role in signposting the structure of and introducing basic concepts in a subject. But you are increasingly expected to become an autonomous evidence-based learner. Thus the ability to find information *autonomously*, and critically evaluate it in relation to the needs of the particular learning task on which you are engaged, are key skills for success.

You must be able to find and critically analyse evidence to support reasoned argument. This emphasis is seen in the increasing use within education at all levels of inquiry-based approaches, including essays, projects, and dissertations, in which you are expected to develop your own evidence-based critique of some topic or problem.

As a higher education student, you are required to engage in *evidence-based* study, and the web is a major source of evidence – or, more precisely, of information that can be turned into evidence by applying your own critical abilities. With appropriate information-seeking, filtering and critical evaluation skills, you can now realistically use the web as a major source of high-quality information to support rigorous academic work. Developing these skills is the principal focus of this book.

Many students arrive at university lacking key skills, particularly those relating to finding, critically evaluating and effectively using information. And you cannot assume that school will prepare you for them. You can often be highly successful at school without necessarily having had to develop and use them. A 2009 report by an independent *Committee of Inquiry into the Changing Learner Experience*, in relation to the great range of resources available via new technology, noted:

> ...significant and strong reservations on the matter of the quality of analysis and critique students bring to bear on those resources, as well as on the extent to which they mine them. Students tend to go no further than the first page or so of a website and, if they don't find what they're looking for there, they move on to another. Not that this behaviour – scanning, 'power browsing' – is particular to students. CIBER's Information Behaviour report for JISC and the British Library points out that, faced with the massive range of sources now available, academics are behaving in precisely the same way: 'Everyone exhibits a bouncing/flicking behaviour ... Power browsing and viewing is the norm for all' ... Unlike their students, however, experienced academics should have sufficiently developed evaluative, analytical and synthetical skills to work effectively in this way. [1]

Yet the information universe available to you offers potential as never before to stimulate and support the development of evidence-based critical thinking. However, both the strength and the weakness of this information universe is the vastness of the information to which it provides access.

---

[1] Committee of Inquiry into the Changing Learner Experience (2009). *Higher Education in a Web 2.0 World*. Retrieved from http://www.jisc.ac.uk/media/documents/publications/heweb20rptv1.pdf

In 2008, *Google* reported that its indexing software was selecting from some 1,000,000,000,000 webpages and the number of webpages was growing by several billion per day.[2] At the beginning of August 2011, the indexed web contained at least 19.4 billion pages.[3]

The internet-based information universe is awash with gold – high-quality information on every topic, subject and discipline under the sun from astrophysics to zoology. The problem is, of course, the vastness of the mud that all too easily hides the gold from view. You need to develop the intellectual equivalent to 'panning for gold' – a metaphor used by Sylvia Edwards in her PhD on web-based information literacy.[4]

Finding the information you need within this information universe can be complex and problematic. You need to be familiar not only with the information universe itself (the different types and levels of information available via the web), but also with the range of search tools and search strategies available to help you in your task.

Many different types of information source are available on the web. These vary in terms of their quality and authority. However, even high-quality sources vary in the extent to which they are appropriate for different learning tasks. You need to be familiar not only with what is available, but also with what is and is not appropriate for the particular type of learning task you are working on at any given time.

There are also a great many different types of search tool that you can use to find these different types of information, of which general search engines like *Google* are only one. Each of these tools generally offers a range of advanced searching options which enable you to maximise the effectiveness of your searching, and you need to be competent in using them to your best advantage. You also need to be aware of their limitations, and of what techniques – and alternative tools – you can use to overcome these limitations.

Information-seeking tools can do a lot to help the information seeker, but the vital ingredient in finding appropriate information is your intimate understanding of your own learning and information needs. You must be able to find appropriate information and process it effectively. However, the processes of finding the right information and processing it in appropriate ways are closely intertwined. Both depend on having a good knowledge of the precise nature of your learning needs. Different types of learning task imply different learning needs, which in turn require different types of information and different ways of processing it. An essay may, for example, ask you to *describe, explain, analyse* or *critically discuss* a topic or problem. Each of these requires engagement in different intellectual processes, and the use of different levels and types of information to fuel these processes.

---

[2]Alpert, J. and Hajaj, N. (2008, July 25). We knew the web was big [Web log post]. Retrieved from http://googleblog.blogspot.com/2008/07/we-knew-web-was-big.html

[3]Kunder, M. (2011). The size of the World Wide Web. Retrieved, August 1, 2011, from http://www.worldwidewebsize.com/. Based on Kunder's Master's thesis at Tilburg University's ILK Research Group.

[4]Edwards, S. (2006). *Panning for gold: Information literacy and the net lenses model.* Adelaide: Auslib Press.

You should also be aware that different people may also approach the same learning task in very different – but equally valid – ways according to their particular learning style. You need to be familiar not only with the precise nature of your learning needs (precisely what type of information processing you are required to engage in), but also of your own individual style of learning. This can help you align the way in which you go about an essay or research project – including the way you seek information at the different stages of your learning – to play to your strengths.

Search tools covered in this book

This book is intended primarily for students registered on courses in universities and colleges. Such institutions are likely to offer access to commercial services such as *SciVerse Scopus* and *Web of Knowledge*, which are major web-based search tools designed specifically to support academic work. These are explored in some detail in the book.

However, the book also introduces *Google Scholar*, a major scholarly search tool that is freely available to anyone via the web. Other search tools covered in this book are also freely available to anyone on the web. Indeed, all the major themes of the book can be supported by freely available web-based tools, meaning that it can also be read to advantage by people who are interested in using the web for learning and research but who are outside the formal educational system.

This book is designed to present in one convenient package what I think you most readily need in order to produce high-quality academic work. But don't forget that each system covered here also has its own help system. Also, a number of tutorials are readily available. Search, for example, for *Google Scholar, SciVerse Scopus* and *Web of Knowledge* or *Web of Science* on *YouTube*.

Your university is also likely to offer training materials and courses in searching for information and study skills. These may be offered via your university library, so check out their webpages and do take advantage of this support. The time and effort you expend on doing so will be richly repaid in terms of time saved in the long run – and greater success in your studies.

A final note before you begin. Search tool providers are constantly working to improve their services. Periodic changes, for example to details of search interfaces, are therefore likely to take place over time. The screenshots used in this book were captured in August 2011. Any changes made after this point will not be reflected in the screenshots. However, except in the case of major revisions, which are relatively infrequent, the basic functions and ways of using the tools remain the same. This is hardly surprising in view of the huge investment of time and effort made by their providers over a long time carefully developing highly sophisticated systems.

TWO

Learning & critical thinking: the essentials

WHY YOU NEED TO KNOW THIS

- What makes a high-quality essay or report? You need to know this to help you to be successful – to produce a piece of work that will gain a really good mark. It is therefore vital to develop your own clear awareness of the criteria of academic quality which will be applied by those who assess your work.
- This knowledge will not only enable you to perform effectively in terms of gaining good marks and leaving university with a good degree. It will also help you develop longer-term goals which are of great importance in higher education – to develop the independent evidence-based learning and problem-solving skills you will need to equip you to be effective in your working and personal life in modern society.
- However, before we can come to grips with the central question of what constitutes quality in academic work, we need to understand the basics of learning and assessment. In order to build advanced knowledge we need firm foundations.
- These foundations include knowing exactly what is meant by terms such as 'learning', 'evidence' and 'critical thinking' and how these will be judged and assessed. This chapter establishes clear working definitions of basic concepts and processes, so that we can progress to explore more advanced issues on a solid basis of shared understanding.

Learning and assessment basics

When you are enrolled on a taught course at university, you are assigned various coursework tasks (e.g. to write an essay or research a project). You are provided with appropriate teaching, advice and supervision, and have to produce end products (a finished essay or dissertation). These are assessed and the marks you receive form the basis for determining your performance, and ultimately your success in being awarded an appropriate qualification. Information informs all of this process (Figure 2.1).

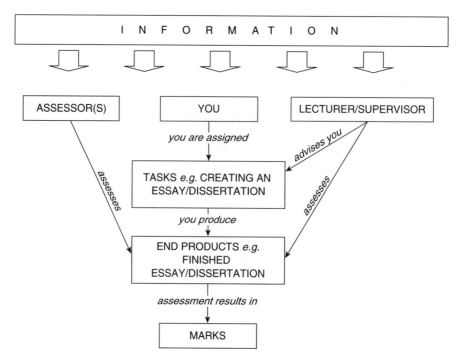

Figure 2.1 The basic academic process

Note that your work may be assessed by more than one person, whom I have termed 'assessor(s)' and 'lecturer/supervisor' in Figure 2.1. Often, your work will be marked by the lecturer who set your essay or who will be supervising your research. Sometimes a second marker may also mark your work – for example in the case of Master's dissertations. At research degree level, an independent external examiner from another university will assess your work. You should also bear in mind that all academic degree programmes have an independent external examiner, whose role is to monitor and maintain academic standards.

Have a look at the box below. Don't continue until you've spent some time over this. It is important to think deeply about these basic concepts.

THINK

If *you* had to mark an essay, project report or dissertation, what are the essential things *you* would look for to give it a 'pass'?

I would look for evidence of...

THE ESSENTIAL GUIDE TO USING THE WEB FOR RESEARCH

Did your answer include any or all of the following terms?

Understanding...

Learning...

Knowledge...

You are certainly expected to show evidence of one or more of these at a basic level. If your essay or report does *not* provide such evidence, then you should not expect to receive a 'pass' mark.

This may seem perfectly obvious, but we need to delve a little deeper. *Knowledge, learning* and *understanding* seem very desirable, but what *exactly* are they? We use these words all the time, but are rarely called upon to define them unequivocally – and in a way that clearly differentiates each from the others.

THINK

Write below exactly what you understand by these words.

Knowledge can be defined as...

Understanding can be defined as...

Learning can be defined as ...

Again, don't continue until you've had a really good think about this.

Bear in mind that there is no uniformly agreed way of defining these terms. They can be defined in different ways at differing levels of complexity. Over the page are the working definitions used in this book...

> *Knowledge* is defined here as *what is considered to be true, or certain* (as opposed, for example, to unsubstantiated beliefs). You can know: *that something is so* (declarative knowledge); *how something is or can be done* (procedural knowledge); and *why something is so* (schematic knowledge).
>
> *Understanding* something is *having knowledge about* it.
>
> *Learning* is *the process of acquiring knowledge* (*coming to understand* something).

Knowing about something enables you to make claims about it. But you can know things with *varying levels of certainty*. This means that you can claim that something *is* so – or you can claim that something *may be* so. In this book I use the term 'assertion' to indicate a claim that something *is* so, and the term 'proposition' to indicate a claim that something *may be* so.

But assessment at higher education level generally entails more than looking for evidence of basic understanding, knowledge or learning. We can discover what else is required if we examine the sort of assessment criteria typically used by lecturers when they mark essays and research projects.

Over and above basic understanding, such criteria require evidence of additional qualities. The following are criteria commonly used to assess students' essays:

Interpretation and scope

Understanding of topic

Use of authoritative literature

Critical analysis

Evaluation of evidence

Synthesis of ideas

Structure and logical development

Here we have some important concepts which go beyond simple *understanding*. Some seem very straightforward – for example, *scope* and *logical structure*. It seems fairly obvious that you should make sure your essay or report is appropriately scoped – that is, it focuses on what you have been asked to focus on. It would also seem self-evident that your work should display a structure that is logical. You would hardly want it to be *illogical*.

But these criteria also include *interpretation, critical analysis, evaluation of evidence, synthesis of ideas* and *authoritative literature*. What exactly do these refer to? They imply that you have to do *more* in an essay or report than simply understand and then describe what you have been told by experts, in lectures and books.

Analysis entails actively breaking something down into its component parts. *Synthesis* entails actively bringing things together to form a whole. *Evaluation* also implies that you have to do more than just understand the information you find or are given. You also need to assess its merits – its strengths, its weaknesses, and its appropriateness for your purposes. And *interpretation* implies that there isn't necessarily just one way of reading something. *Authoritative* literature also implies that there must also be *non-authoritative* literature. ('Literature' in the academic world means more than just literary works like novels – it refers to the complete range of academic writings in an area of study, including books, journal articles, theses, etc., in which ideas are put forward.)

In a nutshell, what is implied by the latter three concepts is the existence of *alternatives* – alternative ideas, alternative interpretations and alternative information sources. Also implied is the fact that you need to be able to assess their relative merits – and to choose and reject them as appropriate. This is the essence of *critical thinking*.

THINK

But if you are at university, then surely what you are paying for is to be provided with up-to-date, accurate information in your chosen subject of study?

If knowledge is 'what is considered to be true', isn't this precisely what you expect to be given to you by your lecturers? Surely the information they give you should already have been thoroughly analysed, synthesised and evaluated by them – the experts?

What's your view on this? Take a few moments to think about it before you continue.

We defined *knowledge* as *what is considered to be true, or certain*. However, what *you* consider as true or certain may not necessarily be considered by someone else as true or certain. There is, therefore, a sense in which we can say that *your* knowledge may be different from *another person's* knowledge.

To complicate matters, we also often use the word 'knowledge' in a less subjective sense to indicate *not* what a particular person considers as certain, but rather what is *more generally* agreed to be certain within a particular community – or in society more generally. From this less subjective perspective, even though *you* may be completely convinced by the evidence available to you that a particular belief is justified (and thereby becomes part of your own knowledge), it does not constitute 'knowledge' in this more general sense unless also accepted as certain by the wider community.

At one level, education is about aligning the two – the subjective knowledge of the individual student with the authoritative knowledge of experts. This applies in cases where what constitutes generally agreed knowledge, shared by experts in the subject area concerned, can be clearly established.

Thus, if I as a novice do not know how to program using the *Flash* graphics software package, I learn how to use *Flash* by interacting with to the knowledge of experts, and attempting to align *my* knowledge with *theirs*. I can tell that the experts' knowledge is 'true' or 'certain' in so far as my programming actually *works* when I apply it.

But often, truth or falsehood cannot be objectively established – particularly when we are dealing with topics and subjects which include *people* and *society* within their focus (as in the arts, humanities, and social sciences). In these areas, it is often more a case of establishing the relative merits of differing – often competing – views of what it is reasonable to believe.

For this reason, producing a piece of academic work on a topic is *not* just a case of showing that you have understood what you have been told by recognised experts (in lectures or books). This *may* apply to some extent where you are new to a subject and need to establish what are its basic tenets – i.e. what are generally agreed by the experts to be the basic concepts and building blocks of the subject.

But when you begin to move beyond the basics, you will generally find that things are less certain – less subject to general agreement. You begin to move to a level in which different people, different experts and different groups make different – often conflicting – claims.

Where things are uncertain, there is always the possibility that for any claim (proposition or assertion), there may be one or more counter-claims. Maybe the evidence on which the claim is based could be interpreted to produce a different claim. Maybe the evidence put forward to support the claim is just not sufficiently strong (or accurate) to justify the claim. Or maybe the evidence given is partial and ignores other evidence that weakens or even discredits the claim.

Any claim – whether it is made by the author of a book or lecture, or by yourself as the writer of an essay or report – should be supported by *evidence*. Your role as a critical thinker is to think:

> *To what extent is this claim truly supported by this evidence?*
>
> *Can the evidence presented be interpreted in a different way – to support a different claim?*
>
> *Is there any counter-evidence that has not been considered?*
>
> *If so, does a different picture emerge when this evidence is also taken into account?*

You should address these questions both to the claims made in the information sources you read and to the claims you make in your own work. Bear in mind that these same questions will be asked about your essay or dissertation by the person who is marking it.

At this level, you need to make yourself aware of, and to evaluate, differing claims in relation to the topic you are writing about. Different claims may derive not necessarily from any errors in evidence (although they *may*), but rather from different (but legitimate) perspectives and points of view. You need not only to be aware of and understand them, but also to weigh up their relative merits and limitations, and decide where *you* stand – and why – in relation to them. This is the essence of critical thinking. It entails considering the evidence supporting different claims.

In the academic world (as indeed in many other aspects of life) we use the notion of evidence as a bridge to enable people to discuss, argue and attempt to convince one another of how strong or reasonable their claims are. Evidence consists of the reasons you put forward to justify your claims. When you write about something for an essay or dissertation, you are expected to put forward *evidence-based* claims – assertions and propositions (saying that such and such a thing is or may be so) backed up by evidence supporting them. By considering this evidence, the reader can weigh up the extent to which he or she considers them to be justified.

In an essay or dissertation, the evidence supporting the claims you put forward will include citations to authoritative sources that support the claims. Thus, there is a big difference – in terms of the quality of your work, and the resultant mark you are likely to receive – between the following versions of the same claim:

'Females tend to be better at expressing positive emotions when using social networking sites.'

'Females tend to be better at expressing positive emotions when using social networking sites (Thelwall, Wilkinson and Uppal, 2010).'

The second version of the claim would link to the following entry in the References section of your essay or dissertation:

Thelwall, M., Wilkinson, D. and Uppal, S. (2010). Data mining emotion in social network communication: Gender differences in MySpace. *Journal of the American Society for Information Science and Technology, 61*(1), 190–199.

As well as making evidence-based claims, you will also need to build evidence-based *arguments*.

THINK

Write down what you think the difference might be between a *claim* and an *argument*.

I use the term *argument* here to refer to a *series of connected claims*. These claims should fit together to form a structured answer to your essay or research question. This is very different from a series of relatively unconnected claims. In fact, as we will see in the next chapter, lack of connectedness is a common problem and cause of low marks in essays and reports.

There are many different types of argument. In the sense in which I am using 'argument' as a 'series of connected claims', analysis, synthesis and evaluation are all types of argument. The following very simple examples express the essence of *analysis*, *synthesis* and *evaluation*. The *argument* in each case is shown in bold. The individual claims (upon which the argument is based, and which themselves will be evidence-based as previously described) are shown in italic.

Analysis:

The main elements of X are ... *The first element is... [details]. The second element is... [details].* Etc.

Synthesis:

X and Y may appear very different... [details of the differences]. However, **they are similar in that...** [details of the similarities].

Evaluation:

X has both benefits and drawbacks. However, **I think that the benefits outweigh the drawbacks because...** *[details].*

If the argument that you are putting forward is someone else's argument – i.e. an analysis, a synthesis or an evaluation that you have found in an authoritative information source – then the 'evidence' supporting it will generally be a reference to that source. However, if you are making an argument yourself, then the 'evidence' supporting it will be its 'reasonableness'. What might count as 'reasonable' is discussed below in relation to each type of argument:

Analysis:

The main elements of X are ... The first element is... *[details].* The second element is... *[details].* Etc.

If it is *self-evident* that the main elements of X are what you say they are, then this 'self-evidence' is your evidence. If it is not self-evident, then you need to explain *why* the reader should accept that it is so, in a logical and defensible way. It is important to play 'devil's advocate' and try to see whether there is any way in which a cynical (but reasonable) person could argue that X cannot be broken down into the elements that you propose – or that the elements you propose are not 'the main' elements as you are arguing. If you can see a possible counter-argument to your own, you will need to think – and say – why the reader should accept *your* analysis.

Synthesis:

> X and Y may appear very different... *[details of the differences]*. However, they are similar in that... *[details of the similarities]*.

> Again, if it is self-evident, then this 'self-evidence' is your evidence. If not, then you need to explain *why* the reader should accept that it is so in a logical and defensible way. As above, it is important to play 'devil's advocate' and try to see whether there is any way in which a cynical (but reasonable) person could argue that X and Y are not similar in the way you argue that they are. If you can see a possible counter-argument to your own, you will need to think – and say – why the reader should accept *your* analysis.

Evaluation:

> X has both benefits and drawbacks. However, I think that the benefits outweigh the drawbacks because... *[details]*.

> If you give logical and defensible reasons why the benefits outweigh the drawbacks, then these constitute your evidence. Once again, try to anticipate any counter-arguments – e.g. that in certain circumstances (maybe that you have not considered) the benefits may not outweigh the drawbacks.

Thus in an essay or dissertation you are attempting to convince those who read it (especially, the person who will mark it) that what you have said is justified. The person marking your work need not necessarily *agree* with what you say. He or she may have a different point of view. But he or she must regard what you say as *reasonable* – that is, supported by appropriate evidence.

One of the key goals of university education is that you learn how to develop effective evidence-based claims and arguments, and to evaluate the strengths and weaknesses of the claims and arguments of other people, for yourself. It is true that you will also need to become familiar with widely accepted beliefs in the topics and subjects you are studying – with what is generally agreed by experts to be firm basic knowledge. But at more advanced levels, you will be expected to explore, and critically evaluate, different claims, arguments, evidence and perspectives.

At a basic level, you are concerned with discovering and coming to understand the key concepts generally agreed by experts as constituting the key building blocks of the topic. As you move from basic understanding to more advanced issues, you generally find differences of views and opinions amongst different writers and experts in the subject – and often conflicting evidence. These differences imply an increasing need to be able to evaluate their merits and limitations, to make choices between them, and to justify your evaluations and choices. This will require increasing involvement in critical thinking – the careful evaluation of alternative claims, arguments, evidence and perspectives.

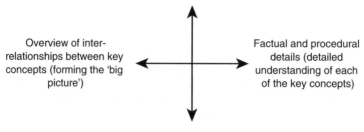

DEVELOP BASIC UNDERSTANDING

The generally agreed basics
(concepts making up the topic)

Overview of inter-relationships between key concepts (forming the 'big picture')

Factual and procedural details (detailed understanding of each of the key concepts)

More advanced issues
(including issues and controversies)

CRITICALLY EVALUATE

Figure 2.2   Basic dimensions of learning

Essential learning components

The vertical dimension of Figure 2.2 shows the different levels of understanding – from basic to more advanced – discussed in the previous section. However, your learning (at all levels of the vertical dimension) will also entail the horizontal dimension shown in the figure.

(a) The left half of the diagram relates to the development of an overall view showing how the main concepts making up the topic interrelate and fit together to form an integrated 'big picture'.
(b) The right half relates to the more detailed examination of the individual components making up the topic.

You need both of these elements. One without the other results in incomplete understanding, and your work would be marked down accordingly.

If the detailed treatment of the individual components (element (b)) is not complemented by a view of how they all fit together to form the bigger picture (element (a)), the result is likely to be 'not seeing the wood for the trees' – fragmented understanding that misses fully appreciating the 'big picture'.

Equally, the overview of how the components interrelate to form an integrated whole (element (a)), if based on only partial or incorrect understanding of the components (element (b)), may result in invalid over-generalisation. Over-generalisation occurs when you present an overview without sufficient supporting detail to validate it. Such an overview may be inaccurate and misleading if examination of the components at a more detailed level fails to support the pattern of interrelationships (the overview) you are claiming.

Figure 2.3 'Description building' is concerned with overall design

Source: http://commons.wikimedia.org/wiki/File:Example_of_CAAD.jpg
Author: Euy. Creative Commons Attribution-Share Alike 3.0 Unported license
(http://creativecommons.org/licenses/by-sa/3.0/deed.en).

Although by no means exclusively, component (a) places particular emphasis on *synthesis*, and component (b) places particular emphasis on *analysis*. As previously noted, analysis entails *breaking something down into its component parts* and examining these in detail. Synthesis entails *looking for ways in which things can be linked together*. It emphasises looking for ways in which they are similar and for things they share.

These different components were termed 'descriptions' and 'procedures' by Gordon Pask, a key figure in research into teaching and learning in higher education.[5] Effective learning in any subject entails both 'description building' and 'procedure building', which he characterised in architectural terms. Description building is like creating the overall design of a building (as in Figure 2.3).

Procedure building, on the other hand, is concerned with the detailed operations and logistics that are necessary if the building is to function, such as plumbing, electrical wiring, and so on (Figure 2.4).

Both description building and procedure building are required to create a successful building. In the same way, both elements are required to build effective understanding in a subject. Description building is all about *relating ideas to synthesise a conceptual overview*. Procedure building is all about *analysing the factual and procedural details that support the overview*.

---

[5]Ford, N. (2000). The increasing relevance of Pask's work to modern information seeking and use. *Kybernetes*, *30*(5/6), 603–629.

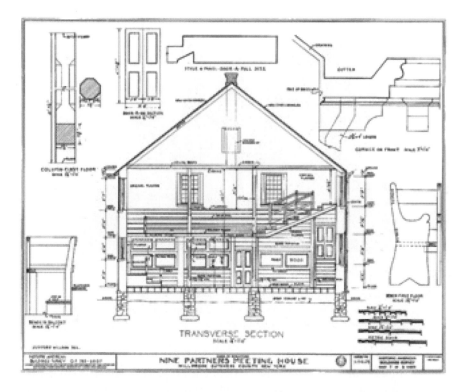

Figure 2.4 'Procedure building' is concerned with detailed operations and logistics

Source: http://commons.wikimedia.org/wiki/File:Nine-partners-meeting-house.png
Author: Wilson, Clifford. Public domain.

We are now about to go on to explore the notion of learning styles. However, if you would like to take a simple test designed to help you identify your own personal style, you should do so before reading the next section, and you should turn now to the Appendix and complete the learning style questionnarie you will find there.

However, although both description building and 'procedure building are necessary components of full understanding, the order in which they take place may vary according to the individual learner. Pask did much work investigating these components of understanding, and he identified distinct learning styles associated with them. Some people, it would seem, have a bias towards (and are more adept at) description building. Others are biased towards procedure building.

The test of learning style in the Appendix is designed to tell you whether you have: a relatively holistic *description-building* style; a more step-by-step *procedure-building* style; or a *versatile* style in which you are able to engage in description building and procedure building in equal measure.

Pask found that a bias towards description building without sufficient procedure building resulted in the distinctive 'over-generalisation' learning deficit previously described. A bias towards procedure building without sufficient description building results in the complementary 'not seeing the wood for the trees' learning deficit.

Even though you may possess skills in both elements of learning, and engage in both description and procedure building, you may still exhibit a stylistic preference for the order in which you do them. Two students may go about learning in stylistically very different ways, arriving at the same end-point (full understanding) via different routes. Even successful, high-achieving university students may display these preferences.

Typically, the student with a description building bias will seek to establish a good overview of the topic or subject early in the learning process. Once he or she has sketched this overall picture of the topic – what its main components are and how they seem to relate to each other – he or she will then go on to explore the details of the components, and the precise logic of how they fit together.

In contrast to this somewhat top-down approach, the student with a procedure building bias will tend to adopt more of a bottom-up, 'brick-by-brick' approach, starting by building up detailed understanding of a part of the subject and, having mastered this aspect, moving on to the next. The 'big picture' will emerge relatively late in the learning process.

Pask found that these biases are also associated with different learning processes. Strong description builders tend to be 'parallel processors', focusing on a number of aspects of the topic at the same time as they broadly – and initially quite speculatively – explore a new topic, trying to gain an overall grasp of what it is all about. Strong procedure builders tend to prefer a more sequential, 'step-by-step' approach concentrating on one thing at a time.

Importantly, there is evidence that if students go about learning in a way that *mismatches* their stylistic preference, their learning may be detrimentally affected, and they may not successfully integrate both components. Conversely, the learning of students working in a way that *matches* their style may be enhanced. As we will see in Chapters 3 and 7, these stylistic biases and preferences also have important implications for the way in which you go about searching for, and using, information for your essays and projects.

Figure 2.5 maps description building (represented by the thumbnail image to the left) and procedure building (the image to the right) on to the dimensions of learning previously presented in Figure 2.1.

The stylistic differences outlined above are reflected in the way in which you move between left and right as you progress downwards from basic to more advanced levels in Figure 2.5. The procedure builder is likely to focus more strongly on the right of

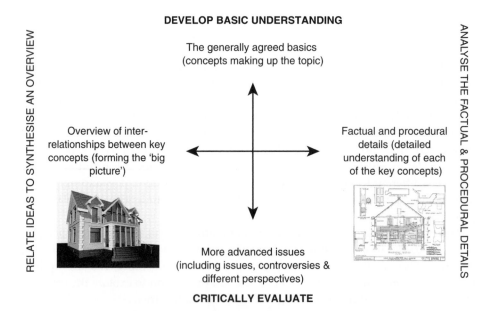

Figure 2.5 Description and procedure building mapped on to the basic dimensions of learning

the figure as he or she progresses downwards. The description builder will focus more on the left. In both cases, this is a matter of degree and not an absolute focus. Both will to an extent dip into elements of both left and right as their learning progresses. We will be further exploring learning styles in relation to how you go about answering your essay or research question (Chapter 3) and the way in which you search for information (Chapter 5).

Summary

In this chapter, we have explored what you need to do to produce a high-quality response to an essay or research question. We have seen that you must go beyond simply demonstrating that you have *understood* the topic you are writing about. You need also to engage in *analysis* and *critical evaluation*, and this chapter discussed what these entail and why they are necessary.

We looked at how you should build an *evidence-based argument*, and went on to explore two fundamental components of understanding: *description building* (essentially, establishing a good conceptual overview of a topic); and *procedure building* (mastering the detailed evidence supporting and validating the overview).

Many people are stronger in one of these aspects of learning relative to the other, and these differences underlie different *learning styles*. How you can assess your own learning style, and the implications of style for how you go about learning and information seeking, will be explored in more detail in Chapters 3 and 7.

The issues explored here are general in the sense of underlying all learning and assessment. The next chapter will focus on specifics – how to analyse the precise requirements of particular pieces of coursework, and how to plan the way in which you will address these requirements in terms of building an appropriate evidence-based response.

THREE

Clarifying what is required of you

Clarifying the nature of your assignment

Different types of essay or project

As you read this, you may be about to start a particular essay or project. One way in which essays and projects may vary is in terms of the characteristics shown in Figure 3.1. For example, you may be working to a topic that has been *provided for you* by your lecturer – for example, you may have had to choose from a list of pre-set essay titles. Alternatively, you may have been asked to come up with a topic *of your own*. Also, your coursework may or may not entail the collecting and analysing of *data* on your part – for example, from a questionnaire or interviews (as opposed to finding information in books, journals, etc.).

Information will be a vital ingredient in all of these cases. In each one, however, the role of information may be slightly different. The four boxes in the figure refer to brief overviews of the role of information relating to these different cases, which immediately follow the figure.

	Topic *provided for you* (by your lecturer)	Topic *decided by you*
It does *not* entail collecting and analysing *data*	See section **A** below	See section **B** below
It *does* entail collecting and analysing *data*	See section **C** below	See section **D** below

Figure 3.1   Characteristics of different types of essay and project

---

A. You have *been provided with a list* of essays/topics from which to choose (rather than having to think of one yourself), and the work will be *based on your reading* (i.e. it will not entail collecting data such as from questionnaires or interviews).

Essays and projects that fit this category are very common in higher education. As your studies become more advanced, you will often be able – indeed expected – to exercise more freedom in coming up with a topic to study (see box B). Typically in later undergraduate years, and at Master's level, you will also engage in more work that entails collecting and analysing your own data (boxes C and D).

But from the very start of your studies, even when working on essays provided for you by your lecturers, you are expected to engage in independent research. That is, you are expected to search for and find information for yourself. This is not just a case of collecting a load of information about the topic and shovelling it into your essay or report. You have to use information as fuel to generate an evidence-based response to your essay question. You therefore need to really think about what it is that you are being asked to do, and what you have to deliver. We'll be looking a little later on in this chapter at precisely what 'evidence-based' actually means.

B. You have to *think of an essay/project topic yourself* (rather than choosing from a list), and the work will be *based on your reading* (i.e. it will not entail collecting your own data such as from questionnaires or interviews).

Typically as your studies become more advanced (at second and third year under-graduate and Master's levels) you will be expected to exercise more autonomy in coming up with your own essay or project topic – as well as searching for and using information independently. When you are choosing your essay or research project topic, it is a good idea to formulate a specific *question*. You should think of the essay or project at this level as providing an *answer* to some specific research *question*, rather then just choosing some broad theme and 'writing all you can about it'.

Exploring the literature (books, journals and other sources) can be extremely use-ful in helping you come up with a good topic and related question. You will also be expected autonomously to find information relevant to answering your question. Information will be used as fuel to build an evidence-based answer. We'll be exploring precisely what 'evidence-based' actually means later in this chapter.

At some universities more than others at present, and on some courses more than others, you may be expected to engage in 'inquiry-based' and 'problem-based' learn-ing quite early in your studies. This may entail working with increasing levels of autonomy relating to your choice of topic, as well as to searching out and using information.

C. You have been *provided with a list* of project topics from which to choose (rather than having to think of one yourself), and the project will involve *collecting and analysing data* (e.g. from questionnaires or interviews).

In later undergraduate years and at Master's level, you will usually also engage in more work which entails collecting and analysing your own data. This may be small scale, as in a piece of work as part of an undergraduate module, and where the topic (the research question or problem) is set for you.

You will need skills in research design, data collection and data analysis, which are *not* taught in this book. However, you will *also* need to be skilled at what is a key theme of this book – using the web to find and utilise information from books, journals and other sources. This will be essential to fuel your literature review, where you set your own work in the context of what is known already about your topic. You will also need to refer to the literature when you are discussing your own findings – to assess how they relate to (maybe confirm or maybe conflict with) findings that exist in the literature.

D. You have to *think of a topic or title yourself* (rather than choosing from a list), and the project will involve *collecting and analysing data* (e.g. from questionnaires or interviews).

Box C above related to small-scale exercises entailing data collection and analysis where the research question or problem is set for you. This box (D) relates to larger-scale research such as a full undergraduate project, or Master's dissertation. You will need skills in research design, data collection and data analysis, which are *not* taught in this book.

However, you will *also* need to search the literature to help you formulate a good research question. To come up with a meaningful research question, you will need to produce a literature review which will enable you to know what has been done already in the field – not least to avoid conducting research that duplicates what has already been done. You will also need to refer to the literature when you are discussing your own findings – to assess how they relate to (maybe confirm or maybe conflict with) findings that exist in the literature.

Interpreting/decoding essay questions

Let us first consider essays topics that have been set for you by your lecturers. These are usually very carefully worded. What this means is that you should take a little time and trouble to decode them very carefully, and to work out exactly what you are being asked to do.

Essay topics often use words such as *discuss, compare, contrast, explain, critically analyse* or *assess*. Table 3.1 lists some of these commonly used words – along with an explanation of what they entail.

Table 3.1 Frequently used essay topic terms

Term	Definition
analyse	identify the key aspects/components of...
apply	show an idea, principle or technique at work using a practical example
assess	weigh up the extent/importance of...
compare	identify similarities shared by...
contrast	identify differences between...
critically	*[analyse or evaluate]* with particular attention to any weaknesses or limitations, alternative interpretations and counter-evidence
define	say exactly what is meant by...
describe	give a detailed account of...
differentiate	explain the difference(s) between...
discuss	analyse the key issues involved in... and assess/evaluate them
evaluate	weigh up the strengths and weaknesses (the relative merits) of...
explain	give details of, including (where appropriate) how and/or why...
illustrate	use an example to show...
outline	describe the main features of...
relate	show the connections between...
review	summarise and evaluate...
synthesise	bring together into a unified/coherent form...
summarise	describe the main points/elements of...

Responding correctly to these different words requires you to engage in different types of intellectual process. It is important to avoid responding with an inappropriate type of process. A common example, resulting in poor marks, is being too *descriptive* when *analytic* or *evaluative* processing is required. It is also very important to avoid 'under-analysing' the task requirements, and sliding into a 'write all I can find out about...' mode of responding to the assignment. Bear in mind that the person marking your work will check *whether you have responded appropriately to the requirements of the task.*

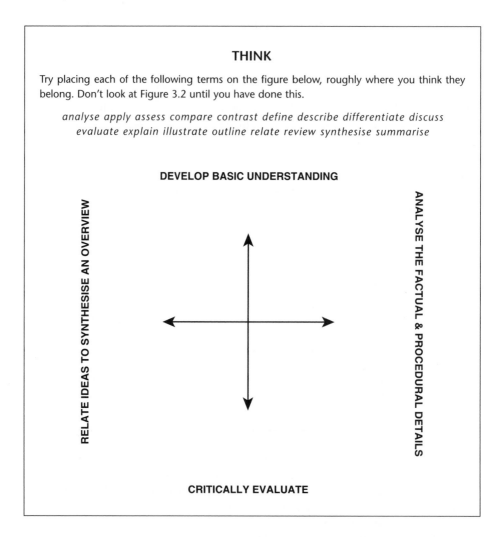

THINK

Try placing each of the following terms on the figure below, roughly where you think they belong. Don't look at Figure 3.2 until you have done this.

analyse apply assess compare contrast define describe differentiate discuss evaluate explain illustrate outline relate review synthesise summarise

DEVELOP BASIC UNDERSTANDING

RELATE IDEAS TO SYNTHESISE AN OVERVIEW

ANALYSE THE FACTUAL & PROCEDURAL DETAILS

CRITICALLY EVALUATE

Figure 3.2 shows my own placing of these words. Don't worry if there are slight differences between your placements and mine. It is quite possible that different people will place some of these words slightly differently, depending on their interpretation

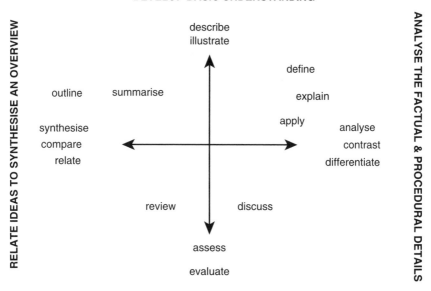

DEVELOP BASIC UNDERSTANDING

Figure 3.2 Mapping intellectual processes on to the dimensions of learning

of their precise meaning. For example, some people may use 'discuss' or 'review' to imply a little less evaluation than is indicated in Figure 3.2.

What's important is that you are clear as to what your tutor expects of you in terms of the broad dimensions of the figure – particularly the vertical dimension. It is particularly important to avoid being overly descriptive when a more active approach is required. Generally speaking, the more analysis, synthesis and critical evaluation you include in your work, the higher the marks you are likely to receive.

Throughout this book, an essay topic or title is referred to as an essay *question*, and the essay that you write in response to it is considered to be an evidence-based *answer* to this question. Clearly, however, essay topics – especially those incorporating the terms we have been exploring here, like *discuss, evaluate, compare* and *contrast* – are often not expressed as questions.

The terms are used here partly as shorthand – it is more economical to speak of 'an answer to an essay question' than 'an appropriate response to the requirements of an essay topic'. However, they are also used in order to help you focus on what you need to *find out* in order to respond appropriately to your essay topic. Table 3.1 emphasised *what you need to do* in response to a range of commonly used essay topic terms. Table 3.2 converts these terms into questions – the answers to which you need to find out in order to produce your essay.

Table 3.2 Essay topic terms rephrased as quesions

Term	Definition
analyse	what are the key aspects/components of...?
apply	how does an idea, principle or technique work (using a practical example)?
assess	what is the extent/importance of...?
compare	what similarities are shared by...?
contrast	what differences are there between...?
critically	*[analyse or evaluate]* with particular attention to any weaknesses or limitations, alternative interpretations and counter-evidence
define	what exactly is meant by...?
describe	what is ... like?
differentiate	what is the difference(s) between...?
discuss	what are the key issues involved in...? What is their extent/importance? What are their strengths and weaknesses (their relative merits)?
evaluate	what are their strengths and weaknesses (their relative merits)?
explain	how and/or why...?
illustrate	what is a good example of...?
outline	what are the main features of...?
relate	what are the connections between...?
review	what are the main points/elements of...? What are their strengths and weaknesses (their relative merits)?
synthesise	what do ... share and how are they related?
summarise	what are the main points/elements of...?

Posing your own researchable research questions

Master's and undergraduate dissertation topics may sometimes be suggested by your lecturers. Very often, however – although subject to final approval by them – you will be expected to devise a topic of your own.

Generally, it is a good idea to come up with a research *question*. Obvious as this may seem, this should be an actual question – i.e. a proposition with a question mark at the end. I never fail to be surprised at the number of students who put forward as research questions what are essentially general descriptions of research topics – such as: 'This research seeks to investigate knowledge management in universities' or 'This research will explore university students' use of *Facebook*'.

Preferable research questions would be for example: 'What are the benefits and disadvantages of adopting an explicit knowledge management policy, as perceived by university managers?' or 'To what extent do undergraduate and postgraduate university students display different patterns of use of *Facebook*?'

If you start with an explicit question, it is also easier to make explicit the ways in which your research will *answer* it. It will also be easier to judge, and to explain to those reading your work, how effectively you have done so. Formulating a topic as a viable research *question* will enable you to build in at the end of your report an assessment of the extent to which you have answered your question.

Ideas for research questions can derive from a number of sources. An idea may be sparked by something you have read in relation to some other part of your course. Or you may start by identifying a broad topic area that reflects a particular interest you have developed on the basis of your own experience or observations, rather than from your course-related reading. For example, you may be on a communications, education or information science course, and become aware of the increasing use amongst your fellow students of mobile phones. You could decide that you would like to do some research broadly in this area – somehow relating mobile devices with learning and communication.

You could then explore the literature to check whether there has been any previous research (or theoretical writings) relating to the use of mobile phones in these contexts. You may find a combination of empirical research (research in which data has been collected and analysed) and conceptual writings (discussing current thinking) relating to the use of mobile phones in education and/or communication. This reading may enable you to 'home in' on a specific research question.

Or maybe a piece of previous research looked at student use of mobile phones in a particular context – or for a particular purpose – and you would like to study their use in a different context or for a different purpose. Or maybe either the conceptual or the empirical paper suggested questions requiring further research. Many research papers conclude by suggesting new research questions or topics that have arisen from the research reported in the paper.

You should bear in mind that, whether or not it was initially sparked by your reading, your research question should link to existing theory and/or other research reported in the literature. 'Link' in this context means that there should be some existing literature relating to the context in which your research is set. This context will be broader than your specific question. So, for example, literature relevant to students' use of *Facebook* could include any previous studies of patterns of use of *Facebook* more generally (not restricted to students), and students' use of other social networking and sharing sites. It will be advantageous if your research question reflects a gap in existing knowledge, as identified in your literature review.

The advantages of rooting your research question in existing literature (theory and research) is that this will enable you to:

- Justify the value of your research question in that it seeks to fill a knowledge gap in an area important enough to have attracted previous researchers.
- Develop a strong literature review section in your work.
- Develop strong *discussion* and *conclusions* sections to your work. You will be better able to interpret your results in the light of previous research findings, comparing and contrasting them with our existing knowledge in the area. Your findings may thus support, illuminate, extend, modify or refute existing knowledge (other people's findings, models and theories).

- Sustain possible negative findings. For the sake of argument, imagine that someone adopts a crazy, 'off the wall' research question such as: 'Do red haired people search the web more effectively than brown haired people?' This question has no foundation in or links to any existing theory. Thus, if they were to fail to find links between hair colour and web searching, they would not be in a position to generate a discussion comparing their results with those of previous researchers, or seek to explain their findings with reference to existing theory. Nor would their work contribute to knowledge in terms of modifying or refuting existing models or theory. An observer may well think: 'You didn't find any link between hair colour and web searching. *So what*? There was never any reason to expect one.' They would be left high and dry, and this would be reflected in their marks.

If you discover existing research that maps closely on to your own research question, this does not necessarily mean that it should be abandoned for a new one. Obviously you should avoid researching a question that has already been specifically answered, but you may be able to take a different slant on the issue. You would need to discuss this with your lecturer.

You want to choose a topic that has the capacity to enable you to excel and get a good mark. You will need to devise a research question that will allow you scope for analysis, synthesis and critical evaluation. These elements will generally lead to higher marks than more descriptive elements.

But don't be over-ambitious. This is a common error. You need to scope your research question so that the research is doable within the time limit you have. If your original research question is over-ambitious, this may be pointed out to you by your lecturer. Or it may become apparent once you start elaborating it – translating your research question into specific objectives which, if fulfilled, will answer your question. You may need to subdivide a broad research question into sub-questions. Again, this is a good stage at which to consider whether you have bitten off more than you can chew.

Look at previous student work submitted for the same level of course (undergraduate project or Master's dissertation). Some university departments make past dissertations available for viewing. This will enable you to obtain a feel for what constitutes a 'researchable research question' in terms of appropriate levels of breadth and depth.

Planning your assignment

Once you have established your goal – the answer to your essay or project question – you can set about devising a plan for how to get there. Whereas Figure 2.5 showed the main *components* of your understanding of a topic or subject in general terms, Figure 3.3 shows more specifically the *processes* entailed in putting together your essay or project.

DEVELOP BASIC UNDERSTANDING

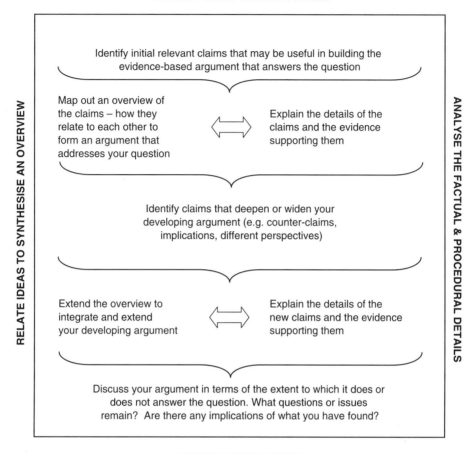

Figure 3.3 'Developing understanding' processes

In answering the essay or project question you are generating an evidence-based argument. Recall that the term *argument* is used here to refer to *a series of connected claims*. Figure 3.4 on the next page presents a simplified example of how claims and arguments could be developed in response to an essay topic.

Figure 3.4 reduces the essay to its essence, to show the basic structure of claims and arguments.

It is important to note that an argument is very different from a series of relatively *unconnected* claims. In fact, lack of connectedness is a frequent cause of low marks in essays and reports. Recall from Chapter 2 our discussion of learning styles. Presenting a series of relatively unconnected ideas is characteristic of learners who fail to complement their procedure building with sufficient levels of description building. The result is that they end up 'not seeing the wood for the trees'.

Claim 1. The web makes freely available an increasingly vast range of information → Details of claim 1, and evidence supporting it

Claim 2. Such rapid access to such vast resources can greatly benefit education → Details of claim 2, and evidence supporting it

Claim 3. However, information found on the web can suffer from serious quality issues → Details of claim 3, and evidence supporting it

Argument 1 (connecting claims 1–3)
Providing students with good access to the web is therefore not enough. We also need to equip them with (a) the ability to evaluate the quality of web materials retrieved, and (b) skills in finding information sources that are authoritative and of high quality.
→ Details of argument 1, and evidence supporting it

Claim 4. Information literacy programmes designed to improve students' skills in effective information seeking, evaluation and use are being developed. → Details of claim 4, and evidence supporting it

Claim 5. However, adoption of information literacy programmes has been patchy and arguably problematic in some universities. → Details of claim 5, and evidence supporting it

Claim 6. Researchers have been working to identify the nature of the problem and develop strategies to improve the situation → Details of claim 6, and evidence supporting it

Argument 2 (connecting claims 1–6)
There are a number of possible ways forward. We need to enhance students' ability effectively to find, evaluate and use information. Ways of doing this include...
→ Details of argument 2, and evidence supporting it

Figure 3.4 A simplified example of claims and arguments in action, in response to the essay topic *'Assess the impact of the web on access to information by higher education students, and discuss implications for information literacy training'.*

The extent to which individual claims are integrated to form a coherent overall argument is also central to the SOLO taxonomy.[6,7] SOLO stands for 'Structure of Observed Learning Outcomes', and the taxonomy is a model developed by Biggs and Collis to assess different levels of students' understanding. The five levels are shown in Table 3.3.

---

[6]Biggs, J. and Collis, K. (1982). *Evaluating the quality of learning: The SOLO taxonomy.* New York: Academic Press.

[7]Biggs, J. and Tang, C. (2007). *Teaching for quality learning at university* (3rd edn). Buckingham: SRHE and Open University Press.

Table 3.3 The SOLO taxonomy of learning outcomes

Level	Description
Pre-structural	Pieces of information are presented in isolation without any unifying structure connecting them. The student has largely missed the point.
Uni-structural	The student has made some simple and obvious connections – but these relate to only one aspect of the topic.
Multi-structural	The student has grasped a number of aspects of the topic, but these are presented separately and are not integrated into an overall coherent argument.
Relational	The student has integrated all the parts into a coherent whole.
Extended abstract	The student has made connections beyond the immediate topic – e.g. generalising the ideas to another context. This entails making connections at a higher level of abstraction.

Recall that in Chapter 2 we likened the building up of understanding to the design of a building. Atherton uses a similar analogy to illustrate the different SOLO levels.[8] Figure 3.5 overleaf is loosely based on his illustration.

The extent to which students succeed in connecting ideas and integrating them into a coherent whole will be a key criterion of quality used by your lecturers when marking your work – whether or not they use the SOLO taxonomy explicitly.

The precise way in which you go about the activities shown in Figure 3.3 may vary from individual to individual. For example, you may already have some familiarity with the subject matter, and your first response to the question may be: 'I already know what I think about this'. In this case, the first stage 'identify initial relevant claims that may be useful in building the evidence-based argument that answers the question' may entail seeking authoritative evidence to support the conclusion that you feel you already have. However, it is important to keep an open mind since, as you delve deeper and begin to build support for your conclusions, you may find that the detailed evidence does not support your initial view, or causes you to modify or qualify it in some way.

On the other hand, you may not feel that you immediately know what you think about the question. In this case, you will need to explore the evidence and see where it leads you in terms of suggesting an answer to the question. The first stage in Figure 3.3 will entail searching for sources that help you decide what lines of argument might be productive.

As previously discussed, the balance of emphasis and sequence between activity towards the left and right of Figure 3.3 may vary according to your preferred learning style. The pronounced *procedure builder* will focus, relatively early in the learning process, on the right of the figure – seeking to build up detailed understanding of individual components before fully integrating them to form the bigger picture. Compared to their description building counterparts, typical procedure builders will prefer to

---

[8]Atherton, J.S. (2010). Learning and teaching: SOLO taxonomy. Retrieved from http://www.learningandteaching.info/learning/solo.htm

Pre-structural (elements not linked)

Uni-structural (connections made but relating to only one aspect – in this case, the windows)

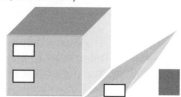

Multi-structural (connections made relating to several aspects – in this case, windows and door)

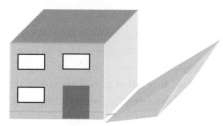

Relational (all the parts are connected to form the whole)

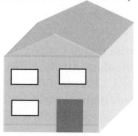

Extended abstract (the house is put into a broader context – in this case as part of a hamlet)

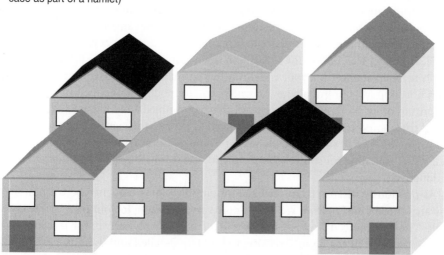

Figure 3.5 Illustration of the SOLO taxonomy (after Atherton)

proceed, from the start, on a much narrower but less tentative and exploratory basis. They tend to prefer a 'one thing at a time' approach, attempting to master one aspect of the topic before moving on to the next. This 'brick-by-brick' approach means that a solid level of detail is established relating to certain aspects of the topic – but the 'big picture' fitting them all together emerges relatively late in the learning process.

The pronounced *description builder* will focus first on getting a feel for the bigger picture – to establish a clear conceptual overview before focusing more narrowly on the details of the individual components. Typical description builders will prefer to start by engaging in broad, relatively tentative exploration – mapping out the territory in broad terms before committing themselves to a more narrowly focused examination of the details. They tend to want to establish a good conceptual overview first, then fit in the more detailed bits into this overall framework. They like to adopt a holistic, 'many things at once' strategy, exploring a number of different aspects of the topic at the same time (rather than concentrating on one aspect, mastering it before moving on to the next). They obtain the 'big picture' early in the learning process, and the details are fitted into this relatively late in the learning process.

However, although these are differences that have been widely observed amongst learners, this does not mean that everyone necessarily has a strong tendency to one or the other. It may be that you find it more productive to switch between broad exploration and detailed study more flexibly than is suggested by the descriptions of the styles above. As discussed in Chapter 2, both description building (overview) and procedure building (details) are necessary to achieve full understanding. The stylistic differences relate to the predominance you give to one relative to the other at different stages of learning about a new topic.

Figure 3.6 overleaf summarises the differences between procedure building and description building learning styles.

These different stylistic approaches will entail different sequences of information seeking. The type of information you need in the initial stages of reading your way into a new topic will be different if you are adopting a broad exploratory approach compared to the information you need if you are adopting a narrower, more focused approach. The implications, for seeking and using information, of building evidence-based arguments and of the different stylistic approaches to doing so described here will be explored in detail in Chapter 7.

Summary

Coursework may vary in the extent to which you are expected to devise your own essay or research question, and the extent to which you are expected to gather and analyse your own original data. We saw how finding appropriate information is central in all cases, but the way in which it is used may differ according to the nature of the assignment.

We went on to explore in detail how to decode the wording of essay questions to ensure that you know exactly how best to answer them. Lecturers use a wide variety of terms to describe what they would like you to do, which differ subtly in their meaning – for example: *discuss, explain, compare, assess*, etc. This chapter defined what terms commonly found in essay titles actually require you to do in terms of the type of intellectual processing involved.

TYPICAL DESCRIPTION-BUILDING STYLE	**TYPICAL PROCEDURE-BUILDING STYLE**

Focus first on building a broad overview of the topic – what are its main sub-topics and how do they fit together? How does the topic fit within a broader context? How does it relate to other topics? Why is it important?

Recognise the 'big picture' – how all the various components of the topic fit together; and set the topic in its broader context – establish how it relates to other topics. Thus add understanding of the 'big picture' to mastery of the details.

Begin to explore the details of different parts of the overview by focusing on selected aspects in more detail.

Build detailed understanding of the next most closely related sub-topic, and so on, until all aspects are covered.

Build detailed understanding of the parts making up the overview.

Build detailed understanding of the entry point sub-topic.

Add mastery of the details to the conceptual overview to achieve both 'big picture' and detailed evidence supporting it.

Focus first on identifying an entry point (a sub-topic) for study of the topic.

Figure 3.6 Characteristic approaches of procedure builders and description builders

The chapter also provided guidelines to help you devise your own essay or project question. As you progress through university, you will be required to do this more and more, and it is essential to know how to choose a question that will enable you to excel and produce high-quality work.

Finally, we looked in detail at how to build an *evidence-based answer* to your essay or research question, and at how important it is to deliver an integrated, as opposed to fragmented, argument. People with different learning styles may approach this in characteristically different but equally valid ways.

In the next chapter, we will turn to the problems associated with finding the information you need to build such an evidence-based answer, and the tools and techniques available to help you do so.

FOUR

Finding high-quality information

WHY YOU NEED TO KNOW THIS

- Whatever the type of assignment on which you are engaged – whether a basic level essay or an advanced research project – you need to find and make use of authoritative information.
- Some of this information may be provided for you by your lecturers, for example in the form of recommended reading lists. However, as you progress from basic to more advanced levels of study, you will increasingly be expected to be able to find high-quality (relevant and authoritative) information for yourself.
- First, you need to know exactly what is meant by 'authoritative' information. Those marking your work will expect you to know this, and to avoid the use of information that is not appropriately authoritative.
- You also need to know how to find it. Whilst it is easy to find large volumes of information, it is more difficult to find the type of high-quality information you require for your academic work.
- You need to be aware of the problems and potential pitfalls of information seeking so that you can avoid and overcome them. This chapter explores the nature of such difficulties. Tools, techniques and strategies for countering them will be introduced in Chapters 5 to 8.

This chapter will define what is meant by 'authoritative' information, and will explore the processes entailed in effectively finding it. But before we go any further...

THINK

What exactly is *information* – and how does it relate to knowledge and learning?

As is the case with the terms *understanding, knowledge* and *learning* presented in Chapter 2, it is important to note that *information* can be defined in many ways, for different purposes, and from different perspectives.

The following is the working definition that I have adopted for this book. As stressed in Chapter 2, the important thing is not to attempt to present some universal definition of these terms upon which everyone can agree (an impossible task), but to ensure that both you as reader and I as writer have a shared understanding of how they are used in this book. Here, then, is my working definition of *information*, and how it relates to *knowledge* and *learning*.

Information is the expression of (a part of) someone's knowledge. Information may be expressed in recorded form (e.g. a book or video) or communicated live (e.g. a lecture or conversation).

If learning is the process of acquiring new knowledge, then information is the raw material fuelling this process.

Information is transformed into knowledge via the process of learning.

There is a universe of information sources 'out there' accessible to you via the web, many of which are freely available. Others require payment. However, your university will have subscriptions to a wide range of such sources as well as its own library collection of resources. A key skill required of you is to be able to effectively navigate the range of information sources available to you both from your library and freely over the web. We will be examining the range of different types of information source available to you later in this chapter. There is also a range of different types of search tool that can enable you to find these different types of information. Again, we will be exploring these later in this chapter.

But first, let us explore the notion of *authority* in relation to information. You will recall from the discussion of evidence-based claims and arguments in Chapter 2 that *authoritative* sources should be used to support assertions and propositions that you present in your work. In the discussion of *critical thinking* in the same chapter, we noted the need to distinguish between *authoritative* and *non-authoritative* sources.

Defining 'authoritative' information

At all levels, from basic understanding of a new topic to the critical analysis of controversial issues, you need to make use of authoritative information. This is necessary since the person marking your essay or project will be asking:

What evidence have you put forward in this essay/dissertation to convince me that what you are saying is reasonable?

There are plenty of information sources, on every subject under the sun, written by well-meaning (and sometimes not so well-meaning) people. However, if you don't know anything about them it is perfectly possible that the information is flawed. It may be poorly argued or it may be partially or completely inaccurate.

But how do you know if information is of high quality, especially if you are new to the topic? Well, in the academic world a key concept relating to quality is *peer review*. Peer-reviewed information is information that has the stamp of credibility because it has been subjected to *independent review by experts*.

Books, journals and conference proceedings published by scholarly publishers or professional organisations will generally be peer reviewed. This means that before a book, book chapter, journal article or conference paper is accepted for publication, it will be sent to independent reviewers who are expert in the topic area. Frequently these reviewers will recommend or require certain changes to be made before the work is accepted. This is a way of ensuring that high academic standards are met. Theses and dissertations produced for an academic qualification are also peer reviewed in that they are examined by independent examiners chosen for their relevant expertise.

Figure 4.1 integrates the notions of *quality* and *credibility* relating to information sources into the model previously presented. These appear as the new dimension labelled on the top face of the figure.

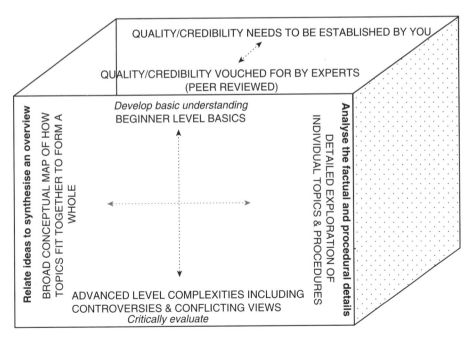

Figure 4.1 Credibility of information sources

Finding and using peer-reviewed information is important in relation to your study at both the top and the bottom of Figure 4.1 – i.e. whether you are just beginning a new topic/subject or are at a more advanced stage.

In the early stages of your learning about a new topic or subject, you are trying to discover what are generally agreed by experts in the field to be the key facts, ideas and arguments making up the topic or subject. At both basic and advanced levels, it is important that what you say is based on authoritative sources. In other words, you need to back up what you say in your written work by referring to these sources. By choosing those that are peer reviewed you can be assured of a certain level of academic quality.

At a basic level, you should refer to these sources to support your claims and arguments. Recall the example given in Chapter 2 of the quality difference between the two claims:

'Females tend to be better at expressing positive emotions when using social networking sites.'

'Females tend to be better at expressing positive emotions when using social networking sites (Thelwall, Wilkinson and Uppal, 2010).'

where the paper by Thelwall, Wilkinson and Uppal was a peer-reviewed source.

At more advanced levels you will probably come across a range of different arguments, views and perspectives on your topic. At this level, you will be expected not just to present these, along with references to where you found them but also to assess them – to compare and contrast them in terms of their contribution and limitations in relation to answering your essay or project question. You will also need to present your own considered view, made in the light of this possibly conflicting evidence.

At this level, being peer reviewed does not indicate that an argument or view is necessarily 'correct', but rather that it is reasonable – i.e. evidence-based. You can still find diversity of opinion in peer-reviewed sources. You may disagree with a particular view, but to argue against it you will need to present counter-arguments and appropriate evidence. You may find such counter-arguments and evidence in other peer-reviewed sources.

In Chapters 4 to 7 we will explore how to use the web to find information that has the authority stamp of peer review. However, non-peer-reviewed sources, such as blogs or websites of individuals and organisations, can at times be useful – but with appropriate caution and evaluation. When you are using sources that are not peer reviewed, you will need to establish for yourself their credibility. You will also need to establish and justify to your reader the credibility of these sources and the reasons why you have used them rather than a more conventional peer-reviewed source.

So why, indeed, would you want to use a non-peer-reviewed source? Well, knowledge generally progresses via the interplay between old and new ideas. New claims, arguments, evidence and perspectives emerge that may challenge as well as build on previous ones – even those previously well established and widely regarded as authoritative. However, leading-edge ideas may not always be readily available in traditional peer-reviewed sources. This may be due to the lead-in time required to get an article reviewed and published in a peer-reviewed journal. Also, it may sometimes be relatively difficult to get a highly controversial article published in a top journal, especially if the article runs counter to accepted wisdom in terms of content or approach.

Thus, there is a constant tension between consensus and novelty in the generation of new knowledge. Creativity entails forging links between concepts in previously unthought of ways. Extreme consensus-based thinking (strongly emphasising convergent thought processes), in which you only ever use ideas that have been thoroughly tried and tested, will at best result in the slow, steady accumulation of knowledge, but is likely not to result in the discovery of really new ideas and directions. Extreme novelty-based thinking (emphasising divergent thought processes) may spark new ideas and directions, but at the risk of generating instead ideas that are so 'off the wall' that they have little value.

This is reminiscent of Pask's learning styles. Recall that procedure building unconstrained by complementary description building led to fragmented learning – failing to see the wood for the trees. Description building unconstrained by complementary procedure building led to over-generalisation – essentially similar to overly divergent thinking in which concepts are linked in previously unthought of, but ultimately spurious, ways.

An important question is to what extent should you…

- 'play safe' in your essays and projects, and keep strictly to peer-reviewed authority sources and well-established information; or
- be creative and try to forge new connections between ideas?

In relation to research projects where you are gathering and analysing your own data, you can generate genuinely new knowledge. However, you are not normally expected to come up with genuinely new knowledge in more basic essays. Rather, you are expected to show mastery of the subject matter in terms of being aware of the key concepts and issues, and to show that not only have you understood and analysed them, but that you have thought critically about them and formed your own view based on the available evidence.

So my advice is – be cautious in using non-peer-reviewed sources. If you feel that they would contribute usefully to your essay or project, you should first evaluate their credibility (see Chapter 9 for details of evaluation criteria and how to apply them), then consult your lecturer before proceeding.

Information seeking

There may be times when a quick and easy search using a general search engine like *Google* is perfectly adequate and retrieves just the information you need. The major search engines have developed sophisticated techniques to enable quick and easy searches to retrieve much useful information.

Some basic problems

However, as we saw in the previous section, *Google* and the other main search engines are not the only tools you can use to find information. Nor are they always the best. Much depends on the nature of the information you need. It is all too easy to get into the *Google* habit and almost automatically use it for all yours searches. However, depending on what you are searching for, there can be problems with this.

Search tools

THINK

There is a place somewhere in the world called 'Place'. Use the web to find out where it is. [Starting in *Google*, this information can be reached within four clicks.]

'Place' is located ... [where?]

Searching using *only* a search engine such as *Google, Yahoo, Bing*, etc., is likely to prove extremely difficult in a case like this. You should bear in mind that, although this particular example may seem rather contrived, it is illustrative of a very common problem that can affect your searching.

Most documents indexed by the search engines using the word 'place' are about places – not specifically places called 'Place'. Although documents that *do* talk about the place 'Place' will *also* be indexed, they will be completely hidden in the wealth of documents dealing with the more common meaning of the word. On the first page of hits, *Google* reports:

'About 1,260,000,000 results'

The key is knowing about and using a more appropriate search tool. In this case, you need a tool that specialises in place names. So if, rather than searching for 'Place' we search for, say:

search world place names

we retrieve a list of sites that allow us to engage in a more specialised search by a tool that 'knows' that we are wanting place names. Figure 4.2 shows the results of our search.

Figure 4.2 Search for *search world place names* in *Google*

The first item on the list will take us to a site that will enable us to search specifically for place names. Search for 'Place' and we will discover exactly where it is.

As noted above, this rather extreme example illustrates a very common and pervasive problem – namely, that the precise information that you want may be hidden by less relevant information. This happens when you can't tell a search tool *exactly* what it is that you need. You can tell *Google* that you want information on 'Place', but you can't specify that you only want to use it as a *proper noun* and not in the more general sense.

Similarly, you might want to search for information on, say, *e-government* using *Google*, but you can't specify that you only want high-quality authoritative information suitable for an academic essay. You certainly get an interesting list of sources (see Figure 4.3), but you can't limit the hits only to high-quality academic sources. You end up with a mixed bag in terms of quality. Again, it is a case of not being able to sufficiently and accurately specify to *Google* exactly what you need.

As shown in Figure 4.3, *Google* has found some interesting sources relating to *e-government*, but they are by no means all suitable for use in an academic essay or dissertation.

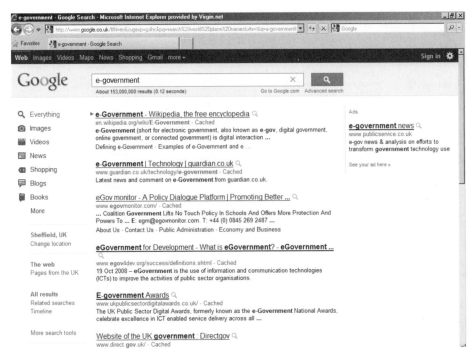

Figure 4.3 *Google* search results for *e-government*

THINK

Can you think of a way to search for *e-government* using *Google* – but in such a way as to get only good-quality academic sources?

If you thought that you should use some other tool – you're right. There are a number of tools designed to help you find high-quality academic sources. Some, like *Web of Knowledge* and *SciVerse Scopus*, are subscription-based, but your university will provide access to these or equivalent tools. *Google Scholar*, however, is freely available on the web. It is, as its name suggests, a scholarly alternative to the general *Google* search engine. Search for *e-government* in *Google Scholar* and you will retrieve good quality academic sources (Figure 4.4).

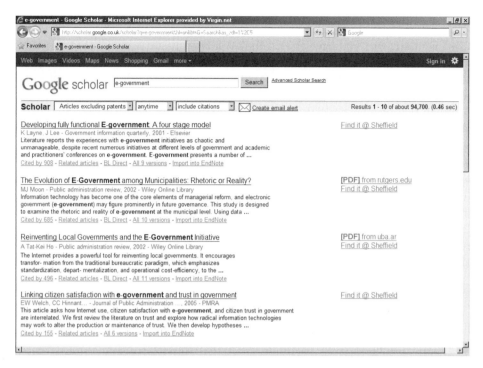

Figure 4.4 *Google Scholar* results for *e-government*

As we will see in Chapter 8, we can refine our searches in *Google Scholar* to specify, for example:

- The most recent information sources;
- Those within a particular discipline (Social Sciences as opposed to Environmental Science, for example);
- Those written by a particular author;
- Those written in a particular year or between certain dates;
- Those available freely to anyone online via the web;
- Those available online to members of our particular university via the web;
- Those not available online but available in our particular university library;

and more…

We will be looking in detail at a range of such tools in Chapter 8. The point here is that you need to be aware that a vital component of effective information seeking is choosing the most appropriate search tool. Before rushing to a general search engine, you should first make sure that there is not a more appropriate tool that would provide you with much more effective results.

Search strategies

Even assuming that you have chosen the most appropriate search tool to use, there are problems that can all too easily hinder effective searching. These potential problems mean that it is well worth your taking a little time to think about your *search strategy*.

When two people speak, they can easily establish the fact that they are talking about the same thing. In other words, they can negotiate any small differences in the wording they use almost without having to think about it. For example, if a student is studying effects of *poor school attendance* and his lecturer knows that there is an excellent book called *The Effects of School Truancy*, she has no hesitation in recommending it. For both lecturer and student, *poor school attendance* and *school truancy* are to all intents and purposes synonymous.

However, we cannot assume that such a translation necessarily takes place in a search engine. Let us perform two searches in *Google*. In the first, we will enter the keywords:

the effects of poor school attendance

In the second, we will enter:

the effects of school truancy

Figure 4.5 shows the results of the two searches – the first at the top and the second below it. This figure was produced by a website (http://www.thumbshots.com/Products/ThumbshotsImages/Ranking.aspx) which allows you to compare different searches in the same search engine – or indeed, the same search in different search engines. The top row of balls represents the first 60 information sources retrieved by *Google* in response to the first search (*the effects of poor school attendance*) and the bottom row shows items retrieved in response to the second search (*the effects of school truancy*). Each ball represents an information source. The balls representing any *common* information sources (i.e. ones retrieved in *both* searches) would be indicated by a line linking them across the top and bottom rows (an example of this is shown in Figure 4.6).

The fact that there are no lines linking any of the balls on the different rows means that, in the first 60 hits, no common information source was retrieved by both searches. (Since search engines are constantly updating their indexes, you may get different results from those obtained at the time of writing.)

A similar result is obtained if we search for:

looking for information

and:

seeking information

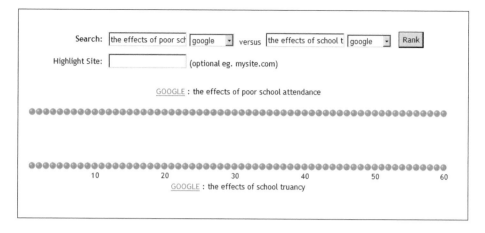

Figure 4.5 Comparison of *Google* results for two searches using only a slightly different way of expressing essentially the same topic

Different results may also be obtained when *exactly the same search* is performed using *different search engines*. Searching for:

the effects of poor school attendance

in both *Google* and *Yahoo* produces only five items in common – and they are not ranked in the same position. The results are shown in Figure 4.6. As previously noted, lines between the retrieved items indicate that they are identical. The position of each ball in the row reflects its position in the list of hits.

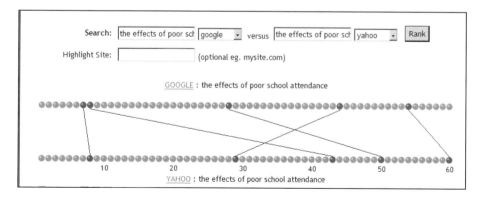

Figure 4.6 Comparison of results for exactly the same search using *Google* and *Yahoo*

To understand how this happens you need to know something about how search engines work. If you are aware of their limitations, you can take steps to compensate for these weaknesses and work around them.

What you need to know about search engines

Search engines compile huge indexes of the information to which they provide access. These are compiled automatically by computer programs that trawl the web looking for new documents posted on websites.

When they find a new document, they copy words that the document contains and put these into their index, along with a link to the document. When you search, you type words (search terms) into the search box of the search engine, describing what it is you are looking for. These search terms are matched by the search engine with words in its index. Those documents that contain the terms that match your query are the ones that are shown to you. This process is shown in Figure 4.7.

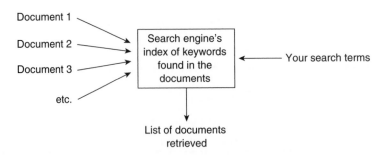

Figure 4.7 Basic search engine indexing and retrieval

At the simplest level, what this means is that if a document is indexed by a search engine using the word *school truancy*, and you search for it using the words *poor school attendance*, there will be no match between index entry and search query and the document will not be retrieved (as shown in Figure 4.8).

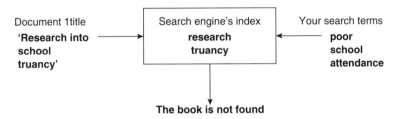

Figure 4.8   A mismatch between search engine index terms and a user's search terms

As we will see in Chapter 7, search engineers have developed – and are continuing to develop – techniques to lessen this limitation. Their goal is to enable search engines to act more intelligently so that they behave a little more like the lecturer mentioned at the beginning of this chapter, who was able to recommend a book on *school truancy* to the student searching for information on *poor school attendance*. A number of such techniques will be introduced in Chapter 7. The basic idea is shown in Figure 4.9.

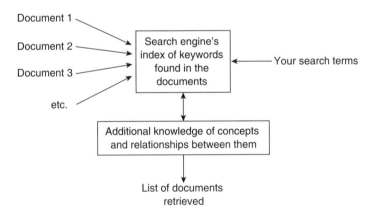

Figure 4.9   Enhanced search engine indexing and retrieval...

If we can provide the search engine with some of the basic common-sense knowledge that humans possess – in this case, the fact that *truancy* and *attendance* are closely related topics, and people searching for one are likely to be interested in the other – it will behave a little more intelligently, as shown in Figure 4.10 overleaf.

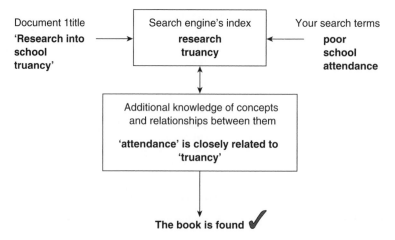

Figure 4.10 ... leading to improved search performance

Many search tools offer a range of features designed to try to help the information seeker find the most relevant information for his or her needs. Research is also
ongoing to try to build even greater levels of intelligence into search engines – for
example, making use of ontologies and semantic web developments.

However, you should be aware that, for the moment at least, the ability of search
engines to make intelligent connections is limited. There is still a need to develop
your own search skills – for example, to figure out what alternative words and
phrases might be used by authors writing about what it is you need to know, and to
try different ones as necessary to refine and improve the effectiveness of your search.
Figure 4.11 shows some of the obstacles that can stand in the way between you and
the information that you need.

Between column 1 (the gap in your knowledge requiring information to fill it) and
column 8 (an author's knowledge that can potentially fill your knowledge gap), there
are many factors that can intervene to prevent you finding the information you need.
However, one way in which you can mitigate some of these problems is to develop
effective information-seeking skills. These include being able to:

- identify the type of information most appropriate to answering your essay or research
  question;
- select the search tools best suited to finding this information;
- devise a search strategy that will make best use of the facilities offered by the search
  tools in order to maximise the effectiveness of your searching; and
- monitor, evaluate and where necessary improve your searching over time.

These skills will enable you not only to be aware of the limitations and strengths of
different search tools, but also to know how to compensate for their limitations and
exploit their strengths to your advantage. The following chapters will explore how
you can develop these skills.

YOU AND YOUR INFORMATION NEED		SEARCH TOOLS				AUTHORS AND INFORMATION SOURCES	
1	2	3	4	5	6	7	8
What you *don't* know that you *need* to know (your knowledge gap)	The information that will fill your knowledge gap (your information need)	The search tool(s) most appropriate to finding the needed information	The words you type into the search tool (your query)	The search facilities provided by the search tool	The words used by the search tool to describe information sources (index terms)	The words used by the author to express his/her message	What the author wishes to communicate (the author's message)
It can be difficult to specify precisely what it is that you *don't* know that you *need* to know.	You need to find information that is appropriate to your needs and avoid getting bogged down with irrelevant information.	Certain search tools will be more appropriate to your search than others.	The particular words you use may not necessarily be the same as those used by the author and/or the search tool to represent the same information.	These may be different in different search tools.	These may be different in different search tools.	The author may not necessarily use the particular form of words that *you* may use to search for the same information.	The author may have a particular type or level of reader in mind – but this is not necessarily information that is made available to the searcher by the search tool.

Figure 4.11 Obstacles that can prevent you from finding the information you need

Summary

In this chapter, we defined what is meant by *authoritative information*. This is important since establishing the authority of the ideas you put forward in your work is a necessary feature of academic work. *Peer review* is a mechanism for establishing the authority of an information source, and you should generally find and use peer-reviewed sources.

However, if you are exploring the latest cutting-edge new ideas relating to a topic, these may often be not yet available in peer-reviewed sources. There may be a trade-off between novelty and creativity on the one hand, and consensus and established authority on the other. Unless you are working at an advanced level, you are advised to err on the side of caution and to use peer-reviewed sources wherever possible. Where you do make use of less authoritative sources, you will be expected to justify this use, critically evaluating the sources and providing evidence yourself of why they are valid and appropriate to put forward as evidence in your work.

The chapter went on to explain some of the problems potentially preventing you from finding the information you are looking for. Some of these problems are inherent in the way search tools index the information to which they provide access.

You need to be aware of these limitations so that you can develop your own information skills in order to compensate for them. These skills include being familiar with the range of search tools available to you, and knowing which are most suitable for helping you find the type of information you need. Different search tools also offer a variety of sophisticated techniques for maximising the power and efficiency of your searching, and you need to know what these are and how to use them. These issues will be introduced in Chapters 5 to 8.

FIVE

How to do a literature review

WHY YOU NEED TO KNOW THIS

- Whether you are working on an essay or a research project, finding relevant authoritative literature (journal articles, books and other resources) is a key element of your work.
- You need to be able to show evidence of having searched effectively for the most appropriate literature relating to your topic. It is important not to miss any key sources that the expert marking your work would expect you to have included.
- You also need to be familiar with appropriate techniques and strategies for conducting the systematic review of existing literature that will be expected of you, and for avoiding the problems and pitfalls of information seeking introduced in the previous chapter.
- This chapter will take you through the process of conducting a review of literature relevant to your topic, from initial exploration to more systematic and focused searching.

As noted in Chapter 2, *literature* in this context refers to the complete range of academic writings in an area of study, including books, journal articles, conference papers, research theses, etc. The nature and extent of a *literature review* will differ according to whether you are writing an essay or are engaged in research.

Essays

In the case of most types of essay, information found in the literature will form the main building blocks of your work. You will be expected to design the building, arrange the building blocks accordingly, and provide the cement to bind the whole thing together.

You need to analyse the question and structure your essay around claims and arguments answering it supported by evidence from the literature. The claims and arguments themselves (as well as the supporting evidence) may be found in the literature – particularly at more basic levels. The amount of 'you' (added value) that you put in the essay may depend on your level or knowledge in the topic and/or the extent to which you can apply your own analysis, critical evaluation and synthesis to what you find in the literature – i.e. think for yourself about the relevant arguments and evidence.

A basic-level essay (which is usually on a topic that is not as controversial or problematic as one forming the focus of a more advanced-level essay) may ask you essentially to find from the literature what is mainstream thinking in relation to some topic and to demonstrate understanding of this. For example:

> *What is a 'community of practice', and what factors are associated with establishing and maintaining a successful one?*

The answer will be largely found in the literature. However, at more advanced levels, you may be expected to find evidence in the literature which you can use to support an answer to a question that may be more controversial – requiring more judgement on your part. You will be marshalling evidence found in the literature to support claims and arguments that are more of your *own*. This will entail pulling relevant evidence together from diverse sources.

The more advanced the level of your study, the more you will be expected to provide your own 'added value' to what you find in the literature – to generate your own argument and support it with evidence from the literature. In *research*, this evidence will also include primary data that you collect and analyses (e.g. from interviews, questionnaires or observations).

An essay may therefore be composed largely of you presenting, analysing, structuring and evaluating what you find in the literature. This is not the same as a 'literature review' as used in the context of a research project (see the next section below). An essay will have a relatively brief *introduction* section, setting the essay question in context and drawing on relevant literature. But the literature will generally be providing much of the answer to the essay question.

Research

Literature in a *research dissertation* or *thesis* assumes a different role in that the research question will, in empirical research, be answered predominantly from your own data gathering, analysis and interpretation. The literature review will form more of a 'container' surrounding your research, setting it in context.

Your research thesis or dissertation (unlike an essay) would normally contain a separate early chapter entitled 'Literature review', consisting of a review of what is already known and published about the phenomenon you are going to research. However, it is not a case of attempting to summarise everything that is known in the subject area in which your research is set. Rather, a literature review should be focused on what is known *that is directly relevant to and informs your research question*. Thus each piece of literature (journal article, conference paper, book or research report) reviewed in the literature review should be described in these terms – how it is relevant to, and what it contributes to, your research question and its possible answer.

A good analytic literature review will also reveal *gaps* in our knowledge – what is *not* yet known. Such gaps can be a good source of research questions. However, if you have already formulated a research question before exploring the literature, a good literature review will be useful as a check that your research question has not already been specifically answered.

It may not be a simple choice between:

- having a research question before going to the literature; and
- basing your research question on a gap in knowledge identified in the literature.

Generating a good research question may often entail a mixture of the two. You may, for example, start with an initial research idea, read around the topic and modify your research question in the light of what has and has not been done already. Equally, you may start by identifying a research topic suggested in the literature, then develop a precise research question that reflects your own particular 'take' on the issue.

The literature is also relevant towards the end of your research report, where you discuss your findings in relation to our existing knowledge. Here you should discuss the extent to which your findings tend to confirm, refute, extend or modify this knowledge. The literature may also be able to help you explain or interpret your results. Table 5.1 summarises the main roles of the literature review.

Initial explorations

If your essay or research topic is very new to you, you may need to spend some time in initial explorations to get a picture of what it is all about at a basic level, and to

Table 5.1 The roles of the literature review

	Literature review	Discussion and conclusions	
SET YOUR RESEARCH QUESTIONS IN CONTEXT	Why is research needed/valuable in the area of your topic?	To what extent do your findings agree with/extend/conflict with existing knowledge in the literature?	SET YOUR RESEARCH RESULTS IN CONTEXT
	What work has been done already? What are the main findings that relate to/inform your own research?	Does anything in the literature help to explain any of your findings?	
	What are the similarities and differences in relation to your research?	What gaps still remain/what new questions emerge from your work that need to be addressed in future research?	
	What are the limitations of the studies you review?		
	What gaps are there in our knowledge? Is your research filling a gap?		

become familiar with terminology so that you can search more specifically in the next, more systematic searching stage. The extent to which and the way in which you do this may vary according to your preferred learning style.

Recall from Chapter 2 that if you have a predisposition to emphasise *description building*, you will be comfortable spending quite a bit of time and energy establishing a broad – and initially relatively tentative – conceptual overview before getting down to a more thorough examination of the specifics and details. This style is associated with a holistic focus from the start, and with a relatively high tolerance of ambiguity and uncertainty, and a parallel-processing, 'many things on the go at the same time' approach. As we will see in Chapter 7, it is well served by a *broad exploratory* approach to information seeking.

However, if you tend to emphasise *procedure building*, you will want to spend relatively less time and energy on such tentative initial explorations, and will be keener to get into more systematic, thorough and detailed investigation as soon as possible – even if this means that the broad conceptual overview may emerge relatively late in the research process. This style is associated with an initially relatively narrow focus and a more systematic, step-by-step approach geared to mastering one aspect of the topic before going on to the next. As we will see in Chapter 7, it is well served by a *specific detailed* approach to information seeking.

If you are a relatively holistic, description building-oriented learner, you are likely to find it useful to spend some time finding and scanning a range of information sources as your first stage of literature searching. This stage of information seeking is characterised by not committing to any source (i.e. not delving into it in great detail or reading it thoroughly) too early. Here are the questions that you are likely to be asking yourself at this stage:

- What is the scope of this topic? What is it all about?
- What are its main components and themes?
- What terminology is used by authors writing about the topic?

It is a good idea at this stage to begin to sketch a rough map of the topic, showing key components and key concepts that you are coming across, and trying to see how they fit together. This may be in note form, but can also be in the form of a diagrammatic mind map or concept map. People differ in the extent to which they find pictorial representations of ideas useful. However, if you feel comfortable with diagrams, a mind map can be extremely useful in helping you get a grasp of the topic. The same map can also be used to plot your main argument. See Chapter 9 for an example of a concept map and for details of free software which you can use to generate such maps.

Search tools that are not specifically academic (e.g. *Google* as opposed to *Google Scholar*) can be useful at this stage:

- To help you establish an exploratory, provisional overview – subject to revision as you begin to explore peer-reviewed, academically strong sources (the subject of the next section in this chapter, 'Strategies for finding high-quality academic sources').

- To help you when your need is primarily for sources that most clearly explain the topic rather than necessarily provide sources that you will ultimately use in your finished work.

Whilst there may be some high-quality authoritative sources in what *Google* finds for you, it is not tuned to prioritise sources in terms of their academic acceptability. *Google* and other general search engines do not specialise in (or even list first in relation to any search) sources that are necessarily suitable for academic work. They do attempt to list high-quality sources first, but quality is not defined in specifically academic terms.

Google, for example, uses a clever technique called *PageRank* to differentiate higher from lower quality information. Basically, the higher the number and quality of web pages that link to a given webpage, the higher is the quality rating given to that page. This will in turn positively affect the quality ratings of pages to which it links. Other factors, such as the number of times the page is visited, are also taken into account. Thus quality is defined to a significant extent in terms of a 'popularity vote' by people choosing to link to and visit webpages.

Clearly, 'quality' in this sense does not necessarily map on to *academic* quality. But academic quality can to some extent be judged by a process that is similar to Google's *PageRank*, but which is based on *academic experts* 'linking' to an information source. They do so by citing it (referring to or quoting it) in their own work. The more a particular information source is cited by other authors, the higher its likely academic quality, in that other authors are building on it to create new knowledge. We will see how to find information sources that are highly cited when we explore academic search tools such as *Google Scholar*, *SciVerse Scopus* and *Web of Knowledge* in Chapter 8.

Google searches will retrieve information from a great variety of sources. It has one of the largest indexes. But bear in mind that no one search engine covers more than a relatively small percentage of web documents 'out there'. You should also bear in mind that a vast amount of material found by *Google* in response to your search will not generally be suitable for using in your academic work – for example, *Wikipedia*, blog posts, twitter feeds, discussion forums, and many websites produced by people or organisations whose academic authority in relation to your topic cannot be established.

However, such sources may well be useful as stepping stones. *Wikipedia*, for example, contains many articles which are up to date and accurate, often providing an excellent current overview of a topic. However, it also contains many that are not. Like the proverbial stopped watch, it is not much comfort to know that it will be accurate twice a day if you can't tell exactly when. Some blogs and discussion forums may contain valuable information about latest developments and thoughts in relation to some topic. You need to be able to take advantage of the potential value of such sources, whilst avoiding the potential pitfalls. It is therefore important to corroborate the information they contain from other sources.

You can not only follow up *Wikipedia*'s own suggested references and links, but also engage in your own independent searching to find corroborating sources that are sufficiently authoritative to be used and referenced in your work. The merits and problems of using *Wikipedia* in academic work are discussed more fully in Chapter 6.

Blogs may also be sources of potentially useful information. In the same way, this *potential* can be converted into *actual* value via the process of verification. Unlike *Wikipedia* articles, many blogs are authored by named individuals, which in some cases can provide an indication of credibility. Take, for example, a blog such as the *Information Literacy Weblog* (http://information-literacy.blogspot.com/). Sheila Webber, the author of this blog (and one of my colleagues at the University of Sheffield) is a recognised authority in the field of information literacy, and her blog is a source of up-to-date and verifiable information on new publications, conferences, developments and activities relating to this field.

To summarise: when you are at this initial 'tentative exploration' stage it is useful to explore a rich variety of sources in 'provisional' mode. As suggested above, there's nothing wrong with going straight to *Google* or *Wikipedia* to find some basic information about your topic, so long as that's not all you do. These initial explorations will be followed by more systematic searching for high-quality sources that you can use in your finished work. Systematic searching will be introduced in the following section. But first, let us see how we might go about this initial exploratory searching stage.

If we simply type, for example, *climate change* into *Google*, we immediately retrieve some useful information (Figure 5.1).

Figure 5.1   *Google* results for *climate change*

The second main link is to a Wikipedia article on climate change. As noted above, *Wikipedia* can be very useful, provided that you corroborate the information from other authoritative – preferably peer-reviewed – sources. Often, sources are listed at the end of *Wikipedia* articles themselves, although you should also engage in your own independent information seeking to find the best ones.

Still within exploratory mode, you can introduce an element of academic quality control by restricting your search to, for example, websites published by academic institutions in the UK and the USA and UK government sites. You can do this by making use of advanced search operators like '*site*': For example, searching for:

global warming site:ac.uk OR site:edu OR site:gov

will retrieve only documents from websites whose address ends in *ac.uk* (which denotes a recognised UK academic institution) or *edu* (the USA equivalent). (The use of this and other search operators will be explored in Chapter 7.)

At the same time you can make the search even more specific by introducing further keywords that may narrow your search to sources useful to you at this initial exploratory stage, such as *overview*, *introduction*, *tutorial*, *primer*, etc. The following search for *global warming* retrieves some potentially useful sources, as shown in Figure 5.2:

global warming overview site:ac.uk OR site:edu OR site:gov

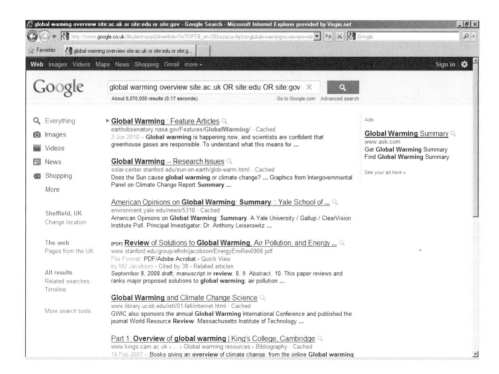

Figure 5.2 Results for *global warming*

Note that all the websites returned are published on websites belonging to UK or USA academic institutions, or governments. This does not mean that the links are to peer-reviewed sources (though some may be). But it does increase the chances that the websites are relatively objective compared, for example, to commercial or lobbying sites. Experiment with using different keywords in your search. As noted in Chapter 4, you are likely to retrieve very different results using different ways of expressing similar or related concepts.

Clicking '*More*' (under '*Shopping*' at the left of the *Google* screen (see Figure 5.2) will give you more options to search for particular types of information including books, places, blogs, discussions and patents. Some are clearly more useful than others in relation to academic work. For example:

News: displays results from *Google News*. News can be searched separately using the *News* link at the top of the page.

> News articles – particularly from the higher quality news sources – can sometimes be used in academic work, depending on the nature of the topic. News reports should be distinguished from opinion pieces. Also, since generally peer-reviewed sources should be used for academic work, you should consult your lecturer if you feel that you need to cite information from a non-peer-reviewed news source.

Books: displays results from *Google Books*.

> *Google* displays only a small number of books (from *Google Books*) if any are relevant to your query. For a more comprehensive search *specifically* for books, you should search *Google Books* direct (http://books.google.com/). *Google Scholar* (http://scholar.google.com/), however, will find other scholarly materials, including journal articles and conference papers as well as books relating to your topic.

Clicking '*More search tools*' (on the left of the screen, see Figure 5.2) will display options which allow you to filter the results shown to you in a number of ways. Potentially useful for academic work are the following:

- **Any time**: results are presented in order of their relevance to your query.
- **Past hour / Past 24 hours / Past week / Past month / Past year**: filters results according to the time period you specify.
- **Custom range**: allows you to specify a particular time period.

> Depending on your topic, there may be a trade-off between up-to-dateness and relevance. If you are needing an introduction to a topic that is new to you, the most up-to-date sources may not always be the best. If the topic is not itself particularly new, and has been written

---

about for some time, the best introductory sources may have been produced some time ago. The best way to find these would be to choose the *Any time* option. The very latest sources can sometimes be rather specialised and more advanced by comparison. This may depend on the topic you are searching for.

As most search engines do, *Google* offers an advanced search page (see Figure 5.3) which allows you to easily input complex queries.

Note that, as you fill in the different sections of the advanced search page, the actual search terms that *Google* will use are shown at the top of the screen. These include the advanced search operators *'allintitle:'*, *'filetype:'* and *'site:'*, which map the choices we have made in the drop-down boxes to *Google*'s query language. These mappings are arrowed in Figure 5.3. Thus, in this example, the search is for:

allintitle: "global warming" results OR consequences OR implications –

greenhouse filetype:pdf site:ac.uk

Figure 5.3 *Google*'s advanced search page

The use of these and other advanced search operators will be explored in Chapter 7.

Further options appearing below the screen in Figure 5.3 are shown in Figure 5.4.

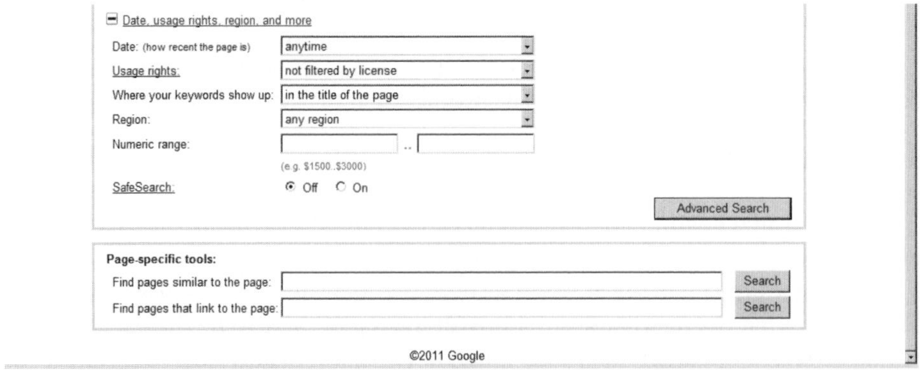

Figure 5.4 Further option from *Google's* advanced search page

If you prefer, you can type such a search – with the advanced search operators – into *Google's* *simple* search box. Note that details of the advanced search operators shown here, and others available in *Google* but not accessible via the advanced search page, are given in Chapter 7, which also introduces advanced search operators used in a variety of the most popular search engines. Advanced searching in scholarly search tools, including *Google Scholar*, *SciVerse Scopus* and *Web of Knowledge* (as opposed to general search engines), is introduced in Chapter 8.

On the default simple search page (Figure 5.5), selecting *Related searches* on the left of the screen displays other searches related to your topic at the top of the centre column of the screen. Clicking any of these related searches links will run the relevant search for you.

Finding related articles, and related searches, can be particularly useful when you are engaged in initial explorations of a topic, when you are wanting to scope it and identify its main components and themes. Another device that can be useful in this initial exploratory stage is the *Wonder wheel* option in *Google*. At the time of writing (July 2011) this feature has recently been removed as part of a redesign of *Google's* interface, and it is not clear whether this is temporary. It is still included here since it represents an interesting approach to finding information which, even if *Google* does not re-offer, may be made available by other search tools in the future. Also, a *Wonder wheel* style interface is still available to *Google Images* (http://image-swirl. googlelabs.com/). The *Wonder wheel* displays your topic (i.e. what you typed into the search box) at the centre of a wheel, with spokes showing topics that are related to it. The results of the search for the topic (i.e. the retrieved websites) are shown at the right of the screen. Figure 5.6 shows the *Wonder wheel* for the topic *global warming*.

Clicking any of the related topics will result in a new wheel being displayed, with the topic you clicked at its centre, with spokes showing topics related to *that* topic, and so on. Search results for the topic at the centre of the wheel are shown at the right of the screen. Figure 5.7 shows the result of clicking on *greenhouse effect* in Figure 5.6.

Figure 5.5 *Google*'s default simple search page

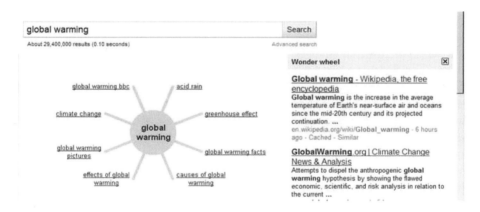

Figure 5.6 *Google's* Wonder wheel

The *Wonder wheel* is of limited value in that the related topics are derived from the co-occurrences of keywords in documents rather than from any human analysis of topics and the relationships between them. But if used in conjunction with the search results shown at the right of the screen, it can be helpful. The examples shown in Figures 5.6 and 5.7 provide links to *Wikipedia* articles. As previously noted, it can

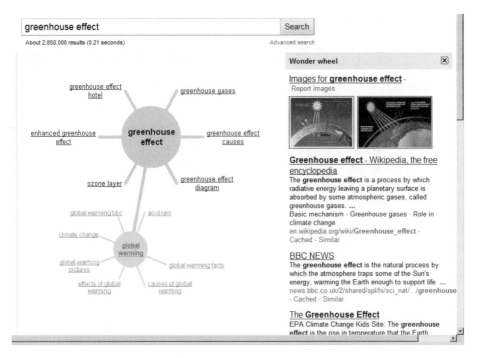

Figure 5.7 The expanded *Wonder wheel*

be useful to scan these to obtain a preliminary overview of a topic. Take a look at the *Wikipedia* article for *global warming*. Look also at the articles for *climate change*, *greenhouse gas*, and *ozone layer*. Compare them. How do they relate to each other? What is the overall picture that emerges?

Bear in mind that when you are in this initial mode, you are exploring tentatively. So it doesn't matter that you are looking at *Wikipedia* articles and possibly other sites that may lack sufficient authority for you to be able to use them in your finished work. You are essentially sampling in order to to get a picture of where multiple sources converge and diverge – rather than putting weight on any one yet.

There are many different types of web search engine, with new ones being developed constantly. Also useful at this initial exploratory stage is a tool like *Yippy* (http://www.yippy.com/) (formerly *Clusty*), which is a *metasearch* engine. A metasearch engine takes your query and searches the web using multiple search engines. *Yippy* not only retrieves documents matching your search terms, but classifies them into higher level clusters, which can be useful in helping you obtain a good overview of the different facets of the topic. Let us try the following search in *Yippy*:

global warming site:ac.uk OR site:edu

The results are shown in Figure 5.8.

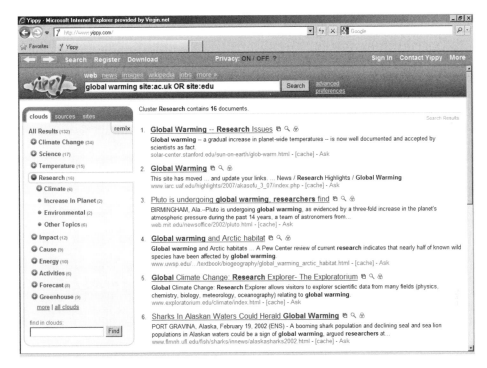

Figure 5.8 A *Yippy* search

At the left of the screen, *Yippy* presents the clusters of retrieved sources. In the figure, **Research** has been expanded to show its sub-categories. To the right of each category is shown the number of sources it contains. Clicking on any of these categories would filter the results shown in the main part of the screen to those sources.

Try searching for:

greenhouse effect

in *Yolink*[9] (http://www.yolink.com/yolink/). This is a 'semantic search engine' which attempts to pull together chunks of text relevant to your search to form an automatically generated summary of the topic (Figure 5.9). By clicking on a given paragraph of text, you can preview (and click to go to, if you wish) the website where that particular chunk of text was found. Again, at the initial stages of your research such tools can be useful in helping you map out the territory.

However, clever though these tools are, they are not the best way of setting about the next stage of your research, which focuses on finding really authoritative academically acceptable information sources. This next stage entails being able to do the following.

---

[9] *Yolink* is a registered trademark of TigerLogic Corporation.

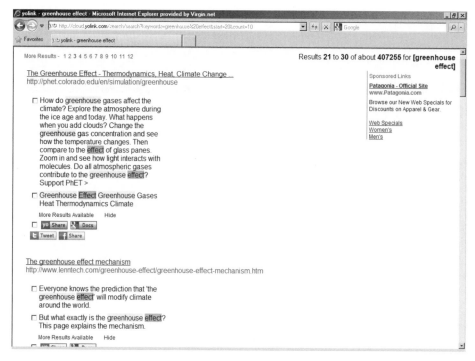

Figure 5.9 A *Yolink* search

- Decide on the best types of information source in relation to your task.
- Choose the most appropriate search tool to find them.
- Devise and put into action strategies for progressively homing in on the sources most relevant to your specific needs.

Let us now turn our attention to doing this – to finding the high-quality academic sources which will help you build an evidence-based answer to your essay or research question, and which you can use and quote in your finished work.

Strategies for finding high-quality academic sources

The initial exploratory search stage described in the previous section is appropriate if you are very new to a topic and need to obtain a provisional view of what it is all about – its main components and themes. This overview may also be useful in helping you plan the next stage of your research, with which this section is concerned, namely: engaging in a more systematic and rigorous search for high-quality information to help you answer your essay or research question. The initial exploratory stage may also help you think of *appropriate keywords* to use in this more focused stage of your searching – and to identify *different facets* of your topic that you need to build in to your searching.

Questions your literature searching will address

The more systematic and rigorous searching described in this section entails targeting high-quality sources that you can use directly as evidence in your work. This stage of your searching aims to answer the following questions.

In the case of an essay

If I have no existing ideas of my own about how I will answer the essay question:

- *Can I find a ready-made answer in the literature?*
  Be careful if you do find a source that seems to answer the question. If you use it, you must acknowledge and reference it, otherwise you will be plagiarising (see Chapter 10). However, your lecturers will not be happy if you simply find and repeat information from one source. Essays are set in order to require you to think, to weigh evidence from different points of view, and not to regurgitate information. Even if you find a source that seems to address your specific question, bear in mind that, except for extremely factual questions (which are not normally set as essay questions), there are likely to be different points of view, and competing claims, arguments and evidence. You should make yourself aware of these and come to your own conclusions about what you think, having weighed the evidence.
- *What information can I find that is relevant to the question, so that I can begin to devise an answer?*
  You should search for information on the key aspects of your question, and map out key concepts, ideas and arguments that emerge. This mapping will be more detailed than the provisional conceptual overview you may have generated in the 'initial explorations' stage discussed in the previous section. As you read, you should ask yourself 'what, if anything, does this tell me that is relevant to my essay/research question?' The more you read, and the more you map, the more the distance between what you are reading and what you need to know to answer the question should diminish. This is an iterative process. Your reading and mapping should begin to give you ideas about how you can go about addressing the question. At the same time, your emerging ideas about how to answer the question will increasingly guide your search for new information.

If I already have some ideas about a possible answer to the question:

- *What evidence can I find in the literature that relates to the components of my tentative answer?*
- *Does the evidence in the literature support or bring into question my ideas about an answer? Does it suggest another line of argument?*

In the case of a research project

If I have only identified a broad topic, and not yet a specific research question:

- *What research has already been done on the topic? What is the current state of knowledge as revealed in the literature?*
- *Do any authors directly suggest topics that need to be researched? If so, are any of these of interest to me – or can I modify any to my own particular interests?*
- *From reviewing the literature, can I identify any gaps in our knowledge that would form a research question?*
- *Can I identify any previously researched topic that I could replicate in a different context? For example, a research project may have explored a particular issue amongst office workers. Could I explore a similar issue but amongst university students?*

If I already have a research question, what sources can I find that I can use:

- *To set my research in context in my literature review?*
- *To justify my research question in terms of emphasising its potential usefulness, and in terms of the research question not having already been answered?*

Also:

- *Can I find information sources relating to research methodology that will help me go about answering my research question effectively?*

  Such sources should be able to:

  - Guide you in selecting an appropriate research approach and methods to help you answer your research question.
  - Enable you to justify your methodological choices and actions (by referring to appropriate methodological literature).
  - Help you apply the research approaches in such a way that you can provide evidence of research quality – e.g. by referencing appropriate methodological literature in your explanation of how you addressed issues of validity, reliability and objectivity (see Chapter 9 for discussion of these quality issues).

You can approach this stage of searching in two ways. You can start by:

- going for 'low hanging fruit'; or
- engaging in controlled systematic searching.

The controlled systematic searching approach is appropriate when you want to maximise your chances of finding *the best* information sources and *minimise the chances of missing potentially important ones*. This approach – and reasons why you should use it – are presented after an introduction to the 'low hanging fruit' approach below.

'Low hanging fruit' strategy

The 'low hanging fruit' approach is suitable when you want quick, least-effort access to some relevant scholarly information sources to get you started. At its most extreme, this approach entails simply typing keywords from your essay or research question into *Google Scholar* which, unlike *Google*, is specifically designed to give you access to high-quality academic sources. Let us assume that your essay question is, for example:

Discuss the effects of TV viewing on children.

You can find suitable peer-reviewed sources in *Google Scholar* via this 'low energy' approach by simply typing the main keywords of your essay question:

effects of TV viewing on children

As shown in Figure 5.10, *Google Scholar* has found some useful sources. The *[PDF]* from msu.edu link to the right of the third source is to a copy of the full text of the document.

There are advantages and limitations to this 'low hanging fruit' approach, particularly using *Google Scholar*.

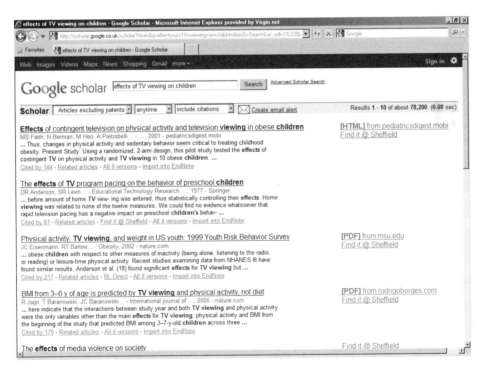

Figure 5.10 *Google Scholar* results

Advantages

- This simple search strategy requires minimum time and effort yet is likely to find some useful sources.
- *Google Scholar* is freely available and offers quick and easy access.
- If you are lucky, some of the documents found by *Google Scholar* will be directly available in full text (like the second item retrieved in Figure 5.10).
- *Google Scholar* is well suited to this approach in that it is more likely to find a good number of documents in response to a naïve query for which other academically specialised search tools, such as *Web of Knowledge* or *SciVerse Scopus*, find nothing or very little. This is because *Google Scholar* indexes the full text of documents. A number of academic search tools, such as *Web of Knowledge* and *SciVerse Scopus,* only index the title, abstract and keywords (descriptive words selected by human indexers or the author to describe the main content of the document). Therefore, if your search terms appear in the full text but not in the title, abstract or keywords of a document, *Google Scholar* is more likely to retrieve it.

Limitations

Whilst the 'low hanging fruit' approach is good at quickly finding you *some* relevant sources to get you started, it is not the most effective approach if you are aiming to find the *best* relevant sources. Whilst the systematic approaches described in the next section are not *guaranteed* to find the best sources, they are arguably less likely to miss them.

To explain why, let us take a simple example. Imagine that we have an essay topic:

> *To what extent can we adapt university teaching styles to match students' learning styles?*

A key source in this debate is an extremely comprehensive and thorough report evaluating learning styles, entitled:

> 'Learning styles and pedagogy in post-16 learning: a systematic and critical review'

This should be essential reading for this particular topic, and certainly comes in the category of one of the *best* sources for this particular essay. However, even if we search in *Google Scholar* for almost the exact title but include *'undergraduate'* instead of *'post-16'* (these two expressions having very similar meanings in practice)

> *learning styles and pedagogy in undergraduate learning critical review*

this particular report does not appear (at the time of writing) in the first 300 hits.

Let's take another example. Search for the subject of Diana Laurillard's seminal book entitled:

rethinking university teaching

and it appears as the first *Google Scholar* hit. However, search for:

re-thinking university teaching

and it is not retrieved in the first 100 hits. A similar problem occurs if you search for, say:

inquiry-based learning

or

enquiry-based learning

You are not likely to retrieve sources in which the author has used one spelling if you search for another. Your list of retrieved sources will be completely different. These are just three examples of a general underlying problem that applies not just to *Google Scholar*.

The argument being made here is this:

- Whether or not a search tool retrieves what may be key essential sources in relation to your search query can depend on the triviality of a hyphen or the accidental choice of one way of expressing an idea rather than another equally valid one.
- There are ways of searching which are designed to minimise, or at least reduce, the chances of you missing important sources in this way. These are the focus of the following section.

Systematic searching

For relatively straightforward topics in which a lot has been written, the 'low hanging fruit' approach can be effective in quickly finding you some useful information sources. However, more rigorous and systematic searching can bring you benefits, and will certainly be required in later stages of relatively advanced-level work when you need to check that you have not missed important key sources. But before outlining what these benefits are, let us briefly consider what exactly is meant by 'more rigorous and systematic' searching. What does it consist of?

Well, basically this entails:

- Analysing what your essay or research question is really asking.
- Identifying the most appropriate types of information source to answer it.

- Carefully selecting amongst different search tools in order to select the best one for finding the information you need. (Search tools differ in terms of what information sources they cover and what search facilities they offer.)
- Devising an explicit search strategy so that you maximise the quality of information you find. (Thinking carefully about exactly how you are going to search can pay dividends.)
- Monitoring and, where appropriate, improving your search strategy as you progress.

Let us explore each of these areas in detail.

Analyse your essay or research question

In the case of an essay question, make sure that you know exactly what it is asking. Sometimes a question may be phrased in such a way as to allow a number of different interpretations. Take the following, for example:

Discuss the effects of TV viewing on children

Initial exploration of the literature might raise a number of questions in your mind as to how you are going to respond to this. Some that come to mind are:

Which children? What age range(s)?

Where? In the United Kingdom or internationally?

Viewing *what?* Specifically children's programmes? TV adverts?

What effects? Effects on behaviour? Effects on dietary health (e.g. of food adverts)?

Etc.

Where an essay allows a range of different interpretations, it is a good idea to seek clarification from your lecturer. If he or she is happy for you to choose your own focus, or take a very general approach, you should explain at the beginning of your essay how you have interpreted the question. For example, that you have chosen to focus on the effects of TV advertising on the dietary health of primary school children in the United Kingdom.

Why do this? It is a good idea to make sure that you are interpreting the question in a way that the person marking it will find acceptable. Having said this, it may be that this person will be all too happy if you express an interest in taking a particular line of interpretation, or in focusing on a particular aspect of the question – so long as you clear this with him or her first.

Identify the best types of information source to answer your question

This will depend on the level of prior knowledge you have of the topic, and the stage at which you are in your research. For example, do you need an *introductory textbook* or a more advanced *journal article*? Do you need a relatively broad *review of research* in the area or a more narrowly focused *conference paper*? (See Chapter 6 for a discussion of different types of information source and how they might be useful in different ways.)

> *Why do this?* Having information that is pitched at the right level, and has the right focus can save you a lot of time and effort, and ultimately enable you to be more effective in your learning and research. Struggling to make sense of a highly specialised journal or conference paper – if what you really need is a clear introduction for beginners – will waste your time and may result in frustration.
>
> Equally, wading through many individual specialised articles describing particular pieces of research – if what you really need is a good integrated overview of research in the area – may waste your time and hinder your effectiveness. Clearly, spending a little time figuring out what type of information you need can pay dividends.

Identify the best search tools to find information

Google Scholar is free and easy to use. However, there are many other academic search tools, such as *Web of Knowledge* and *SciVerse Scopus*, as well as specialised tools covering specific fields of knowledge. Some are free to anyone with an Internet connection. Others are subscription-based. However, if you are working in a university, you will have access to a wide range of such tools.

You should familiarise yourself with the tools available to you – your university will have a list. Those available to registered students at my own university of Sheffield, for example, are listed at http://www.shef.ac.uk/library/cdlists/cdtable.html. You should find a similar listing for your own university. (See Chapter 6 for details of different search tools – their coverage and search facilities.)

> *Why do this?* Whilst there is some overlap in coverage between scholarly tools such as *Google Scholar*, *Web of Knowledge* and *SciVerse Scopus*, such overlap is far from complete. This means that if you use only one, you may miss potentially important sources.
>
> Note that some scholarly search tools (including *Google Scholar*, *SciVerse Scopus* and *Web of Knowledge*) allow you to filter your search according to broad subject categories. Using this facility can be helpful in reducing the amount of irrelevant material you retrieve. For example, searching for information on *transport* in the context of **economics** will filter out the huge range of sources relating to **engineering** aspects, and vice versa.
>
> Using only general search tools when there is a tool that specialises in your topic may mean that you miss potentially important sources. You will find information sources not covered in these general scholarly search tools by searching in tools that specialise in a particular area, such as *MEDLINE* and *CINAHL* in medicine and nursing, the *ACM* or *IEEE* digital libraries for computing and electrical engineering, *Emerald Management Reviews* for management, etc.
>
> Different search tools can also offer different search facilities. For example, individual specialised databases available within *Web of Knowledge* offer their own specialised controlled vocabularies and search fields.

Devise a search strategy to apply when you are using the search tools

Recall from Chapter 4 (in particular, Figure 4.11) that there are potential barriers standing between you and the information that might satisfy your information needs. You need to try to obtain the best match between the words you use to express your information needs and the words used by a search tool's index to describe information sources that might be able to satisfy them. When your topic is complex and the same or similar concepts can be expressed in many different ways, this is by no means necessarily a trivial task. In short, it is a good idea to think about how you are going to search and to devise a strategy.

You should think carefully in order to identify appropriate keywords to describe your topic.

Sometimes, this may be straightforward. But often, you will need to be aware of a variety of terms in order to avoid missing important information. As you begin to explore the topic in the literature, you may become aware of specialist terms that will be useful in finding relevant sources. For example, you may be working on an essay question such as:

> *To what extent is the full potential of the Internet for central and local government being fulfilled in Britain?*

Keywords that immediately come to mind may include: *internet*, *central government*, and *local government*. But as you progressively explore the topic, you may find other terms, such as *e-government*, that are even more effective in your search for relevant information. You should try to identify alternative terms – synonyms, near-synonyms and closely related terms, for example: *digital government*, *e-gov*, *online government*, *e-democracy* and *e-voting*.

Having identified appropriate keywords, think carefully about how you can exploit them to best effect by using advanced search features.

There are several techniques to make best use of the words you have selected to describe the information you need. Chapters 7 and 8 will introduce these in detail. However, some examples are provided here in order to give a flavour of the range available.

As we saw in the previous section, scholarly search tools like *Google Scholar*, as well as most general web search engines, allow you to specify that you want to retrieve documents that contain your keywords in their *title*, rather than just somewhere in the text. They also allow you to search for a *specific phrase* by enclosing your keywords in quotation marks. If I search in *Google Scholar* for:

> *introduction to health care*

I retrieve (at the time of writing) some 2,470,000 documents. Hardly any of the first few hundred give me what I want – an *introduction to health care*. Documents from the first page of hits are shown in Figure 5.11.

Figure 5.11 *Google Scholar* result for *introduction to health care*

My keywords are certainly present in these documents, but take a look at where they appear. *Introduction* appears far away from *health care*. The documents are about aspects of health care, but are not specifically *introductions to health care*.

I can, on the other hand, specify that I want the words to appear exactly as I type them (i.e. the exact phrase), and that I want the phrase to appear in the title of documents retrieved. I can specify that my keywords should be treated as a *phrase* by enclosing them in double quotation marks. And I can specify that they should appear in the *title* of documents by using the advanced search operator '*intitle:*' (note that this and other advanced search operators available in *Google* and *Google Scholar* are introduced in detail in Chapters 7 and 8):

intitle:"introduction to health care"[10]

I retrieve 50 documents, all of which include the phrase in their titles. For example:

'Introduction to health care'

'Caring: an introduction to health care from a humanistic perspective'

'Introduction to health care technology assessment'

Introduction to health care education: a course for new associate of science in nursing faculty

---

[10]When using *intitle*: do not leave a space after the colon. However, a space is permitted after *allintitle:*

'Introduction to health care reform in New Zealand'

'Health and health services: an introduction to health care in Britain'

'Introduction to health care delivery: a primer for pharmacists'

'Introduction to health care management'

'Introduction to health care economics & financial management: fundamental concepts with practical applications'

Words in quotation marks are treated by most search engines as phrases – i.e. they will be searched for exactly. Thus, searching for *"health care"* will not match the phrase *"health and nursing care"* occurring in a document, whereas searching for *health care* without quotation marks would. This technique can be very useful when used in conjunction with other advanced search operators.

Other words and phrases may also produce useful results, depending on what you want. For example:

allintitle: "health care" "review of research"[11]

allintitle: "health care" "advances in"

allintitle: "health care" overview

allintitle: "health care" primer

You can try even more specific phrases, for example:

intitle:"research into health care"

intitle:"issues in health care"

Bear in mind that although searching for *very specific phrases* can be a good technique when you want to find something to help you get started in a topic, it is not a good way of finding a range of relevant material, since by searching for an exact phrase you will be ruling out retrieving other, possibly even more relevant documents that happen to express the same idea using different wording.

There is a trade off. The more specific you make the wording of phrases in your search, the more you risk finding few or no documents. But the greater may be the reward if it does, in terms of a possible quick hit on a highly relevant information source.

The way in which you *combine* words and phrases is also critical. Assume, for example, that we want to retrieve documents that use *either* of the phrases *'digital government strategie'* or *'online government strategies'* in their title, and type the following into *Google Scholar*'s search box:

allintitle: "digital government" "online government"

This finds **no** documents (at the time of writing), despite the fact that there are over 500 documents containing one of these phrases in their title. The reason is

---

[11]Advanced operators including *intitle:* and *allinititle:* will be introduced in detail in Chapter 7.

that *Google Scholar* (as well as *Google* and many other search engines) automatically assumes that, unless you specify otherwise, it should automatically link the words and phrases you type into the search box with **AND**. It thus interprets this search as:

allintitle: "digital government" **AND** *"online government"*

What you have inadvertently asked *Google Scholar* to find is documents *each* of which contains *both* these phrases. But what you really want is documents each of which contains *either* (but not necessarily both) these phrases. The way to search for this is:

allintitle: "digital government" **OR** *"online government"*

Some (by no means all) search tools also allow you to put one or more *wildcards* into your search. An asterisk placed in a *Google Scholar* search for a particular *phrase* will stand for any one or more words. So, for example:

*"introduction to * research methods"*

will retrieve documents containing the phrases:

introduction to qualitative research methods
introduction to behavioural research methods
introduction to social research methods
introduction to quantitative research methods
etc.

Other search tools allow wildcards to be inserted at the end of *words*. In *SciVerse Scopus*, for example:

*comput**

will find *computer, computers, computation, computational*, etc.
The question mark also represents a single character and can be inserted within a word, so:

privati?ation

will find *privatisation* and *privatization*.
Some tools offer more sophisticated search facilities. The following search in *SciVerse Scopus* (which will be introduced in detail in Chapter 8), for example:

TITLE-ABS-KEY(drug W/4 addict*) AND DOCTYPE(cp) AND PUBYEAR AFT 2002 AND SUBJAREA(soci) would retrieve documents which:

- in their title, abstract or keywords
  TITLE-ABS-KEY
- contain the word *drug* appearing within 4 words of any word beginning with *addict* (e.g. *addict, addicted, addiction*)
  drug W/4 addict*
- and which are conference papers
  DOCTYPE(cp)
- published after 2002
  PUBYEAR AFT 2002
- in the area of Social Sciences
  SUBJAREA(soci)

A number of search tools also allow you to restrict your search to particular date ranges and to broad subject areas. From its Advanced Search page *Google Scholar*, for example, allows you to restrict your search to:

Biology, Life Sciences, and Environmental Science

Medicine, Pharmacology, and Veterinary Science

Business, Administration, Finance, and Economics

Physics, Astronomy, and Planetary Science

Chemistry and Materials Science

Social Sciences, Arts, and Humanities

Engineering, Computer Science, and Mathematics

Other tools such as *Web of Knowledge* also allow filtering using finer-grained subject categories, analysing your search results in terms of these narrower categories and allowing you to select one or more to apply as a filter. For example:

Communication

Social work

Demography

Urban studies

Public administration

Imaging science & photographic technology

Telecommunications

Psychology

Materials science

Education & educational research

etc.

Table 5.2 Search narrowing and broadening strategies.

Narrow your search by...	Broaden your search by...
Adding new search terms (linked by **AND**) to make the search more specific	Linking existing search terms using **OR** (and/or adding new terms linked by **OR**)
Combining terms into phrases by surrounding them with quotation marks	Converting phrases into separate words by removing quotation marks
Applying filters (e.g. subject, document type, location of keywords in the document, etc.)	Not applying, or applying fewer filters
	Removing search terms to make the search less specific
	Using wildcards to make the search less specific

You can use these strategies to improve your search over time – particularly if you find that you are retrieving too few or too many results. Table 5.2 summarises how the strategies introduced above can be used to narrow your search to make it more specific (to retrieve fewer but more targeted results) or broaden it to maker it more general (to increase the number of items retrieved).

Different search facilities offered by a range of general search engines are introduced in Chapter 7. Search facilities officered by the scholarly search tools *Google Scholar*, *SciVerse Scopus* and *Web of Knowledge* are introduced in Chapter 8.

Why do this? Working out a strategy for searching will ultimately save you time and is likely to result in a more effective search.

Your choice of search terms can drastically affect the quality of what you find. Also, making effective use of the facilities offered by the search tool you are using can help you target your search more precisely, avoiding searches that are either overly narrow or overly broad.

By thinking about your strategy, and taking the time to learn what search tools have to offer, you can increase your chances of finding high-quality, relevant documents that are appropriate to the needs of your particular essay or research project. You will also be less likely to miss important information.

Search tools offer a lot of powerful features. Why not use them to your advantage?

Monitoring your searching

It is a good idea to keep a record, or audit trail, of your searching. As your search progresses over time, and as you try different keywords and new combinations of them – and different databases and search tools – it is all too easy to lose track of what you have already searched for, where and with what result. If this happens, you can waste a lot of time repeating searches and parts of searches and basically going round in circles. If you are engaging in a systematic search of the literature for an essay or project over a protracted period of time, it is a good idea to keep a clear record of where you search, what search terms you use, and what the results are.

Where there is a lot of literature available and you have to select what to include and what to reject in your literature review, it is also a good idea to keep a record of the criteria you used to select and reject sources.

Why do this? Monitoring your searching will help you effectively modify your searches to be more effective, using the strategies discussed above (and in Chapters 7 and 8). If you find that your results are too narrow (producing too few results or results that are too specific), you can systematically broaden your strategy. If they are too broad (not sufficiently focused), you can systematically narrow your strategy. This should enable you effectively to find targeted relevant information.

At later stages of your work, you will also need to check to make sure you have not missed any important relevant information. If you cannot clearly recall the details of your searches earlier on, you may end up duplicating much of this early searching effort.

Monitoring and recording your searching activity may be helpful in assisting your lecturer in providing instructive feedback on how you could have improved your search, and how you can develop more effective strategies in the future.

Summary

In this chapter we explored the function of a literature review and how to conduct one. We saw how its role differs depending on whether you are engaged in an essay or a piece of original research. In the case of an essay, the literature is a key source of the building blocks you will use to create your answer. In the case of original research, reviewing the literature can often be the source of your research question in that it may reveal a gap in our knowledge that your research can go some way towards filling. It also provides a context in which to discuss your findings.

The chapter then focused on strategies for conducting a literature review, starting with an initial exploratory survey of your topic. At this stage, it can be useful to use a wide variety of search tools and techniques in order to establish a basic overview of what the topic is all about. The next stage, however, is a more rigorous search for high-quality information sources. A number of strategies for conducting this stage of your search were introduced.

This latter stage requires a precise analysis of the information required for your essay or research question, and the selection of the search tools and techniques that are most likely to be able to find it. A number of search strategies were introduced, including ways of narrowing your search if it is too broad and broadening it if it is too narrow. It was also recommended that you monitor your search activity so that you can improve it over time.

The next chapter will examine the different types of information that you can use both in your literature review and more generally in coming to understand a new topic. It will also introduce the range of different search tools that are most appropriate to finding them.

SIX

Information sources and search tools

WHY YOU NEED TO KNOW THIS

- You need to be familiar with the variety of different types of *information source* available to you, ranging from textbooks through journal articles and conference papers to research theses and dissertations.
- You need to know the circumstances in which each of these different types of information source is appropriate. It is important that you identify the types of source that will be most appropriate for the type and level of work on which you are engaged.
- You also need to be familiar with the wide range of *search tools* available.
- Some are more appropriate than others for finding particular types of information, and you need to be able to select those that are most appropriate for finding the information you need at any given time.

Types of information source

The selection of information sources presented here is arranged in order of generality – from least to most specialised.

Social networking sites

Social networking and sharing sites are not a mainstream source of academic content. However, they can be useful for:

- keeping up to date with academic-related news;
- finding and maintaining personal academic contacts; and
- finding some academic content (an increasing amount of educational material is available on academic networking sites and on sites such as *YouTube*).

Social networking and sharing sites are incorporating an increasing amount of educational material. They include social networking sites such as *Academia.edu*, (http://www.academia.edu/) and *ResearchGATE* (http://www.researchgate.net/) where academics can not only post information about themselves and their activities, but also details of and full text copies of research publications. *ResearchGATE* has a scholarly search engine giving access to bibliographic details of over 35,000,000 documents from sources including *Pubmed, Citeseer, IEEE, NASA, RePeC* and *ArXiV*. It also offers a 'similar abstract' search which finds documents that best match an abstract or section of text that you submit to it, and a 'journal finder' which also takes an abstract and finds journals most relevant to the contents of the abstract. Other networks include MyNetResearch (http://www.mynetresearch.com/).

General social networking and sharing sites such as *Facebook* and *YouTube* can also be useful sources of information. *Facebook* can offer academic contacts, news and links to documents – particularly in the form of publically accessible groups set up, for example, by universities, university departments and research groups such as *Methodspace.com: Connecting the Research Community* (https://www.facebook.com/methodspace). *YouTube* also offers academic content. See, for example, *Sage Publications Channel* (http://www.youtube.com/SAGEPublications), which offers research-related videos.

Encyclopaedias

> - Encyclopaedias are particularly helpful if you are new to a topic and want a relatively short introduction.
> - Articles will typically provide an overview of the topic, outlining its main components and themes. This can be useful in helping you map out the topic in broad terms, before going on to focus on aspects in more detail using other types of information source.

Encyclopaedias are publications that contain many articles written on a range of topics. General encyclopaedias cover many different areas of human knowledge. However, there are many specialised encyclopaedias which focus on a particular subject. Encyclopaedia articles may be relatively static or dynamic in relation to the frequency of their updating.

Some encyclopaedias publish the names of the authors of their articles, whilst others are authored anonymously. In some, articles are peer reviewed by experts, whilst in others they are not. Clearly, these differences have important implications for quality and authority, and these are discussed below.

There are an increasing number of *online* general and specialised encyclopaedias. An example of a free, online, specialised, dynamically updated, peer-reviewed encyclopaedia is the *Stanford Encyclopedia of Philosophy* (http://plato.stanford.edu/). This has links from its home page to details of its credentials. Its academic quality and authority are vouched for by the fact that:

- it is hosted by Stanford University (stanford.edu); and
- there is a link from the homepage to details of the Editorial Board, which gives an extensive list of the academic Subject Editors.

Wikipedia is the prime example of a free general (in the sense of covering all subject areas), online, dynamically updated encyclopaedia. However, there has been much criticism of *Wikipedia*, and some university educators advocate avoiding its use for academic work.

THINK

Why do you think some university teachers advise so strongly against using *Wikipedia* for academic work? Do you agree with them? Is there any way *Wikipedia* can be helpful for academic work?

There are a number of distinct problems associated with using *Wikipedia* for academic work. These include the fact that:

- anyone can write a *Wikipedia* article (although they must first register as a user);
- anyone can edit and change a *Wikipedia* article;
- there have been many cases of mischievous and malevolent editing of articles; and
- although strong in some topic areas (e.g. science and technology), it is less so in others.

Therefore, in principle, you can never be sure that a *Wikipedia* article is accurate or authoritative. However, these disadvantages are to some extent countered by the fact that:

- many *Wikipedia* articles have references at the end, so you can 'triangulate' the evidence – in other words, check what is being said by using other sources;
- *Wikipedia* articles can often provide a good current overview of a topic and an excellent starting point – so long as you corroborate the information from other peer-reviewed sources; and
- *Wikipedia* is particularly strong in some areas (e.g. science and technology).

It is worth noting *Wikipedia*'s own caveats:

> Articles are never complete. They are continually edited and improved over time. In general, this results in an upward trend of quality and a growing consensus over a neutral representation of information ... Users should be aware that not all articles are of encyclopedic quality from the start: they may contain false or debatable information ... Others may, for a while, become caught up in a heavily unbalanced viewpoint which can take some time – months perhaps – to achieve better balanced coverage of their subject. [...] Some articles contain statements which have not yet been fully cited. Others will later be augmented with new sections. Some information will be considered by later contributors to be insufficiently founded and, therefore, may be removed or expounded. While the overall trend is toward improvement, it is important to use Wikipedia carefully if it is intended to be used as a research source, since individual articles will, by their nature, vary in quality and maturity.[12]

> Wikipedia's radical openness means that any given article may be, at any given moment, in a bad state: for example, it could be in the middle of a large edit or it could have been recently vandalized.[13]

So should you use Wikipedia *– and if so, when and how?*

Well, the first thing you should do is check with your lecturer about using *Wikipedia*. As noted above, some educators feel strongly that it is not appropriate to use it in academic work. If this is the advice you get, then follow it. At the end of the day, your lecturer will be marking your essay, project or dissertation, and ignoring his or her advice could adversely affect the evaluation of your work – and your mark. If you do not receive such advice, then consider using *Wikipedia,* but not as a source to use directly in your work, but rather as a stepping stone to other sources.

If *Wikipedia* contains an article covering, or relevant to, your coursework topic, then consider it as provisional – potentially useful – knowledge. This is rather like 'pencilling in' a date in your diary for a meeting. You need to confirm it, but the fact that you have provisionally agreed data can actually be very useful, even if subsequently you have to change it.

Follow up the references often given at the end of a *Wikipedia* article. However, also do your own searching to find evidence that corroborates what you have found there. The references you include in your work should be to authoritative, peer-reviewed sources.

---

[12]Using Wikipedia as a research tool (n.d.). In Wikipedia. Retrieved July 28, 2010, from http://en.wikipedia.org/wiki/Wikipedia:About#Using_Wikipedia_as_a_research_tool

[13]Researching with Wikipedia (n.d.). In Wikipedia. Retrieved July 28, 2010, from http://en.wikipedia.org/wiki/Wikipedia:Researching_with_Wikipedia

Handbooks and manuals...

Handbooks and manuals are particularly useful when:

- you are to some extent familiar with the topic and want to consult an authoritative, 'ready reference' source of information on key concepts, and particularly techniques, in an area of knowledge; and
- answering 'How do I do this?' types of query.

Handbooks and manuals are generally single volume, comprehensive compendiums of information on a particular topic. They are designed to provide 'ready reference' access to key concepts, knowledge and techniques in relation to a topic, rather than being designed to be read from beginning to end.

A 'handbook of quantitative research', for example, typically would introduce principles of research design, techniques for data collection and analysis, and key concepts such as validity, reliability, objectivity, etc. Handbooks and manuals can vary from basic to advanced level.

The terms 'handbook' and 'manual' are also often used to mean pretty much the same thing. However, when they are distinguished, 'manual' is often used to signify a source that explains how something works and/or how to use something (i.e. it focuses on procedural knowledge).

Teaching texts

Basic introductory texts are particularly useful when:

- you are new to a topic;
- you want to learn in a structured way from a source specifically designed to teach people who are new to the topic; and
- the topic is broad, well defined and fairly well established (as opposed to more specialised and leading-edge topics typically covered in, for example, conference papers).

Textbooks are books prepared specifically with a teaching function. They adopt a structured, pedagogic approach. They are usually written for a well-established and defined topic. They are often adopted by or associated with a particular course, in which case they are likely to be listed in required or recommended reading lists. If they are core texts for your course, they are likely to be available in multiple copies from your university library.

They are generally explicitly targeted at a particular level of study and this may be indicated explicitly in the text itself. Increasingly, open texts are freely available on the web. For details of how to find open texts, see the 'Types of search tool' section later in this chapter.

Basic texts are often written by one author. This can bring advantages similar to those associated with having a series of lectures delivered by the same lecturer – as opposed to a series of visiting speakers coming in every week. These advantages include the fact that the chapters (like the weekly lectures) may be more closely integrated, each building carefully on the previous ones. One person has carefully selected key aspects of the topic for you to provide a coherent and consistently presented overview of the topic as well as sufficient detail to provide a good introduction.

Advanced texts

More advanced texts are suitable when:

- you want to explore a topic in some detail and at more than a basic level from a book written by experts in the topic;
- you want at the same time to be guided by a knowledgeable editor (or author) who has carefully selected and sequenced the chapters presented to you in the book. This approach may be contrasted with searching on your own for journal articles and conference papers on different aspects of the topic (as discussed below). Using a text is appropriate when you want to benefit from the selection and sequencing of information by a good editor (or author); and
- you also want to explore the area in more detail than is typical with the types of 'reviews of research' discussed below. Advanced texts tend to be longer and more detailed than these.

At more advanced levels, texts may be more specialised, often edited with a series of chapters, each authored by an expert in that particular aspect of the topic. This can bring both advantages and disadvantages. The potential disadvantage is that edited texts may sometimes lack the consistent style and careful cumulative presentation of information that builds carefully from chapter to chapter and is characteristic of a good basic text authored by one expert. Nevertheless, a well edited book does contain a selection of topics carefully chosen by the editor to constitute a coherent view of the state-of-the-art in the topic.

The more advanced a text is, the less identifiable it may be as a *teaching* text. There is a point at which an 'advanced text' shades into just 'a book on a specialised topic' or a research monograph.

Journal articles

Journal articles are particularly useful when:

- you are working at a more advanced level than coming to grips with the basics of a topic (for which textbooks would be more appropriate);

(Continued)

Journal articles are the basic fuel of academic work that requires you to engage in independent research – beyond the basic level where teaching texts and other instructional materials are more appropriate. They can vary in the level of expertise required to read them. Their purpose is generally to communicate the latest research findings and ideas to fellow researchers and practitioners in the field. You would typically use many journal articles in one essay or report.

There is a skill in scanning these to find one at an appropriate level for you. Don't look at some journals and decide they are all too advanced – try others. Having said this, if you really are new to a topic at undergraduate level, then it may be best to start with a textbook since journal articles are not designed to teach, but rather to speak to fellow researchers or practitioners.

They generally present research results relating to a particular topic, or a review of recent research in the topic (see also 'Reviews of research' below). They often contain literature reviews early on to set the article in context. Such literature review sections usually give a good assessment of the state-of-the-art of the subject.

Different journals are devoted to different topic or subject areas and contain articles that all have this focus. There are different levels of journal, from the highly specialised ones aimed at experts to the less esoteric and more accessible ones suitable for less experienced readers.

Each journal article has an abstract of its contents. This means that you can quickly scan through a journal to see if it is at an appropriate level for you and relevant to your interests. If so, identify articles that are useful for your particular needs.

Depending on the nature of the journal, you can sometimes find conceptual articles which present a critical overview of the state of knowledge in a particular topic, along with ideas about future directions. Other articles may present the results of empirical research. You can sometimes find review articles which overlap to an extent with the 'reviews of research' discussed below.

As well as journals requiring a subscription, there are an increasing number of freely available open access journals in a range of subjects.

Reviews of research

- For a more gentle introduction to the topic, and to research in the topic, you should prefer an appropriate textbook or research monograph.
- Reviews of research are also extremely useful in enabling you to identify further, more detailed reading in relation to different aspects of the subject.
- They may also explicitly or implicitly indicate gaps in our knowledge that may provide you with ideas in devising a research question, if you are working in independent study mode requiring you to devise your own question.

Reviews of research may be found in journal articles as well as separately published reviews such as the *Annual Review of Information Science and Technology* or the *Annual Review* series covering many disciplines and subjects (http://arjournals.annualreviews.org/action/showJournals).

You will generally find a review of relevant research literature at the beginning of a journal article, whether this is a conceptual article (discussing ideas and trends) or an article reporting empirical research. These reviews can provide a very useful overview, and enable you to follow up more detailed reading on the various aspects of the topic via the references quoted in them. Generally, reviews of research at the beginning of journal articles – as indeed the articles themselves – are not designed for the beginner, but rather the intermediate to advanced reader.

You will also find reviews of relevant research literature at the beginning of research dissertations and theses. A PhD or Master's thesis or dissertation will generally report a specialised, relatively narrowly-focused piece of research in great detail. However, the reviews of research literature they contain, typically in a separate section entitled 'Literature review', may still be quite broad and useful since one of the functions of the review is to set the work in its broader context.

Conference papers (see below) may also contain a review of relevant research literature – but not necessarily so. Where one is included, it is generally shorter than one found in a journal article. Conference papers themselves are often relatively short compared to journal articles, and are usually specialised with a narrow focus since they are designed to inform other researchers or practitioners working in the field who are already familiar with the context and relevant literature relating to the topic of the paper.

You can often find journal articles whose prime focus is to provide a review of the research literature on a particular topic. In other words, rather than having a literature review at the beginning of an article that goes on to present other information, the review is the main content of the article.

Note that some journals with 'review' or even 'review of research' in their title do not *necessarily* contain reviews of research in the sense just described. Rather, they may contain 'normal' journal articles relating to the subject of the journal.

Conference papers

Conference papers are particularly useful when:

- you want leading-edge thoughts or research results relating to your topic; and
- you want thoughts or research results on specialised topics written by researchers or practitioners for their peers.

They are less useful when:

- you are very new to your topic and want a gentler introduction to it; and
- you want a more general introduction to the topic rather than information focusing on a particular specialised aspect of it.

Conference papers are papers presented at meetings of researchers in a particular field of study or practitioners in a particular profession. They are often published in the 'proceedings' of the conference. Like journal articles, they present original research findings or thoughts relating to a particular current issue. They tend to be specialised – produced by experts (researchers or practitioners depending on the conference) for other experts. They are generally focused on specialised topics for a specialist audience, and present leading-edge thinking and very recent research results from ongoing research projects. They also tend to be shorter than journal articles. Consequently, they may not offer as complete a literature review and context-setting information as you will tend to find in journal articles. Bear in mind that conference papers are not always as self-explanatory as journal articles, since they are often designed to accompany a presentation by the author where questions can be asked.

This is not the case when authors are invited to write an expanded version of their conference paper for publication in the proceedings, when a conference paper may take on more of the characteristics of a journal article. Sometimes the organisers of a conference will, by arrangement with the publishers of a journal, publish such expanded versions of the best papers from their conference in a special issue of the journal.

Research theses and reports

Research theses can be useful in that:

- they present the results of a substantial piece of research on a specialised topic;
- they provide an extensive literature review relating to the topic;

(Continued)

(Continued)

- they also represent a detailed case study of the choice, rationale and successful implementation of a particular research methodology (useful if you are exploring which methodology to use in your own research); and
- they allow you to examine the fine detail of a research project. If you are using the findings of someone else's thesis as a building block in your own research, particularly if you are working at PhD level, you may need to examine detailed aspects of it – e.g. to evaluate its validity in relation to your own work.

Research theses are not appropriate if you are are new to a topic, and require a gentler, less specialised introduction to or overview of a topic.

Research theses and dissertations are reports of original research conducted by people working for a recognised academic qualification. The terms 'thesis' and 'dissertation' are sometimes used to differentiate between (a) undergraduate or Master's and (b) PhD (doctoral) level work. However, the terms may be used conversely in different academic institutions and countries to indicate these different levels. When you are searching for research theses or dissertations, the details you find should indicate whether they are Master's or PhD level. Undergraduate theses/dissertations are not generally indexed by the major search tools.

A thesis (or dissertation) is a report of a substantial piece of original research. It will present the results of some focused research on a specific topic. A PhD thesis will report a more extensive and rigorously assessed piece of research extending over a number of years. A Master's thesis is often undertaken as part of a one-year programme of studies that also entails teaching. It is therefore not as extensive – or of such an advanced level – as a PhD thesis.

A thesis will generally include a relatively long and comprehensive review of related literature. It will include an abstract, a 'conclusions' section, allowing relatively quick access to knowledge of what the thesis is about and what the main results are, and usually a section outlining the implications of the research for what future research needs to be done. This may be useful when you are exploring possible topics for your own research.

Often, you may encounter PhD research in the form of a journal article or conference paper summarising the research or some aspect of it. If having read this you wish to 'drill down' to explore the details of the research, you may be able to access the full thesis. If this is not immediately available in your university library, you may be able to obtain it on inter-library loan.

If you are yourself engaged in PhD or advanced Master's level work, and a research thesis you have found presents findings that are important to your own work (e.g. your research question is derived from them or you wish to build on them), you may need to examine the research in detail (e.g. to learn about or critically assess some aspect of the methodology used).

Note that the term 'research report' is used more loosely and can refer to almost any kind of report of a piece of research. These can vary from short and relatively easily intelligible reports to more esoteric and highly detailed reports of research conducted by an organisation or an individual. The term does not imply that the report has been peer reviewed or that the research has been subject to academic scrutiny, although it may well have been. Scholarly search tools such as *Google Scholar, SciVerse Scopus* and *Web of Knowledge* are likely to retrieve peer-reviewed reports. General search engines like *Google* are equally likely to find research reports, but of more mixed quality. You should even more carefully evaluate the authority and credibility of a research report if it is not an academic thesis/dissertation or published in a peer-reviewed source.

Datasets and data analyses

Data are of course central to research.

- In many cases you will encounter analyses and interpretations of data in journal articles, conference papers, research theses and books.
- However, you may also find it useful to find and present data in a less already-interpreted form, and to interpret them yourself in order to build an argument.
- For research at Master's and PhD level, you will normally be expected to gather your own original data. However, theses based on the analysis of existing datasets are by no means uncommon. You should discuss any such plans with your lecturer.

Data are available via the web in various forms. They may be quantitative (e.g. the United Nations Economic Commission for Europe (UNECE) *Statistical Database* at http://w3.unece.org/pxweb/Dialog/) or qualitative (e.g. the Economic and Social Data Service's *Qualidata* website at http://www.esds.ac.uk/qualidata/). Data may be available in analysed and summarised form (e.g. the UK National Statistics' *Publication Hub Gateway to UK National Statistics* at http://www.statistics.gov.uk/hub/index.html) or as datasets available for you to download and analyse yourself (e.g. the UK government's data website http://data.gov.uk/).

Types of search tool

You should be aware of the range of different types of search tool so that you can use the ones most appropriate to your particular needs. Some of the different types of tool are given in the overview classification shown below. The rest of this section will describe each type of tool shown in the classification. The tools described are freely available over the web, except for those marked '[subscription-based]' or '[commercially available]'.

A. General (not specifically academic) web-based sources

    a. Directories
    b. Search engines

        i. Single search engines
        ii. Metasearch engines

    c. Searchable (not specifically academic) encyclopaedias

B. Academic sources

    a. Directories (allowing access by browsing)
    b. Search engines/databases (allowing search by keyword)

        i. Multi-source (journals, conferences, academic books, etc.)

            1. Allowing search across all subject areas
            2. Allowing filtering by subject area

        ii. Specific to particular types of source

            1. Journal articles

                a. Multi-publisher
                b. Particular publisher

            2. Books
            3. Conference papers
            4. Reviews of research
            5. Research theses
            6. Data
            7. Other types of source

    c. Searchable academic encyclopaedias

A. General (not specifically academic) web-based sources

There are a number of search tools that are general in the sense of not focusing exclusively on scholarly information sources. Whilst they may retrieve some high-quality academic sources, they are not optimised so to do. As noted in Chapter 5, such sources can be useful when you are very new to a topic and want to establish a provisional overview of what it is all about – before going on to concentrate on high-quality sources that you can use as evidence in your work.

a. Directories

Directories allow you to browse pre-defined subject categories of information generally pre-selected by human editors. The number of information sources to which they enable access is less than that available via search engines which automatically index vast volumes of information. Examples include the *Open Directory Project* (ODP) (http://www.dmoz.org/), and the *Yahoo Directory* (http://dir.yahoo.com/).

b. Search engines

There are a great many general search engines designed to find information on the web, displaying a range of different search facilities and techniques. A number of these will be discussed in Chapter 7.

i. Single search engines

Single search engines compile their own indexes of information on the web. Examples include *Google* (http://www.google.com/), *Bing* (http://www.bing.com/), *Exalead* (http://www.exalead.com/search/), etc.

ii. Metasearch engines

Metasearch engines essentially provide a single interface to a number of other search engines. Examples include *Yippy* (formerly *Clusty*) (http://search.yippy.com/), *Dogpile* (http://www.dogpile.com/), *Excite* (http://www.excite.com/), *Metacrawler* (http://www.metacrawler.com/), etc.

c. Searchable encyclopaedias (not specifically academic)

There are a number of large searchable general encyclopaedias online, the best known and largest of which is *Wikipedia* (http://www.wikipedia.org/). Other online encyclopaedias exist, such as *Encyclopedia.com* (http://www.encyclopedia.com/) and *Infoplease* (http://www.infoplease.com/encyclopedia/).

B. Academic sources

A range of search tools focus specifically on scholarly information sources, and these are the tools that will help you find high-quality sources that you can use and reference directly in your work.

a. Directories

Like general directories, academically focused directories give access to sources that have been selected by humans – rather than crawled and indexed automatically by machine as is the case with the large search engines. Academically focused directories include *Intute* (http://www.intute.ac.uk/), which as well as enabling browsing by subject headings also allows keyword searching. However, although still available, the website is no longer being updated after July 2011 due to the discontinuation of Joint Information Systems Comittee (JISC) funding. It is still included in this book as an interesting example of an academically focused directory offering browse and search access to human-selected resources.

b. Search engines/databases

There are a number of academically focused search tools which provide access to high-quality scholarly information.

i. Tools covering multiple types of information source

A number of these will search across a range of types of information source, including journal articles, conference papers, books and research theses.

1. Multi-subject tools

These allow you to search across all subject areas, for example *Google Scholar* (http://scholar.google.com/), *SciVerse Scopus* [subscription-based], *Web of Knowledge* [subscription-based] and *Intute* (http://www.intute.ac.uk/) which, as noted above, allows directory-based browsing as well as keyword searching. Also as noted above, it is no longer being updated. *Scirus* (http://www.scirus.com/) and *Scientific WebPlus* [subscription-based] are science-specific scholarly search engines. *OpenDOAR* (http://www.opendoar.org/) and the *UK Institutional Repository Search* (http://irs.mimas.ac.uk/demonstrator/) provide single interfaces to search a range of open access academic digital repositories across all subject areas.

2. Subject-specific search tools

A range of tools allow you to restrict your search to particular subject areas. As well as allowing multi-subject searching, the tools listed in the previous section also allow the option of restricting search by subject.

Google Scholar (http://scholar.google.com/) allows you to filter your search using the following categories:
> *Business, Administration, Finance, and Economics*
> *Physics, Astronomy, and Planetary Science*
> *Chemistry and Materials Science*
> *Social Sciences, Arts, and Humanities*
> *Engineering, Computer Science, and Mathematics*

Web of Knowledge allows the following subject filters:
> *Science & Technology*
> *Social Sciences*
> *Arts & Humanities*

However, it also analyses your search results into finer-grained subject categories and allows you to filter the results by one or more of these.

SciVerse Scopus subject filters are:

    Life Sciences
    Health Sciences
    Physical Sciences
    Social Sciences & Humanities

Like *Web of Knowledge*, *SciVerse Scopus* also analyses your search results into finer-grained subject categories.

Intute (http://www.intute.ac.uk/) allows the following choices[14]:

All subjects	Humanities
Agriculture, food and forestry	Law
Architecture and planning	Mathematics and computer science
Biological sciences	Medicine including dentistry
Business and management	Modern languages and area studies
Communication and media studies	Nursing, midwifery and allied health
Creative and performing arts	Physical sciences
Education and research methods	Psychology
Engineering	Social sciences
Geography and environment	Veterinary medicine

Additionally there are a large number of search tools which are specific to particular subject areas. Consult your library's website. An example from my own university can be seen at: http://www.shef.ac.uk/library/subjects/

ii. Tools specific to particular types of source

A number of search tools allow you to filter your search according to the type of information source, for example, books, journal articles, conference papers or research theses.

1. Journal articles

(a) Multi-publisher

Intute (http://www.intute.ac.uk/), *SciVerse Scopus* [subscription-based], *Web of Knowledge* and *Web of Science* [subscription-based] and *Scirus* (http://www.scirus.com/), *OpenDOAR* (http://www.opendoar.org/) and the *UK Institutional Repository Search* (http://irs.mimas.ac.uk/demonstrator/) all allow you to filter your search results by document type, including, journal article. *OpenDOAR* and the *UK Institutional Repository Search* provide access to academic repositories. The *Directory of Open Access Journals* (http://www.doaj.org/) allows searching of freely available open access journals that are subject to peer review or editorial quality control.

---

[14]As noted on page 94, *Intute* is no longer being updated.

(b) Particular publishers

A number of individual publishers offer search tools covering their own publications. Although other resources may be included, they offer searching across a large range of their own journal titles. *Wiley Online Library* (formerly *Wiley InterScience*) (http://onlinelibrary.wiley.com/), for example, is a collection of resources covering the humanities, social science and life, health and physical sciences. It offers a *document type* filter, including journals. Emerald's *Advanced Search* (http://www.emeraldinsight.com/search.htm) allows searching by journal.

2. Books

Google Books (http://books.google.com/) is a book-specific search engine. It allows some searching within books and, where permitted, displays snippets of text to show your search terms in context. In some cases more extensive sections of text are shown. *Scirus* (http://www.scirus.com/) allows searches to be restricted to books.

Don't forget your own *university library catalogue*, which will enable you search for books that are available in your own university. In many cases, you can find out online if a copy is available. You can also request books and other items not in stock via inter-library loan. You should check with your library for procedures and restrictions relating to this service.

It is also possible to search for books in other libraries using search tools such as *Copac* (http://copac.ac.uk/), which gives access via a single interface to the collections of member institutions of Research Libraries UK (RLUK). These include the British Library, the National Library of Scotland, the National Library of Wales, and the National Art Library at the Victoria and Albert Museum. *OpenDOAR* (http://www.opendoar.org/) and *the UK Institutional Repository Search* (http://irs.mimas.ac.uk/demonstrator/) allow searches across academic repositories to be filtered according to document type, including books. *WorldCat* (http://www.worldcat.org/) allows you to search for books in more than 10,000 libraries worldwide and locate the library nearest to you that holds a copy.

Individual university library catalogues are also accessible online, such as that of Cambridge University Library (http://www.lib.cam.ac.uk/newton/). Reference management software such as *EndNote* (http://www.endnote.com/) [commercially available] also allows searching of remote libraries from a single interface. Reference management software is discussed in Chapter 12.

An increasing number of freely accessible 'open textbooks' are becoming available. An example of a catalogue of open textbooks may be found at the *Student Public Interest Research Groups* website at http://www.studentpirgs.org/open-textbooks/catalog. *Intute* (http://www.intute.ac.uk/) also allows searching specifically for *e-books* and *learning materials*. The *Open Educational Resources Commons* (http://www.oercommons.org/) allows searching for open leaning resources by subject area and educational level.

One way of locating handbooks and manuals is to search a scholarly search tool such as *Google Scholar* for documents with *handbook* or *manual* plus the topic in the title. For example:

allintitle: handbook OR manual psychology

3. Conference papers

SciVerse Scopus [subscription-based], *Web of Knowledge* [subscription-based] and *Web of Science* [subscription-based], and *Scirus* (http://www.scirus.com/) all allow you to filter your search results by document type, including conference paper. In *Web of Knowledge,* the appropriate document type is *Meeting. Web of Science* offers the document types *Proceedings paper, Meeting abstract* and *Meeting summary. OpenDOAR* (http://www.opendoar.org/) and *the UK Institutional Repository Search* (http://irs.mimas.ac.uk/demonstrator/) allow searches across academic repositories for conference papers.

4. Reviews of research

SciVerse Scopus [subscription-based], *Web of Knowledge* [subscription-based] and *Web of Science* [subscription-based] all allow you to filter your search results by document type, including *Reviews. Intute* (http://www.intute.ac.uk/) allows searching for the document type *Systematic reviews*, which tend to relate to health and medicine. Its *Review* document type does not retrieve documents restricted to reviews of research.

Another way of locating reviews of research is to search a scholarly search tool such as *Google Scholar* for documents with '*review of research*' plus the topic in the title. For example:

allintitle: "review of research" psychology

5. Research theses and dissertations

Scirus (http://www.scirus.com/) allows the option of searching specifically for *Theses and Dissertations*. Other search tools use the *Scirus* search engine to provide a search interface devoted to electronic thesis and dissertations, such as the *Networked Digital Library of Theses and Dissertations (NDLTD)*'s *Scirus ETD search* (http://www.ndltd. org/serviceproviders/scirus-etd-search). *Index to theses* [subscription-based] covers higher degree theses from universities in Great Britain and Ireland. *Dissertation abstracts* [subscription-based] covers American theses. *OpenDOAR* (http://www. opendoar.org/) and *the UK Institutional Repository Search* (http://irs.mimas.ac. uk/demonstrator/) allow searches across academic repositories for theses and dissertations.

6. Data

The Economic and Social Data Service's *Qualidata* website (http://www.esds.ac.uk/ qualidata/) offers access to social science qualitative datasets. *OpenDOAR* (http://

www.opendoar.org/) allows searching across academic repositories for datasets. *Intute* (http://www.intute.ac.uk/) offers the option of filtering searches to one or both of the document types *Datasets* and *Statistics*. UK government statistics can be found at the UK National Statistics' *Publication Hub Gateway to UK National Statistics* (http://www.statistics.gov.uk/hub/index.html) and the UK government's data website (http://data.gov.uk/).

Other notable websites offering access to data and statistics include: the UK Data Archive, covering data from research institutions, public organisations and companies and government departments (http://www.data-archive.ac.uk/); EDINA, the JISC national academic data centre (http://edina.ac.uk/); the *Census Dissemination Unit* (http://cdu.mimas.ac.uk/) and *Census.ac.uk* (http://census.ac.uk/), which provide access to UK census statistics; the European Commission's *Eurostat* website (http://epp. eurostat.ec.europa.eu/portal/page/portal/eurostat/home/), covering European statistics; the United Nations Statistics Division *Statistical Databases* website (http://unstats. un.org/unsd/databases.htm); the International Monetary Fund *Data and Statistics* website (http://www.imf.org/external/data.htm); the World Health Organisation *Data and Statistics* website (http://www.who.int/research/en/); and the United Nations Economic Commission for Europe (UNECE) *Statistical Database* website (http:// w3.unece.org/pxweb/Dialog/).

The U.S. Census Bureau offers a software package called *DataFerrett* (http:// dataferrett.census.gov/) which allows access to the *DataWeb* – a network of online data libraries covering demographic, economic, environmental, health (and more) US-based datasets.

7. Other types of source

Some tools allow you to choose from a wide range of filters which include other types of information source. For example, *Web of Knowledge* [subscription-based] allows you to refine your search results by limiting them to one or more document type categories including:

Abstract	*Government publication*
Art and literature	*Legistation*
Article	*Letter*
Bibliography	*Meeting*
Biography	*News*
Book	*Patent*
Case report	*Reference Material*
Clinical trial	*Report*
Correction	*Retraction*
Editorial	*Review*
	Thesis/Dissertation

Web of Science [subscription-based] allows you to apply the following filters. You can specify a document type as part of your search and also filter your search results by one or more.

Article	Meeting Abstract
Art Exhibit Review	Meeting Summary
Bibliography	Meeting-Abstract
Biographical-Item	Music Performance Review
Book Review	Music Score
Chronology	Music Score Review
Correction	News Item
Correction, Addition	Note
Dance Performance Review	Poetry
Database Review	Proceedings Paper
Discussion	Record Review
Editorial Material	Reprint
Excerpt	Review
Fiction, Creative Prose	Script
Film Review	Software Review
Hardware Review	TV Review, Radio Review
Item About An Individual	TV Review, Radio Review, Video Review
Letter	Theatre Review

SciVerse Scopus [subscription-based] document type filters include:

Article	Erratum
Article in press	Letter
Business article or press	Note
Conference paper	Review
Conference review	Short survey
Editorial	

Intute (http://www.intute.ac.uk/) allows you to filter your search by the following resource types:

Archives	Government publications
Arts projects	Images
Associations	Interactive resources
Bibliographic databases	Journals – contents and abstracts
Bibliographic material	Journals – full-text
Biographical material	Law reports
Blogs	Learning materials
Case studies	Lecture notes
Collections	Legislation
Companies	Libraries
Datasets	Mailing lists and discussion groups
E-books	Maps
Events	Moving images
Exhibitions and galleries	Museums
Field guides	News
Field studies	Non-bibliographic databases
Government bodies	Non-profit organisations

(Continued)

(Continued)

Other organisations
Papers/reports/articles/texts
Patents/standards
Patient information leaflets
Practice guidelines
Primary source
Product information
Professional organisations
Reference sources
Research centres and projects
Resource guides and directories

Reviews
Secondary source
Sequence databases
Software
Sound
Specimen databases
Statistics
Systematic reviews
Think tanks
Treaties
Tutorials

Scirus (http://www.scirus.com/) offers the following filters:

Abstracts
Articles
Books
Company homepages
Conferences

Patents
Preprints
Scientist homepages
Theses and dissertations

OpenDOAR (http://www.opendoar.org/). Searching the contents of the multiple academic repositories covered by *OpenDOAR* does not allow filtering by document type. However, you can search for repositories (which you can then access and search) using the following categories:

Articles
Books
Conferences
Datasets
Learning objects
Multimedia

Patents
References
Software
Special
Theses
Unpublished

The UK *Institutional Repository Search* (http://irs.mimas.ac.uk/demonstrator/) offers the following filters:

Art object
Article
Artifact
Audio
Book
Book part
Case study
Communication
Conference object
Contribution to periodical
Crystal structure
Dataset
Design
Dictionary

Doctoral thesis
Exhibition
Image
Journal
Learning object
Manual
Manuscript
Map
Master thesis
Moving image
Musical score
Patent
Performance
Plan

(Continued)

Preprint	*Sound*
Presentation	*Text*
Project	*Web site*
Report	*Working paper*
Software	

It also allows filtering according to whether the sources are:

Non peer reviewed

Not known/not applicable

Peer reviewed

c. Searchable academic encyclopaedias

Wikipedia (http://en.wikipedia.org/) contains many articles likely to be of value in academic work. However, see pages 83–84 for a discussion of the problems and limitations as well as the benefits associated with using *Wikipedia*. An example of subscription-based online access to reference works including specialised academic encyclopaedias is *Sage Reference Online* (www.sage-ereference.com/) [subscription-based].

One way of locating encyclopaedias is to search a scholarly search tool such as *Google Scholar* for documents with *encyclopaedia* plus the topic in the title. For example:

allintitle: encyclopedia psychology

or

allintitle: encyclopedia OR encyclopaedia psychology

Figure 6.1 maps broad types of information source and search tool on to the 'Credibility of information sources' model previously presented in Figure 4.1.

Examples of search tools shown in the side panel to the right in the figure are selected to illustrate differences in the extent to which they enable the finding of *peer-reviewed* information. General search engines appear towards the back of the fig-ure since, even though they *may* find peer-reviewed information amongst what they retrieve, they are not particular geared to this type of search.

General directory-based tools are characterised, as previously noted, by selection and review by human editors. However, although this does introduce an element of quality control, it does not equate to peer review. The human editors involved are often enthusiastic amateurs rather than recognised experts in the subject areas for which they are responsible.

Academic search tools such as *Google Scholar*, *Web of Knowledge*, *SciVerse Scopus*, *Scirus* and *Scientific WebPlus* are specifically geared to finding good quality academic sources. As noted in the previous section, *Google Scholar*, *Scirus* and *Scientific WebPlus* are freely available on the web. *Web of Knowledge* and *SciVerse Scopus* are fee-based, but universities will generally subscribe to these or equivalent tools. *Google Scholar*, *Web of Knowledge* and *SciVerse Scopus* will be introduced in detail in Chapter 8.

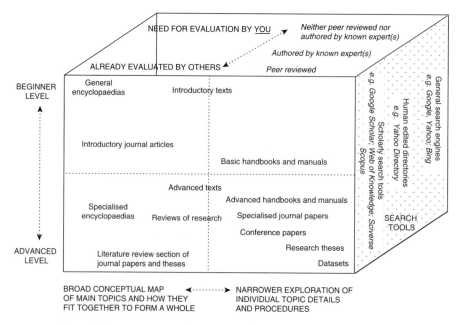

Figure 6.1 Types of information source and search tool

Summary

Different types of information source may make different types of contribution to your academic work. For example, textbooks generally present knowledge that is well established and widely agreed upon by experts in the topic. It is usually presented in a way that is accessible to people relatively new to the topic. Conference papers, on the other hand, represent leading-edge information and address a specialist audience of experts already working on the area.

The suitability of different types of information will depend on whether, for example, you are writing a basic-level essay or an advanced critical review. This chapter introduced a wide range of such types of information, and indicated their different potential contribution to your academic work.

The chapter went on to introduce a range of different types of search tool, including both general search tools and academic search tools that specialise in finding high-quality scholarly information. The academic search tools were categorised in terms of the different types of information source to which they are particularly suited to finding. Figure 6.1 mapped types of information source on to levels of study (beginner to advanced) and on to the previously introduced components of learning (description building and procedure building).

The next chapter will explore in detail the search facilities available within both scholarly and more general search tools. If you take the time to become familiar with them, this can greatly improve both the speed and effectiveness of your searching.

SEVEN

Mapping search approaches & techniques to information needs

WHY YOU NEED TO KNOW THIS

- Just as different types of information source (introduced in the previous chapter) are appropriate to different levels and stages of your work, so are different search approaches.
- You need to be familiar with the different approaches available to you, and to be able to map them on to the different levels and stages through which you will pass as you generate your essay or research project report.
- Within these broad search approaches, there is a variety of more specific search techniques that you can use, available in different search tools. Being familiar with these will help you find the information you need more easily and more effectively.
- Ultimately, you need to be able to choose the most appropriate search approach and search techniques for the task on which you are engaged.

Depending on both the type of work you are undertaking (essay or research project) and the stage you are at in working on it, your learning needs will differ, as will the type of search you need to conduct in order to satisfy them. Figure 7.1 maps four broad categories of search approach on to the model of the basic dimensions of learning previously presented in Figure 2.5. The four different search approaches shown in the boxes in Figure 7.1 are introduced below. We will then explore a number of specific search *techniques* that are particularly appropriate to these different search approaches.

Broad search

The left half of Figure 7.1 represents searching for information to satisfy description-building aspects of your research – that is, where you are focusing on relating ideas to

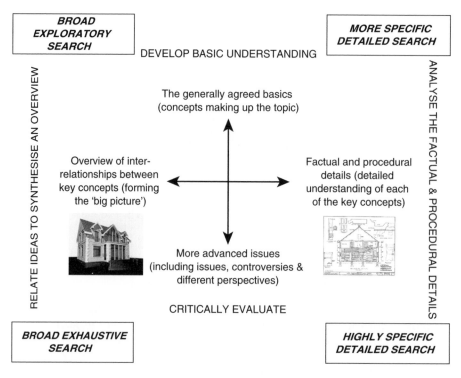

Figure 7.1 Search approaches mapped on to the basic dimensions of learning

synthesise the 'big picture' in relation to your topic. The function of relatively broad searches is to establish a good conceptual map of the topic, in which the individual components are interlinked to form a coherent whole (recall the 'relational' level in the SOLO taxonomy introduced in Chapter 3), and to set the topic into its broader context (recall the 'extended abstract' level in the SOLO taxonomy).

A *broad exploratory* search is suitable when you want to build an overview or conceptual map of the topic – to figure out what it is all about and what are its component parts. This will entail exploring the literature broadly but not too deeply to form an initial (provisional) overview. It entails adopting a wide-ranging, relatively speculative focus as you gather what is essentially a collection of candidate information sources for subsequent more detailed consideration. These candidate materials are selected by a process of *relatively* superficial scanning as you build a provisional framework of the main components of the topic and how they fit together to form the big picture. The candidate information sources can then be sampled and read in more detail, as you move into procedure-building mode in order to validate (provide detailed evidence to support) your provisional overview. This approach is particularly suitable for people with a description-building learning style (see Chapter 2 for discussion of learning styles).

A *broad exhaustive* search is most appropriate later in the research process, and will need to be conducted by people with either a description-building or procedure-building learning style. Its purpose is to help you check that you have not missed any important component of the topic, or any important wider implications or broader contextual aspects of the topic (i.e. making sure that you have avoided an overly narrow treatment of the topic). This type of broad search will be more systematic – you are systematically checking that you have covered the necessary ground and have not left any important stone unturned, rather than exploring new territory.

Specific search

The specific searches to the right in Figure 7.1 represent searching for information to satisfy procedure-building aspects of your research – the close examination of details and evidence supporting the overview established during your description-building stages.

The type of search shown at the top right of the figure is termed *more specific detailed search* in order to draw a comparison with the broader more general type of search shown at the top left in the figure. The function of this more narrowly focused type of search is to find sources suitable for a detailed study of the specifics of the components making up the topic. Its purpose – rather than to build up a wide collection of information sources in order to sketch a provisional overview – is to seek out one or a small number of detailed sources to act as an authoritative starting point. This entails finding literature that provides sufficient depth for you to build understanding of the details.

For the person with a procedure-building style, starting with this type of search may provide sources which themselves provide links to other sources. This type of search may also be repeated to find detailed information on other components or aspects of the topic, as your understanding broadens as well as deepens. Progressing in this way may be sufficient for the person with a procedure-building style to engage in the level of description building necessary to integrate the details into a coherent overall framework – without the need for engaging in much broad exploratory searching. But broad *exhaustive* searching will still be needed at later stages of the research process.

Highly specific detailed searching is particularly appropriate at more advanced stages of your research when you need to find information on very specific and detailed aspects of your topic. It is also relevant at the later stages of your research when you are checking that you have not missed anything – but in this case (compared to broad exhaustive searching), in terms of depth rather than breadth. Are your claims and arguments thoroughly supported by your evidence? Do they stand up to detailed scrutiny? You need to be able to exercise great control over your search in order to specify what it is you need with high levels of precision. This search approach is likely to be needed by people with either a description-building or procedure-building learning style.

Search tools offer a great variety of different techniques to help you search effectively. Some of these are especially helpful in relation to particular types of search discussed above. In Figure 7.2, a number of key techniques offered by different search tools are mapped on to the broad search approaches just discussed.

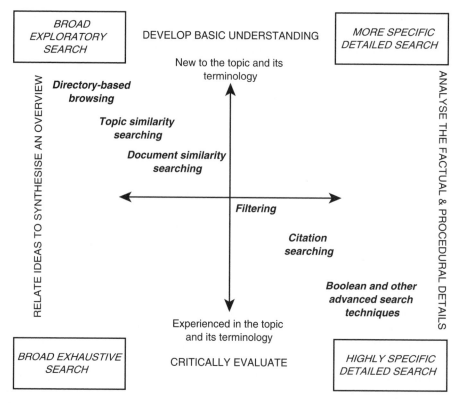

Figure 7.2 Search techniques mapped on to the dimensions of learning and search approaches

Figure 7.2 adds two further labels to the vertical dimension: *New to the topic and its terminology* at the top and *Experienced in the topic and its terminology* at the bottom. Being familiar with the terminology of the topic you are researching is a key factor in effective searching.

As we saw in Chapter 4, the more you can achieve a match between the words you use to describe what it is you need and the words used by the author of the information that will fulfil your need, the more effective your search is likely to be. However, this can be problematic even at advanced levels of study since experts in the subject can also often struggle to find exactly what they want.

At beginner level, the problem is much worse. If you are not familiar with the words likely to be used by the authors of information sources that you need, how can you describe your needs in such a way as to find these sources? Luckily, there are a variety of techniques available to help you in this process – at both advanced and beginner levels. These techniques are the focus of the present chapter.

Techniques towards the top left in Figure 7.2 are particularly helpful for people who are very new to the topic they wish to explore. Techniques towards the bottom right are particularly appropriate for people who are familiar with the terminology of their topic, and who want to use their knowledge in order to exercise very precise control over their searches. In this way they can specify in great detail exactly what they want the search tool to find – and what they want it to exclude in their search.

Now let us explore each of these in detail. We'll take a look at what the technique entails and when you might want to use it. We will also explore its relative advantages and disadvantages.

Directory-based browsing and searching

Quick view

What do they do?

Directories will allow you to do the following:

- They offer you a list of broad subject categories generally arranged alphabetically, e.g. *Arts, Business, Computers,* etc.
- They allow you to browse from the general to the more specific, by clicking on any of these categories to see what sub-categories it has, and again clicking on a sub-category to see what sub-sub-categories it has, and so on.
- They also allow you to click in the reverse direction, to explore from the specific to the more general.
- At each point, you can see the information sources that are listed under the particular sub-category that you have clicked on.
- In some directories, such as the *Open Directory,* you are also shown *related* topics. These are topics that are neither broader nor more specific categories in relation to the topic you are looking at, but which may nevertheless be of interest. For example, a category:

    Business > Management > Ethics

    may be related to other categories including:

    Home > Consumer Information > Complaints
    Society > Philosophy > Ethics > Applied > Professional Ethics

- You can search within a directory using your own keywords. In some directories, such as the *Open Directory*, as well as being shown information sources containing the words you searched for, you will also be shown the category to which it is assigned in the directory. Clicking on this category takes you into the directory at that point – from which you can navigate to explore broader, narrower and related topics. When you are looking at a particular sub-category, you can also choose to do a keyword search *only within that particular category.*

- Note that the subject categories, and the way search results are presented to you, are different in the different directories (those of *Google* and *Yahoo*, for example).
- Information sources included in a directory are generally evaluated, selected and assigned to categories by human editors.

> Where can I find them?

Examples of search tools that offer directory-based browsing include:

- The *Open Directory* (http://www.dmoz.org/)
- *Yahoo Directory* (http://dir.yahoo.com/)
- *Intute* (http://www.intute.ac.uk/)

> When should I use them?

Directories can be useful when you are new to a topic or subject and are not particularly familiar with its terminology, or how it is broken up into sub-topics. The general directories such as the *Open Directory* and the *Yahoo Directory* are not scholarly search tools (unlike *Intute*), and although the selection of sources is made with human judgement, the editors are not academic subject experts.

> What are their benefits?

- The information you find in a directory should be of reasonable quality. This is because the websites listed in a directory have generally been selected by a human editor (as opposed to a computer algorithm). However, as noted above, in the case of general as opposed to scholarly directories, 'quality' is not determined by academic subject experts, and the sources are not selected primarily on the basis of their suitability for academic work.
- Information sources on the same topic will be listed together regardless of whether they use different terminology to describe it. This means that you may be able to find linked resources without having to search using alternative terms. This is because a human indexer decides which category a particular information source should be assigned to (again, as opposed to a computer algorithm, as applies in the case of non-directory based search engines).
- Even if you are not sufficiently familiar with its terminology to search specifically for a topic, you can 'home in' on it by starting with the broad top-level categories (like *Arts, Business, Computers*, etc.) and exploring sub-categories and sub-sub-categories.
- Directories are generally based on human-generated classification schemes. These can provide useful supportive structures in which to explore topics, especially for people new to them (see next bullet point).

- You can explore by moving from the general to the specific, and from the specific to the more general. In the *Open Directory* and the *Yahoo Directory*, at each point, you are shown *related* topics (topics that may be of interest, even though they are neither more general nor more specific). This allows you to explore a new topic, its main features, and its relationship with other topics, without having to be familiar with its terminology (as you would have to be to perform effective keyword searches).
- You can combine searching with browsing a directory. The large general directories will allow you to do a keyword search within the directory as a whole or restricted to a particular category or sub-category. For example, if you search for 'research' within the *Business* category of the *Open Directory*, you will retrieve information sources concerning research only in relation to business. This allows you to narrow your search and avoid retrieving large quantities of irrelevant information.

> What are their drawbacks?

- The number of information sources offered by a directory is not as great as that offered by a general search engine, since each resource has to be selected and indexed by a human editor.
- The resources contained in a general directory are not particularly geared to the requirements of academic work. Whilst they do reflect quality judgements by human editors, these judgements may be made on the basis of what is most useful to the widest range of web users. The editors are not academic subject experts.
- For these reasons, depending on the nature of your essay or dissertation, the resources you find in a directory may not be sufficiently deep or focused to be useful beyond initial familiarisation with the topic and its main features.
- The subject classification schemes provided by different directories may be different and do not necessarily map on to subject divisions most useful for academic purposes.

Topic similarity searching

Quick view

> What does it do?

- Topic similarity searching entails finding topics that are similar to the one(s) for which you are searching.
- They may be displayed graphically – for example, as in *Google's Wonder wheel*[15]. (Figure 7.3 shows the *Wonder wheel* for a search on *learning style*.)

---

[15]As previously noted, at the time of writing, the *Wonder Wheel* is unavailable, and it is not clear whether it will return. A *Wonder Wheel* style interface is still available to *Google images* (http://image-swirl.googlelabs.com/).

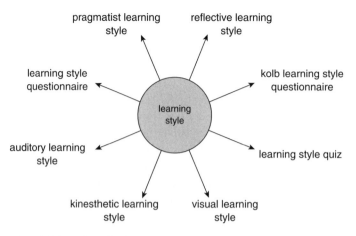

Figure 7.3   *Google's Wonder wheel*

Figure 7.4   *Exalead's* related terms

- Or they may be displayed textually, as for example topics listed under *Google's* Something different heading (bottom ref in Figure 7.4).
- They may also be presented as *query expansion* suggestions as you type in your search terms, as shown in Figure 7.5.

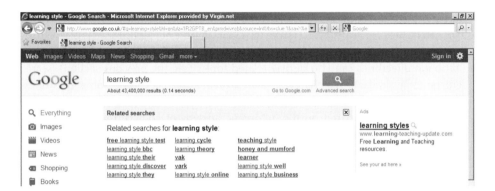

Figures 7.5 & 7.6 *Google's* query expansion (top) and related searches (bottom) for *learning style*

- Or as *related searches,* as shown above in *Google,* relating to a search for *learning style* (Figure 7.6):

> Where can I find it?

Examples of search tools that offer them include:

- *Google* (http://www.google.com/): the *Wonder wheel[16]*, related searches and query expansion.
- *Ask* (http://ask.com/): query expansion and related searches.
- *Bing* (http://www.bing.com/): query expansion and related searches.
- *Yahoo* (http://yahoo.com/): related topics.

---

[16]As previously noted, at the time of writing, the *Wonder wheel* is unavailable, and it is not clear whether it will return. A *Wonder wheel* style interface is still available to *Google Images* (http://image-shirl.googlelabs.com/).

Topic similarity searching is useful when you want to explore a new topic broadly, particularly in terms of how it fits within a broader context of related topics. It can be particularly useful when you are new to a topic and not already familiar with its scope, its different facets, and/or its terminology.

- Topic similarity searching identifies and presents related topics without you having to know about them in advance, or search for them explicitly.
- This can be useful in helping you explore topics that you are not particularly familiar with, by suggesting related topics and terminology that you may not have come across otherwise.
- Although directories can also display related topics (see the previous section), search engine topic similarity searching can offer a greater diversity – and sometimes unexpectedness – since it is not based on a pre-existing human-generated classification system. Rather, it is based on the automatic analysis of co-occurrences of terms in documents. This can sometimes suggest interesting new directions for your thinking and further exploration.

Unlike in directories, relationships between topics are not generated by human judgement, or on the basis of consulting a classification or ontology. They are based on the automatic statistical analysis of word co-occurrences. This is not the same as a human expert identifying the relationships of a topic to other topics. As noted above, this can sometimes be effective. But it can be hit and miss. For example, Table 7.1 shows the different response by *Exalead* to two very similar searches – one for "cognitive styles" and one for "cognitive style".

'Columbia Disaster', 'Edward Tufte' and 'Powerpoint presentation' are in fact relevant terms since Edward Tufte wrote a well-publicised book *The Cognitive Style of PowerPoint*, suggesting that *PowerPoint* imposes a particular cognitive style. He argued that it is unsuitable for complex technical briefings, using the Columbia space shuttle

Table 7.1 Response by *Exalead* to two similar searches

"cognitive styles"	*Related terms:* Higher Education; Individual Difference; Information Processing; Learning Style; New York; Review of Educational Research; Social Sciences; Style Inventory.
	Related Searches: Cognitive Process; Cognitive Psychology.
"cognitive style"	*Related terms:* Beautiful Evidence; Columbia Disaster; Edward Tufte; Individual Difference; Powerpoint Presentation.
	Related Searches: Cognitive Process; Learning Style; Cognitive Ability.

disaster as an example. Some may find these *related topics* useful, suggesting new lines of investigation; others may find them quirky and less useful. The system certainly gives a very different response to very similar queries.

Document similarity searching

Quick view

What does it do?

- Assuming that you have found a document that is relevant to your needs, similarity searching enables you to find other documents that are similar to it.
- This is done automatically for you. For example, in *Google Scholar* (Figure 7.7), having found a useful document, you simply click *Related articles* and the similarity search will be performed automatically for you.

Let us assume that we are searching in *Google Scholar* for documents on the topic *serendipity in information seeking*, and retrieve the items shown in Figure 7.7.

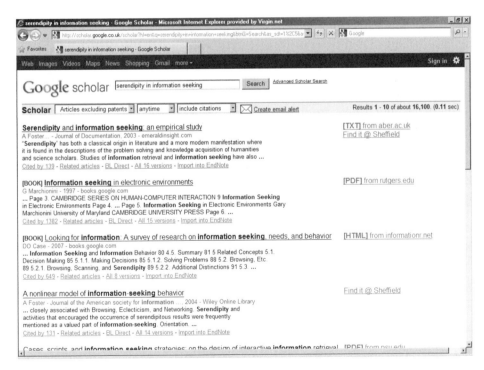

Figure 7.7 *Google Scholar* search for *serendipity in information seeking*

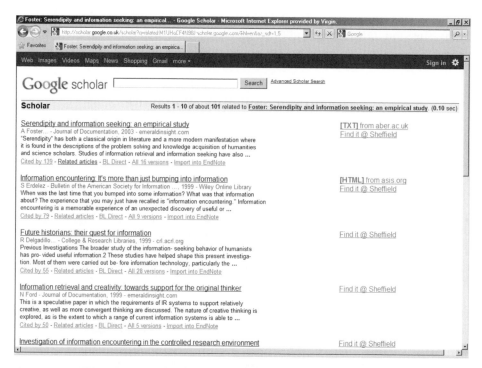

Figure 7.8 *Google Scholar* related articles search

The first item looks very relevant, so we click on *Related articles*. The related search retrieves the items shown in Figure 7.8.

The items found here are indeed related. The original paper ('Serendipity and information seeking: an empirical study') reports a study of information seekers who included historians. The automatic similarity searching mechanism has picked this up without our being aware of it (item three). Clearly, the information seeking of historians was talked about in the original paper, and the mechanism has found another paper about information seeking that also talks about historians.

The third item on the screen is also relevant. Although we did not search specifically for *creativity*, serendipity is linked in much of the literature to *creativity*, and again the similarity search has picked this up. Also, *information encountering* is often used as synonymously with *serendipity*, and again the similarity search has picked this up in items two and four.

Where can I find it?

- *Google Scholar* offers a *Related articles* option that finds documents that share terms and ranks them in order of relevance to your query. It is not as explicit as *SciVerse Scopus* or *Web of Knowledge* about precisely how this is done.

- *Google* offers a *Similar* link after the brief details of items it retrieves. Clicking the link will result in a search for similar documents based on textual similarities and relevance to your query.
- *SciVerse Scopus* offers considerable control over how similarity is calculated. It provides a *Find related documents* option that allows you to choose the basis on which documents are considered to be related. You can choose to find documents that are related on the basis of shared references, shared keywords, or shared authors. The references, keywords and authors relating to your 'source' document are displayed to you in the different options. You can select *all* references or *select* from the list of references presented to you. Similarly, you can choose *all* or *selected* keywords, and *all* or *selected* authors.
- *Web of Knowledge* offers a *Related Records* link when viewing the details of a particular article. This will find articles on the basis of *references* that they share with the original document.

> When should I use it?

Similarity searching is useful when you have identified a document that is relevant to your topic and you would like to find more documents that are similar to it. This can be a good way of finding related documents without having to think of and type in more search terms. The system automatically analyses the document you have given it, and searches for other documents that share similarities.

> What are its benefits?

The automatic calculation of similarities between documents:

- can be more subtle than your own manual searching;
- may find documents that you may not have been able to find through manual searching;
- can suggest to you words describing and relevant to your topic that you may not have thought of; and
- can occasionally reveal a document that takes your research or thinking in a new direction that you hadn't anticipated.

> What are its drawbacks?

- The process is automatic, based essentially on analysing the co-occurrences of features in different documents. This process will not necessarily pick up important relationships between documents that would be recognised by a human.
- Although some systems, such as *SciVerse Scopus,* allow you to explicitly choose the basis on which similarity is calculated (e.g. shared references, shared keywords or shared authors), others, such as *Google Scholar,* adopt more of a 'we know best' approach (which may nevertheless often be effective).

Filtering

Quick view

Filters allow you to restrict your search, for example, to particular subject areas or particular types of documents, by selecting from pre-defined categories offered to you by the search tool. This may be in the form of a dropdown list, checkbox, radio button or other selection device. *Google Scholar*, for example, from its advanced search page allows you to select one or more of the following subject areas by clicking checkboxes. The subsequent search will be restricted to those areas.

Biology, Life Sciences, and Environmental Science

Medicine, Pharmacology, and Veterinary Science

Business, Administration, Finance, and Economics

Physics, Astronomy, and Planetary Science

Chemistry and Materials Science

Social Sciences, Arts, and Humanities

Engineering, Computer Science, and Mathematics

Other search tools allow you to restrict your search to particular types of document – for example, conference papers, journal articles or research theses.

The filters described here are of two types: pre-search and post-search.

- Pre-search filters allow you to select one or more pre-defined categories at the time of searching.
- Post-search filters cluster your search results into higher-level categories (e.g. subject areas, types of source, websites retrieved from, etc.). By selecting a category, you can filter your view of your results to documents in that category.

Advanced search operators are commands that can be added into the wording of your search such as *"intitle:"*. There is some overlap between the filters introduced here and those introduced in the section 'Boolean and other advanced search engine operators' on page 119, since a number of selectable filters are also available as advanced search operators. In these cases, they are included in both sections.

Most search tools offer some sort of filtering, for example, by date. Some search tools also offer filtering by other categories, such as subject and document type. Examples include the following:

- *iSeek* (http://www.iseek.com/) offers post-search clustering. Depending on the results, clusters include: *Topics/People/Places/Organisations/Date and time/Abbreviations/Date published/Source.*
- *Google Scholar* (http://scholar.google.com/). See Chapter 8 for a list of the pre-search filters offered.
- *SciVerse Scopus.* See Chapter 8 for a listing of the pre-search and post-search filters offered.
- *Scientific WebPlus* [subscription-based]. Pre-search. The following filters are available from the search page: *Topic/Person or Author/Organism/Gene/Drug.* Post-search. Filters offered are: *Source* of the documents (Repository results, News results, Blog Results)/ *Domain* (e.g. .com, .org, .net, .edu)/*File format.*
- *Intute* (http://www.intute.ac.uk/) offers the following pre-search filters: *Subject/Resource type/Country of origin.*
- *Web of Knowledge* and *Web of Science.* See Chapter 8 for a listing of the pre-search and post-search filters offered.
- *Scirus* (http://www.scirus.com/). Pre-search (from the advanced search page): Filter by *Dates/Information types/File formats/Content sources* (journal titles, preferred web sources, the rest of the scientific web)/*Subject areas.* Additionally, the following are available from the advanced search page: AND, OR, ANDNOT, phrase search, location of search terms in the document (article title, journal title, author name, author affiliation, International Standard Serial Number (ISSN), keywords, URL or part of it). Post-search: *Content sources* (journal sources, preferred web sources other web sources)/*File format/Keywords.*
- *Exalead* (http://www.exalead.com/search/). Pre-search: the following are available from the advanced search screen: *Phrases/Essential terms* (i.e. terms that must be present, even if stop words[17])/*Optional Terms/Exclude Terms /Prefix Search/Proximity Search/ Boolean* (AND, OR)/*Phonetic Search/Approximate spelling/Language/Site/Title/URL/ Link/ Search before a date/Search after a date.* Post-search: *Site type* (e.g. blog, forum)/ *Multimedia* (e.g. audio, video)/*File type/Related terms* (a related term can be clicked to add it to the search, which will be run automatically – clicking it again will deselect it and again run the search)/*Languages/Countries.*
- *Yippy* (http://www.yippy.com/). Pre-search: the following advanced search operators are available from the advanced search page: *Host/Language/File type.* Post-search: *Topics* (called 'Clouds' in *Yippy*)/*Sources* (e.g. *Ask, New York Times, Yahoo*)/*Sites* (e.g. .com, .uk, .edu).

When should I use it?

- Both pre- and post-search filtering are appropriate when you know that you are not interested in documents from particular subject areas (e.g. you want information on *drug addiction* but in a *public health policy* and not *medical* or *biological* context), of a particular type (e.g. conference papers), outside a particular date range, etc.

---

[17]'Stop words' are common words like 'a', 'the', 'to', 'from', etc., that are normally ignored by search tools.

- Using a search tool that offers post-search filtering is appropriate if you are interested in seeing how your search results (and by implication, your topic) are analysed by the search tool into different facets.

What are its benefits?

- Filtering can save you time and effort in not having to wade through irrelevant documents trying to identify the ones meeting your requirements.
- Post-search categories result from an analysis of what has actually been found. This can sometimes provide an interesting and useful analysis of the different facets of the topic as found in the literature.
- Post-search categories produced by tools such as *Web of Knowledge* can be fine-grained and detailed, allowing you to rapidly home in on what is most relevant.
- Post-search filtering, in which results are clustered into higher level subject (and other) categories, can make it easy to see potentially interesting search results which, if presented as the normal single sequence of items listed in order of relevance to your initial query, might appear very far down the list and be missed.

What are its drawbacks?

- Pre-search clustering represents a way of trying to ensure that you only find what you know you need. But sometimes you don't know what it is that you need until you see it. Post-search filtering to some extent mitigates this danger (compared to pre-search filtering) since although you can still choose to filter unwanted categories, it is extremely easy to preview them by category to see if anything looks interesting.
- Filtering categories offered by different search tools may differ. Some may be less useful to you than others.

Citation searching

Quick view

What does it do?

Citation searching shows you – in relation to a particular document that you specify – other documents that have cited it in their references.

Where can I find it?

Examples of search tools that offer it include:

- *Google Scholar* (http://scholar.google.com/)
- *Web of Knowledge*
- *SciVerse Scopus*

When should I use it?

Citation searching is useful when you already know of a key source (e.g. a book or journal article) that is centrally relevant to your topic, and want to find more recent sources that build explicitly on this original source. This can introduce you to the latest work relating to the topic. It is a way of asking 'What later work has built on this previous work?'

What are its benefits?

- Citation searching enables you to find closely related sources without you having to do a subject search for them. All you need is details of a key source. This bypasses the problem of terminology since the process does not rely on you using search terms that match the words used by authors to describe a topic.
- It is a good way of finding the most up-to-date sources that have built on the source you specify.

What are its drawbacks?

- Occasionally a source may have cited the original book or article that forms your starting point as an incidental rather than central influence. In this case, the discovered source may not be particularly useful. However, it may often be easy to identify such a source as not relevant from its title and/or abstract.

Boolean and other advanced search engine operators

Note: advanced search operators available in *Google Scholar*, *SciVerse Scopus* and *Web of Knowledge* are covered in Chapter 8 where each of these scholarly search tools is introduced in detail. This section details advanced search operators available in a selection of **general web search engines**. Note that the advanced search operators attributed to *Google* below also work in *Google Scholar*.

Quick view

Most search tools offer advanced search options. These allow you to make your searches more precise in order to avoid retrieving information that is not relevant to your needs. For example, you may want to specify that you require information on *jaguars*, but specify that you are interested in the *animal* and not the *car*. In many search engines, the minus sign (–) signifies NOT, as in the following example:

jaguar – car

Or you may want documents about research into *learning styles*, *learning strategies* or *learning approaches*, with *Kolb* in their title, and which are found on the websites of UK or USA academic institutions:

research ("learning styles" OR "learning strategies") (site:ac.uk OR site:edu) intitle:Kolb

There are a great many options available to you. Many are common across the major search engines, but others are specific to particular ones. Also, occasionally the same commands must be specified slightly differently in different search engines. These differences are listed below in relation to the seven search engines presented here. Also, different search tools may interpret *AND* and *OR* in a different order, which can have serious implications for searches containing them. These differences are introduced in 'Advanced search operator precedence' on page 128.

A selection of advanced search operators is listed below. For each, a brief illustration is given to show how it may be useful, along with details of its availability in a range of different search engines, and how to actually use it.

Seven search engines have been selected for detailed treatment in this section. These are: *Ask, Bing, Yippy, Exalead, Google,* and *Yahoo*. They have been chosen to represent major search engines and also a range of available search techniques.

Why and how to use them

AND

How is this useful?

AND simply combines your search terms. A search for:

teaching AND sociology AND university

will find documents each of which contains all these words.

How do I use it?	Most search engines automatically interpret two or more keywords together as though they were linked by **AND**s, and therefore don't require you to state it explicitly – e.g.

e-government effectiveness research

would be interpreted as:

e-government AND effectiveness AND research

However, the words do not have to appear in the same order that you typed them. So documents containing any of the following phrases would all be retrieved:

research into the effectiveness of e-government

research into e-government effectiveness

e-government research effectiveness

Bear in mind a common error. We often use the word 'and' in normal conversation when, strictly speaking, we mean 'or'. For example, when we say:

'I'm interested in e-government and e-health'

we often mean that we would consider as relevant documents about e-government and also other documents about e-health. But a search for:

e-government AND e-health

will only find documents containing both these terms – in other words, documents *each* of which is about *both* e-government *and* e-health. This would restrict your search in a way that you didn't intend. So don't use **AND** when you really mean **OR**.

Also, be careful combining **AND**s and **OR**s in a search. For more information see the 'Advanced search operator precedence' section on page 128.

Available in...	Ask	Bing	Exalead	Google	Yahoo	Yippy

Include...

How is this useful?	This is useful when you want the search to include common words like 'a', 'the', etc., which are normally ignored by a search engine (i.e. are included in its 'stop list').
How do I use it?	Use the plus sign + to indicate that the word *must* be present.

    fish +and chips

Putting words between quotation marks (thus making them into phrases) has a similar effect, e.g. "fish and chips". The effect is similar, but not exactly the same, since without quotation marks, the search would also retrieve *chips and fish.*

Available in...	Ask	Bing	Exalead	Google	Yahoo	Yippy

(Continued)

(Continued)

NOT

How is this useful?	You may want to <u>exclude</u> a certain word or phrase from your search. For example, you may be interested in teaching – but <u>not</u> in relation to higher education. The following search: *teaching –"higher education"* will retrieve documents which contain the word *teaching* but which do <u>not</u> contain the phrase *"higher education"*.

How do I use it?	Use the minus sign – before (with no space) the word you want to exclude. Only some search engines accept the word **NOT**. Therefore it is safer generally to use the minus sign.
	
	    In *Exalead* the minus sign can only be used to exclude individual words and not phrases. *Exalead*, however, also accepts **NOT**, which *can* be applied to phrases as well as words.
	
	    NOTs are usually processed after **AND**s and **OR**s. For more information see the 'Advanced search operator precedence' section on page 128.

Available in...	Ask | Bing | Exalead | Google | Yahoo | Yippy

OR

How is this useful?	**OR** allows you to search for different combinations of search terms. This helps you avoid missing a relevant document because the words the author used to describe what you are looking for was different from how you described it to the search tool. For example: *styles OR strategies* will find documents containing either word.
How do I use it?	Link search terms with the operator **OR**. Be careful combining **AND**s and **OR**s in a search. For more information see the 'Advanced search operator precedence' section on page 128.
Available in...	Ask | Bing | Exalead | Google | Yahoo | Yippy

Phrase searching

How is this useful?	You may want to specify a search in which the order of the words is important (e.g. <u>bike sports</u> and not <u>sports bike</u>).
	
	    "bike sports"
	
	will retrieve documents containing the *exact phrase*. Without the quotation marks, documents on *sports bike* would also be retrieved.
	
	    Or you may want to search for an *exact phrase*. To take an extreme but illustrative example of the problem, the search:
	
	    "dog sinks battleship"

(unsurprisingly) retrieves no documents in *Google*. But take the quotation marks away and:

> *dog sinks battleship*

retrieves over 72,000 documents. These include, for example, the item:

> "Scurvy **Dogs** 2 2.0 – Fun and challenging ship combat game (not a **Battleship** clone). Outwit your opponent to **sink** him."

How do I use it?	Enclose your search terms in quotation marks. In *Exalead*, using the minus sign with phrases does not work – but using **NOT** does.
Available in...	Ask | Bing | Exalead | Google | Yahoo | Yippy

Proximity searching

How is this useful?	You may want to specify that your keywords appear within a certain distance of each other – for example, within the same sentence or within three words of each other.
How do I use it?	*Exalead* offers the operators NEAR and NEXT.

> *cognitive NEXT strategies*

will retrieve documents in which these terms occur next to each other.

> *allintitle: cognitive NEXT strategies*

will find documents with the adjacent words in their title.

> *cognitive NEAR strategies*

will find documents with the terms occurring within a few words of each other. You can control exactly how many words – for example:

> *strategic NEAR/8 instruction*

would find documents with the words *strategic* and *instruction* occurring within eight words of each other. A more complex example:

> *allintitle: strategic NEAR/2 instruction NOT intitle:"strategic instruction"*

would find documents with *strategic* occurring within two words of *instruction* but not with the exact phrase 'strategic instruction' in the title. Note that the use of **NEAR** qualified by a number is not (at the time of writing) documented in *Exalead's* Advanced Search or Help pages. As noted in the section above, the operator **NOT** is required if you wish to exclude a phrase. The minus sign only works with individual words, not phrases.

Available in...	*Exalead* Proximity options are available in *Web of Knowledge* and *SciVerse Scopus*. See Chapter 8 for details.

(Continued)

(Continued)

Wildcard

<table>
<tr>
<td>*How is this useful?*</td>
<td>In *Google* the asterisk * can be used as a 'wildcard' – i.e. a symbol that can stand for one or more missing words. Note that in *Google* this can only be used within a phrase. This can increase the flexibility of your search, for example, if you want the search engine to suggest different terms to fill in blanks you leave. Thus:

" * to research methods"

will retrieve, for example:

<u>Introduction</u> to research methods
<u>Guide</u> to research methods
<u>Introductory guide</u> to research methods
etc.

Exalead allows * to stand for zero, one or more letters (not words, as in *Google*), but only at the end of a word stem. So:

comput*

would successfully retrieve *computers, computing, computation*, etc., whereas:

wom*n

would not retrieve *woman* and *women*.
Whilst *Google* does not permit the asterisk to be used in this way, it does apply this type of word stemming automatically if it considers that this will improve a given search.</td>
</tr>
<tr>
<td>*How do I use it?*</td>
<td>In *Google*, place the asterisk within a phrase, with spaces before and after it. In *Exalead*, add the asterisk on to a word stem – e.g. comput*</td>
</tr>
<tr>
<td>*Available in...*</td>
<td>*Google | Exalead*
Web of Knowledge and *SciVerse Scopus* offer a number of wildcard options. See Chapter 8 for details.</td>
</tr>
</table>

File type

<table>
<tr>
<td>*How is this useful?*</td>
<td>You may want to restrict your search to a particular type of file, e.g. PowerPoint presentations, PDF files, Word documents, etc. For example, official forms (e.g. visa applications or local government forms) are often available for download in PDF format. Thus searches for, for example

visa application form filetype:pdf

Leeds City Council "application form" filetype:pdf

will retrieve some relevant forms.</td>
</tr>
<tr>
<td>*How do I use it?*</td>
<td>Include:

filetype:pdf

in your search. To search for other file types, replace *pdf* with the appropriate code shown in bold type in the table below, which lists the different file types supported by the different search engines.</td>
</tr>
</table>

Note: not all search engines advertise *all* the formats they allow (for example, *Ask* does not give access to any *filetype* from its advanced search page form, although it does support a number of these if you type the *filetype*: command in your search box – see below).

Available in...   Ask | Bing | Exalead | Google | Yahoo | Yippy

See below for a list of common file types that can be searched for using the different search engines (as of August 2011).

	Ask	Bing	Exalead	Google	Yahoo	Yippy
HTML .htm, .html	✓			✓	✓	
Adobe Acrobat PDF .pdf	✓	✓	✓	✓	✓	✓
Adobe Postscript .ps	✓			✓	✓	✓
Autodesk DWF .dwf	✓	✓		✓	✓	✓
Google Earth KMZ .kmz	✓			✓	✓	
MS Excel .xls	✓	✓	✓	✓	✓	✓
MS Excel .xlsx	✓		✓	✓	✓	
MS PowerPoint .ppt	✓	✓	✓	✓	✓	✓
MS PowerPoint .pptx	✓		✓	✓	✓	
MS Word .doc	✓	✓	✓	✓	✓	✓
MS Word .docx	✓		✓	✓	✓	
Rich Text Format .rtf	✓	✓	✓	✓	✓	✓
RSS/XML .xml	✓			✓	✓	✓
Shockwave Flash .swf	✓		✓	✓	✓	
Text format .txt	✓	✓		✓	✓	✓

(Continued)

(Continued)

Find my search terms in...

How is this useful?	You can often make your search more specific by specifying that the search engine should look for your search terms in a particular part of the documents it is searching. For example, if *copyright law* is found in the *title* of a document, this may be a better indicator that the document is mainly about copyright law than if these words had just been mentioned somewhere in it. The title is only one of the areas of a document that you can specify – as shown below.

The sections below contain details of the different operators available in the different search engines (as of August 2010) and how to use them. Note that advanced search options in *Google Scholar*, *SciVerse Scopus* and *Web of Knowledge* are introduced in Chapter 8.

How do I use them?

Title

The search:

intitle:sociology

will retrieve documents containing the word *sociology* in their *title*. There must be no space after the colon in *Yippy*, *Google* and *Yahoo*. *Ask*, *Bing* and *Exalead* accept queries with or without a space after the colon.
For multiple words, you could search for:

intitle:public intitle:policy intitle:research

but in *Google* and *Exalead* a quicker way is to use the operator **allintitle:**

allintitle: public policy research
allintitle: "inquiry-based learning" OR "enquiry-based learning"

Google and *Exalead* accept the operator with or without a space after the colon. *Ask*, *Bing*, *Yippy* and *Yahoo* do not accept **allintitle:**

URL (web address)

The Uniform Resource Locator (URL) is the address of a file on the Internet. It consists of the following elements:

http:// www.all-about.com /define/index.html

↑ ↑

The domain

The location and name of a
document at this domain

inurl: specifies that one search term must be in the URL. Thus:

inurl:sheffield

will retrieve documents from, for example:

www.sheffield.gov.uk	*www.sheffield.anglican.org*
www.sheffield.ac.uk	*www.travelsouthyorkshire.com/*
www.shu.ac.uk/sheffield	*timetables/sheffield*
en.wikipedia.org/wiki/Sheffield	*www.sheffield.nhs.uk*
www.sheffield-internet.co.uk	*etc.*

It is accepted in *Ask, Bing, Yippy, Exalead, Google* and *Yahoo.*

allinurl: specifies that multiple search terms must be in the URL. For example:

   allinurl: sheffield steel

It is accepted by *Exalead* and *Google*, with or without a space after the colon. It is not accepted by *Ask, Bing, Yippy* or *Yahoo.*

Domain

site: will restrict your search to a particular website. For example:

   site:www.sheffield.ac.uk admissions

will find documents containing the word *admissions* located at *www.sheffield. ac.uk.*

Note that you must include the last part of the domain name. For example:

site:sheffield.ac.uk	will retrieve items from *sheffield.ac.uk*
site:ac.uk	will retrieve items from any *.ac.uk* site
site:uk	will retrieve items from any *.uk* site

But:

site:www.sheffield.ac	will retrieve nothing
site:www.sheffield	will retrieve nothing
site:sheffield	will retrieve nothing

If you want to search for a word that appears as part of a web address, use **inurl:** instead.

site: is available is all the search engines selected here: *Ask, Bing, Exalead, Google, Yippy* and *Yahoo.*

Only *Yippy* and *Exalead* will accept a space after the colon.

For further search information, including details of other advanced search operators, see the following links:

- *Ask* – http://about.ask.com/en/docs/about/adv_search_tips.shtml
- *Bing* – http://onlinehelp.microsoft.com/en-us/bing/ff808535.aspx
- *Exalead* – http://www.exalead.com/search/web/search-syntax/
- *Google* – http://www.google.com/help/features.html/

The following unofficial Google guide is also very useful – http://www.googleguide.com/advanced_operators.html

It lists a number of advanced search operators which are not officially declared by Google, and which therefore may change or be withdrawn.

- *Yahoo* – http://help.yahoo.com/l/uk/yahoo/search/basics/basics-04.html
- *Yippy* – http://search.yippy.com/help-searchsyntax

Advanced search operator precedence

Search tools differ in the way they interpret search queries that use a combination of **ANDs**, **ORs** and **NOTs**. For example, *Ask* and *Google* (along with *Google Scholar*) will process **ORs** *before* **ANDs** and **NOTs**. What this means is that, for example:

research learning styles OR strategies OR approaches Kolb OR Mumford

will be interpreted as:

research
AND learning
AND (styles OR strategies OR approaches)
AND (Kolb OR Mumford)

If a document does not contain either the word *Kolb* or the word *Mumford*, <u>and</u> at least one of the words *styles*, *strategies* and *approaches*, <u>and</u> the word *learning* <u>and</u> the word *research*, it will not be retrieved.

However, other search engines, including *Bing* and *Exalead,* will interpret exactly the same query very differently as:

(research AND learning AND styles)
OR strategies
OR (approaches AND Kolb)
OR Mumford

In this case, documents will be retrieved if, for example, they simply contain the word *strategies* – and *none* of the other words. Other documents will be retrieved if they simply contain the word *Mumford*. This can make a very big difference to the effectiveness of your search.

In the case of *Bing* and *Exalead*, you can use brackets to control the order in which **ORs** and **ANDs** are processed, and to override the search engines' default order of precedence. Thus, the following search:

(vehicle emissions) OR pollution

would retrieve information on *vehicle emissions* and *pollution* of all types – not just from vehicles. However:

vehicle (emissions OR pollution)

would retrieve documents about *vehicle emissions* and *vehicle pollution*. You cannot control *Ask, Yippy, Google* (or *Google Scholar*) in this way.

The following table explains, with an example, how each of the seven selected search engines handles these search operators in terms of (a) its default order of precedence in processing them, and (b) whether it allows you to override this default order of precedence by using brackets.

Ask	
Order of precedence	*Example*
OR	*cognitive styles OR independent learning*
AND	is interpreted as:
NOT	*cognitive AND (styles OR independent) AND learning*

Brackets **cannot** be used to override the default order of precedence.

Bing	
Order of precedence	*Example*
( )	*cognitive styles OR independent learning*
AND	is interpreted as:
OR	
NOT	*(cognitive AND styles) OR (independent AND learning)*
	But you can use brackets to override the default precedence:
	cognitive (styles OR independent) learning
	is interpreted as:
	cognitive AND (styles OR independent) AND learning

Brackets **can** be used to override the default order of precedence.

(Continued)

(Continued)

Exalead

Order of precedence	Example
( )	cognitive styles OR independent learning
AND	is interpreted as:
OR	(cognitive AND styles) OR (independent AND learning)
NOT	But you can use brackets to override the default precedence:
	cognitive (styles OR independent) learning
	is interpreted as:
	cognitive AND (styles OR independent) AND learning

Brackets **can** be used to override the default order of precedence.

Google

Order of precedence	Example
OR	cognitive styles OR independent learning
AND	is interpreted as:
NOT	cognitive AND (styles OR independent) AND learning

Brackets **cannot** be used to override the default order of precedence.

Yahoo

Order of precedence	Example
OR	cognitive styles OR independent learning
AND	is interpreted as:
NOT	cognitive AND (styles OR independent) AND learning

Brackets **cannot** be used to override the default order of precedence.

Yippy

Order of precedence	Example
( )	cognitive styles OR independent learning
OR	is interpreted as:
AND	cognitive AND (styles OR independent) AND learning
NOT	But you can use brackets to override the default precedence:
	(cognitive styles) OR (independent learning)
	is interpreted as:
	(cognitive AND styles) OR (independent AND learning)

Brackets **can** be used to override the default order of precedence.

Summary

Different information needs are best served by different search approaches. *Broad exploratory searching*, for example, is most suitable when you are building a preliminary overview of your topic. *More specific detailed* searching is required as you move from overview to a more focused examination of the precise details of your topic.

As you seek to increase the depth of your understanding of the topic, your searching will become more *highly specific* and *detailed*. *Broad exhaustive* searching will be useful in the later stages when you need to check that you have not missed any important aspects of the topic, or failed to appreciate fully how it interrelates with other topics within the bigger picture. As previously noted, the order in which you engage in these different types of searching may to some extent depend on your learning style.

The chapter then mapped these search approaches on to different types of search facility available in different search tools. These search facilities include *directory-based browsing, similarity searching, filtering, citation searching, Boolean techniques* and *advanced search operators*. Not all search tools offer all of these facilities. The chapter went on to explain what each of these offers, how to use it, and in which search tools it is available.

The next chapter will explore in detail three of the principal search tools designed specifically to find high-quality scholarly information.

EIGHT

Scholarly search tools in detail

WHY YOU NEED TO KNOW THIS

- General web search engines like *Google* can take you so far. But you need to be aware of other search tools that are better able to find the high-quality academic information that you require for your essays and research reports.
- These search tools are very different from general web search engines in that they are specifically geared to finding high-quality *scholarly* information – books, journal articles, conference papers, research theses and more.
- High-quality scholarly information is the essential fuel for your academic work, and these tools are specifically designed to find them.
- This chapter focuses in detail on three such tools – *Google Scholar*, *SciVerse Scopus* and *Web of Knowledge*. *Google Scholar* can be accessed freely by anyone over the web. *SciVerse Scopus* and *Web of Knowledge* are subscription-based. However, many universities subscribe to one or both of them.
- These are major scholarly search tools, and you need to be familiar with what they have to offer and how to use them.
- There are differences between these tools, and you also need to know when it might be more appropriate to use one rather than another.

When to use which search tools

No one search tool covers everything, and to achieve as comprehensive coverage as possible it is a good idea to use a variety of search tools. Although there is considerable overlap in coverage between them, *Google Scholar*, *SciVerse Scopus* and *Web of Knowledge* will also each retrieve unique documents not found in the others.

Having said that, each has its own particular strengths and weaknesses, which may make one more appropriate to use at different stages of your work, depending on your level of knowledge of your topic and what you are wanting to achieve from the search you are doing at the particular time you are doing it. Although you may eventually want to make your search as comprehensive as you can, this stage may come relatively late in the process of producing your work. At earlier stages, you may find it more appropriate to use one tool rather than another.

This section is designed to give some general guidelines which may help you decide on which tool(s) to use at different stages of your research.

If you are new to your topic, Google Scholar *may be a good starting point.*

Why? Because *Google Scholar* is less likely to find no or few hits. It will usually come up with something to get you started. One of the main reasons is that *Google Scholar* (unlike *SciVerse Scopus* or *Web of Knowledge*) indexes the full text of documents, so if your search terms or phrases are found in the text of a document but not in the title, abstract or keywords (the fields indexed by *Web of Knowledge* and *SciVerse Scopus*), *Google Scholar* is more likely to retrieve the document than the others. *Google Scholar* also offers a search interface that is arguably easier and more intuitive.

If your topic is complex, and you know what you want, then Web of Knowledge and SciVerse Scopus *offer you higher levels of control.*

How? Web of Knowledge and *SciVerse Scopus* allow you more control in precisely specifying exactly what you want in the case of complex searches. They offer a range of more sophisticated search facilities, including:

- More flexible wildcards (both '?' and '*' to stand for missing characters). *Google Scholar* only allows the wildcard '*' in phrases.
- More pre- and post-search filters to make your search more specific.
- Controlled vocabularies.
- Authority lists (authors and affiliations).
- Proximity operators.
- More control over how 'related' is defined in related document searching.

These allow you to be both more precise and more exhaustive in your searching, as you wish.

If you want to achieve as broad coverage as possible in order not to risk missing possibly important sources, you should use a range *of scholarly search tools such* as Google Scholar, Web of Knowledge *and* SciVerse Scopus *– not just one of them.*

Why? None of them covers all the literature. A number of useful sources are likely to be found in one but not the others. *Web of Knowledge* and *SciVerse Scopus* tell you exactly what they index. *Google Scholar* is less transparent. This allows you to be more systematic in terms of knowing exactly what you have searched for and what you have not yet searched for, in terms of their coverage of information sources.

If you want to narrow down the list of retrieved items systematically using progressive filtering, **Web of Knowledge** *and* **SciVerse Scopus** *are more sophisticated than* **Google Scholar.**

Why? Relative to *Google Scholar, Web of Knowledge* and *SciVerse Scopus* enable more sophisticated systematic narrowing down of your search if you retrieve a large list of items and want to refine it by adding filters (e.g. particular types of document, particular subject areas, etc.). *Web of Knowledge* and *SciVerse Scopus* also allow more flexibility in how your search results are displayed, allowing you to choose whether you want to display them in order of, for example, date, relevance, number of citations, author order.

The following sections explore each of these tools in detail.

Google Scholar

Google Scholar, like *SciVerse Scopus* and *Web of Knowledge*, is one of a number of search tools that are specifically geared to helping you to find scholarly academic information sources. So just by selecting one of these tools, you are easing your task of discovering high-quality information that you can use directly in your work. Unlike *SciVerse Scopus* and *Web of Knowledge*, which you can only access if your university subscribes to them, *Google Scholar* (http://scholar.google.com/) is completely free for anyone to use.

Coverage

Google Scholar covers scholarly literature. This includes peer-reviewed journal articles, conference papers, research theses, books and citations. It provides access not only to freely available information on the websites of universities, professional societies and open-access journals, but also, importantly, to information about sources only available from publishers via payment. The latter category forms a vast ocean of high-quality peer-reviewed information, including, for example, thousands of journal titles covering the whole range of academic subjects.

Much of this information will be available to you since your university will have subscribed to a large number of journals and will have purchased large numbers of books. *Google Scholar* will indicate whether you have access to particular sources via your library, and will allow you to directly access the full text of journal articles if they are available, assuming that your university has configured it to do this.

Some information sources will also be freely available via full-text copies of pre-prints (pre-publication versions of an article or paper) from university repositories or authors' personal websites. *Google Scholar* will also indicate beside an item it has found whether there is a free full-text version available. Where this is the case, you can simply click it to view or download it. Examples of how *Google Scholar* indicates whether information is available to you will be given in the next section.

Google Scholar covers a huge volume and range of scholarly material, and is a major search tool for finding high-quality information. However, unlike *SciVerse Scopus* and

Web of Knowledge, it does not explicitly publish details of exactly which publishers and which publications it covers.

Searching in *Google Scholar*

Google Scholar's default search page is shown in Figure 8.1. Note that you can use all the advanced search operators available in *Google* (see Chapter 7). For example:

allintitle: "review of research" OR "progress in" "mental health"

However, in addition to the advanced search operators discussed in relation to *Google*, *Google Scholar* offers an operator which will find documents by a particular author, for example *author:entwistle*. If you wish to specify an author's first as well as last name(s), enclose them in quotation marks. It is also advisable to use initials rather than full first names, e.g. *author: "nj entwistle"*. Note that a search for *author: "nj entwistle"*, will not necessarily retrieve documents indexed as being by 'n entwistle', but searching for *author: "n entwistle"* will retrieve documents by 'nj entwistle' as well as 'n entwistle'.

Available from the default search page (Figure 8.1) is the option to search for:

- Articles ('articles' includes not only journal articles, but also other documents including books and conference papers); or
- Articles including patents; or
- Legal court opinions and journals.

Figure 8.1   *Google Scholar*'s default search page

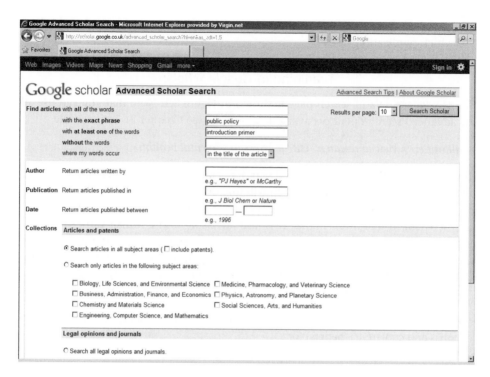

Figure 8.2   *Google Scholar's* advanced search page

Available from *Google Scholar's* advanced search page (Figure 8.2) are additional options. The boxes provided here enable you to use advanced search operators without having to type them into the search box. Filling in the form shown in Figure 8.2 is equivalent to typing the following into the search box shown in Figure 8.1:

allintitle: introduction OR primer "public policy"

However, there are other features available from the advanced search page which cannot be accessed via advanced operators. These include the ability to limit your search to a particular journal (or journals containing particular words in their title) by using the '*Return articles published in*' box. You can also limit your search to documents published in a particular year, between certain dates, or since a certain date by using the '*Return articles published between*' box. To find documents published since a particular year, enter that year in the first box and leave the second box blank. To find documents published in a particular year, enter the year in both boxes (e.g. *from 2009 to 2009*).

You can restrict your search to one or more of the following broad subject areas:

- Biology, Life Sciences, and Environmental
- Science Medicine, Pharmacology, and Veterinary Science

- Business, Administration, Finance, and Economics
- Physics, Astronomy, and Planetary Science
- Chemistry and Materials Science
- Social Sciences, Arts, and Humanities
- Engineering, Computer Science, and Mathematics

You can search specifically for legal court opinions and journals, and for opinions of particular types of court, and courts in particular US states.

Finding information that is directly available to you

Google Scholar can tell you which of the documents it has found are directly available to you. Figure 8.3 shows an example of search results with different levels of immediate availability. In this case, *Google Scholar* has been set up to flag items:

- Available freely online to anyone;
- Available online to members of the University of Sheffield Library (you can create your own list of one or more libraries to which you have access); or
- Available from your selected library but not necessarily online.

You can set up *Google Scholar* to do this via *Scholar Preferences* available from the cogwheel *Options* icon to the right of *Sign in* at the top right of the screen.

Type the name of your chosen library into the *Library Links* box, click the **Find library** button, and available libraries will be shown (Figure 8.5).

Tick the relevant box, but don't forget to click the **Save Preferences** button to confirm your choice. If you wish, you can add a number of libraries to your list.

Figure 8.3 *Google Scholar* search results

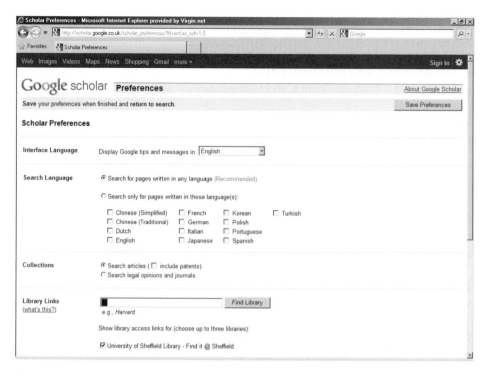

Figure 8.4 The *Google Scholar* preferences page

Library Links
(what's this?)

Sheffield   Find Library

e.g., *Harvard*

Show library access links for (choose up to three libraries):

☑ University of Sheffield Library - Find it @ Sheffield
☐ Sheffield Hallam University - Full Text via SHU Links

Figure 8.5 Setting up your library links

Citation searching

Citation searching allows you to find documents that cite an earlier document. If you are aware of a really key source that is highly relevant to your essay or project, and want to see who has done more recent work in the same area, building on this key source, you can use the source as a starting point in a citation search. In the example below, we have searched *Google Scholar* for a key paper by Webber and Johnston on *information literacy*. This may have been recommended to us as a key influential paper in the field, or we may have found it as a result of a search and decided that it was

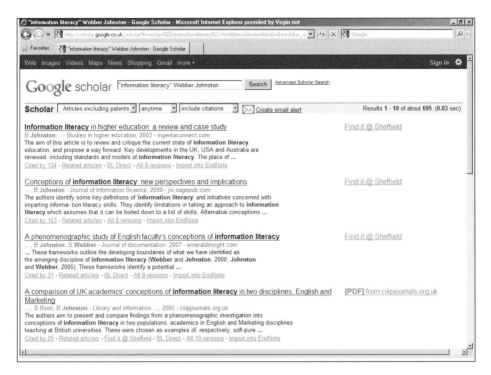

Figure 8.6 *Google Scholar* results page

highly relevant to our interests. Citation searching is available from the *Google Scholar* results page (Figure 8.6).

Note that at the bottom of the first reference, there is a link *Cited by 134*. Clicking this link will take us to another page displaying the documents that cite the work by Webber and Johnston in their bibliographies.

The same citation searching procedure can be applied to any of the sources appearing on the new page. It means that you can find potentially relevant sources without having to know their authors – or even explicitly search for them.

Exporting citations

Google Scholar also offers the option to export citations. For this to work, you need to have installed appropriate reference software such as *Mendeley* or *EndNote*. Reference software will be introduced in Chapter 12. Basically, it works in conjunction with search tools like *Google Scholar* and word-processing tools like *Microsoft Word*. It allows you to create your own database of information sources directly from the results pages of search tools.

In Figure 8.6, note the *Import into EndNote* link that appears at the end of each retrieved item. This example assumes that you are using the *EndNote*

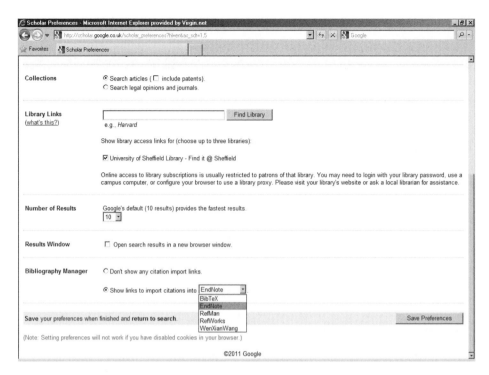

Figure 8.7 The *Google Scholar* Preferences page

reference software and have set up *Google Scholar* to offer the appropriate format for export (see below). When you click on the *Import into EndNote* link, a full reference to the item will be automatically inserted into your *EndNote* database. You can then read sources from your database directly into your essay or dissertation at the click of a button. The software will automatically create correct references in your text, and a correctly formatted bibliography at the end of your work.

You can set this up – and choose the particular format in you would like references to be exported – from the *Google Scholar Preferences* page (Figure 8.7).

See the final section in this chapter for details of the relative strengths of *Google Scholar*, *SciVerse Scopus* and *Web of Knowledge*.

SciVerse Scopus

Although it is not freely available on the web, *SciVerse Scopus* is a major search tool and is available to students in many universities. It offers searching across its own huge database of some 44.4 million items across scientific, technical, medical, social sciences and arts and humanities literature. It is updated daily, and claims[18] to cover almost 18,500 titles with 16,500 peer-reviewed journals and "Articles-in-Press" from over 3,750 journals, 400 trade publications, 300 book series and 4.4 million conference papers. It integrates searching for web-based information via Elsevier's own scientific web search engine *Scirus*, which indexes 315 million scientific web pages (this can also be accessed separately, and freely, at http://www.scirus.com/).

SciVerse Scopus is integrated into Elsevier's *SciVerse* platform. The *SciVerse* hub is designed to offer a single point of access allowing searching across not only *SciVerse Scopus*, but also *ScienceDirect* and *SciTopics*. *ScienceDirect* is a database of over 10 million journal articles and book chapters. *SciTopics* is a database of authoritative summaries of research on a range of scientific topics.

Check your university library website for details of the search tools it offers you to see if *SciVerse Scopus* is included. If it is not, then it is possible that *Web of Knowledge*, another of the major scholarly search tools, is available. *Web of Knowledge* is introduced in the following section. Both may be accessed via a web browser.

Although these databases give access to many of the same information sources covered by *Google Scholar*, there are important differences. The bottom line is that different search tools cover only a proportion of what is out there. You need to use more than one. Perform the same search in *Google Scholar*, *SciVerse Scopus* and *Web of Knowledge* and, although there will be considerable overlap, there will also be items found uniquely in each. The unique items *may* be the ones that are best suited to your needs, so it really is worth the effort of using multiple databases.

Also bear in mind that expensive subscription tools such as *SciVerse Scopus* and *Web of Knowledge* tend to offer more sophisticated search options and to allow you greater control over your searches. This can pay dividends.

Searching for documents

Figure 8.8 shows the *SciVerse Scopus* basic **Document search** search page. It is a good idea to use the singular form of words when searching in *SciVerse Scopus*. If you do so, it will automatically, for most words, also search for plurals and other common forms.

Also, you should be aware that *SciVerse Scopus* (unlike *Web of knowledge*) ignores 'stop words' when it searches. Stop words are common words that you may put in your search but which do not add a lot of meaning. According to the *SciVerse Scopus* help system, stop words include: personal pronouns (e.g. *we*, *she*, *he*, *they*), most articles (e.g. *a*, *the*), most forms of the verb *to be* (e.g. *is*, *was*, *were*), and some conjunctions (e.g. *if*, *when*, *because*).

If you include a stop word in your search, it is ignored unless you specifically stipulate that it should be included, for example by enclosing it in double quotation marks. Stop words will also be included if they appear within a phrase that you are searching for, a phrase also being indicated by being enclosed in double quotation marks. (However, in *Web of Knowledge*, stop words are ignored even if they appear within a phrase.)

---

[18]Sciverse Scopus (April 2011). Content coverage guide. Retrieved from http://www.info.sciverse.com/UseFiles/sciverse_scopus_content_coverage_O.pdf

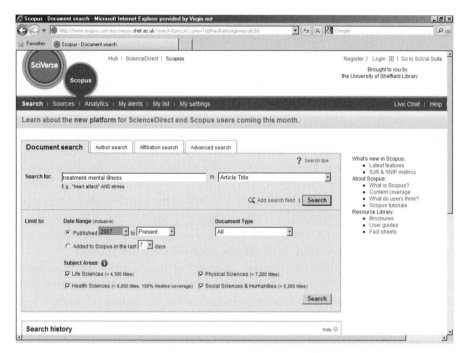

Figure 8.8   The *SciVerse Scopus* basic search page

Let us assume that we are searching for articles on *the treatment of mental illness*. As shown in Figure 8.8, we can further specify that we want to find articles that contain these keywords *in their title* (which indicates their importance in the sources). Instead of *Article title*, choices we could have made include:

All fields	Keywords
Article title, abstract, keywords	Affiliation
First author	Language
Authors	References
Source title	Conference
Article title	Article title, abstract, keywords, authors
Abstract	

We can also specify the type of document we want to retrieve. Choices include:

All	Conference review
Article or review	Letter
Article	Editorial
Review	Note
Article in press	Short survey
Article or conference paper	Business article or Press
Conference paper	Erratum

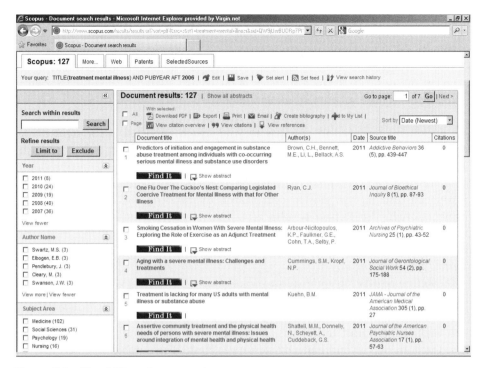

Figure 8.9   The *SciVerse Scopus* results page

We can build a more complex search if we wish. Clicking the *Add search field* option would open a new 'search for' box, allowing us, for example, to specify, additionally, that the word *policy* should also occur in the <u>abstract</u>. Further search boxes can be added and linked to previous ones using AND or OR or AND NOT. We have not done so in the example shown.

We can also specify that we want to find materials published from 2007 to the present. As you can see from Figure 8.8, we could also have filtered the search according to one or more broad subject categories (Life Sciences, Physical Sciences, Health Sciences and Social Sciences & Humanities). The default, selected here, is to search in all these categories.

Clicking *Search* will display the page shown in Figure 8.9. This tells us that *SciVerse Scopus* has found a number of items that it has classified into five types: **Scopus** (127 items found); **More**; **Web**; **Patents**; and **SelectedSources**.

- **Scopus** is the main category, consisting of items indexed by *SciVerse Scopus* itself.
- **More** includes references from documents indexed by *SciVerse Scopus*, but which are not necessarily themselves available on *SciVerse Scopus* (documents not available are marked with an icon).
- **Web** refers to references found from a *Scirus* search of the web. *Scirus* is a specialised search engine designed to find scholarly scientific information and filter out more

general and lower quality sources. You can access it directly (i.e. not only from within *SciVerse Scopus*) at: http://www.scirus.com/.

- **Patents** are, as the name suggests, patents.
- **SelectedSources** are sources from a specific category of *Scirus* search that may be set up by your particular library. For details of the criteria used to define selected sources you should contact your library administrator.

The documents retrieved in response to your search are listed at the right of the screen. By clicking on the appropriate column heading, you can display them in order of their *date* of publication, their *relevance* to your search, *author name*, *title of the source*, or the *number of times each has been cited* by other authors.

You can also narrow down your search by filtering the results using the information in the **Refine results** box. This shows an analysis of the documents that match your search query by *Year, Author Name, Subject Area* (and not shown in Figure 8.9) *Document Type, Source Title, Keywords, Affiliation, Source Type and Language*.

The **Refine results** categories allow you to narrow down your search, which is useful in searches where a large number of items are retrieved. You can choose to limit your results to one or more of the categories shown by ticking the appropriate box(es) then clicking the **Limit to** button. Conversely, you can choose to exclude one or more categories from your results by clicking **Exclude**. The number of items retrieved for each category is shown in brackets after each one. Figure 8.10 below shows the effects of limiting the search to include **Nursing**[19] sorted by *relevance*.

If you select the first item by clicking its title, you are shown details of this particular document (Figure 8.11).

Note that you are able to view the 48 references used by the authors in this document by clicking the *View references* option.

How to obtain documents and save their details

If you have a **Find It** button (appearing above the title of the document in Figure 8.11, and below the title in Figure 8.10), your university has configured *SciVerse Scopus* to find the document directly. Click the **Find It** button, and you will be told whether your library has the information source. If it has, and the full text is available electronically (e.g. an article in an online journal subscribed to by your library), you should be able to access it immediately. If it has the item but it is not available electronically (e.g. a book), you will be taken to the library catalogue record for the item.

---

[19]In Figure 8.11 *Scriverse Scopus* has automatically added OR LIMIT-TO (SUBJAREA, "MULT") to the query. This is an automatic "catch all" which is redundant when using the **Refine results** option.

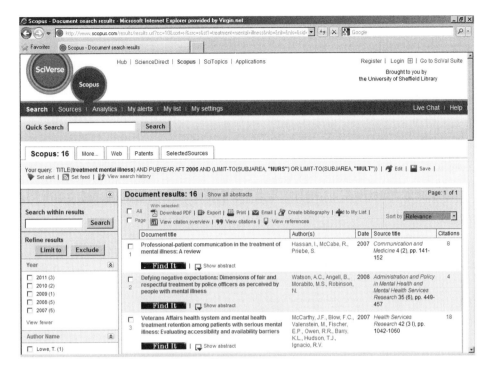

Figure 8.10 Limiting your search results

In Figure 8.11 there are other buttons available to you.

- **Library Catalogue** also searches for details of the document in your university library catalogue, assuming that *SciVerse Scopus* has been configured to enable this.
- **Copac** searches for the document in the combined holdings of members of Research Libraries UK (RLUK) and tells you which libraries have copies.
- **1st Author PubMed** performs a search for publications by the first author of the document

You may also want to save the bibliographic details of documents you find using *SciVerse Scopus*. Don't forget that full bibliographic details of the sources you refer to in your work will need to appear in the bibliography of your document (see Chapter 10 for details of citations and bibliographies).

SciVerse Scopus allows you to do this very easily via a number of options shown in Figures 8.10 and 8.11. If you are looking at the details of a particular document (as in Figure 8.11), you can simply click one of these options. If you are looking at the list of retrieved items (as in Figure 8.10), you will need to select one or more documents via the check boxes before you do so. These options are:

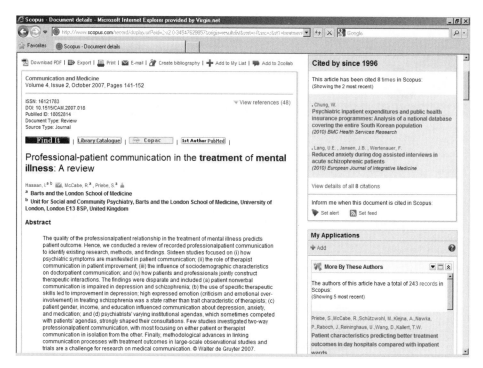

Figure 8.11   Document details page

- **Download** a PDF version of the document if this is available, and an abstract if it is not.
- **Export** details of the selected document(s) in one of the following formats: *text file*, *comma-separated file* (suitable for opening in *Excel*, for example), *RIS format* files suitable for reference management software such as *EndNote*, *ProCite* and *Reference Manager*, *RefWorks* direct export, and *BibTeX*.
- **Print** details of the selected document(s).
- **Email** details of the selected document(s).
- Create a **bibliography** of the selected document(s) in a *Word*, *RTF*, *HTML* or *text* file.
- **Add to My List** enables you to create a running list of documents to which you can add during your *SciVerse Scopus* search session. You can at any time go to this list via the **My List** tab at the top and bottom of the *SciVerse Scopus* screen, and apply the options listed above to all or selected items on your list. The list will not persist after you have closed your *SciVerse Scopus* session. You can save lists between sessions if you register personally (this is free) and are logged on to your personal account.

Advanced search

Advanced search allows you to exercise more control. Figure 8.12 shows the *SciVerse Scopus* **Advanced search** page, available as a tab on the **Search** page.

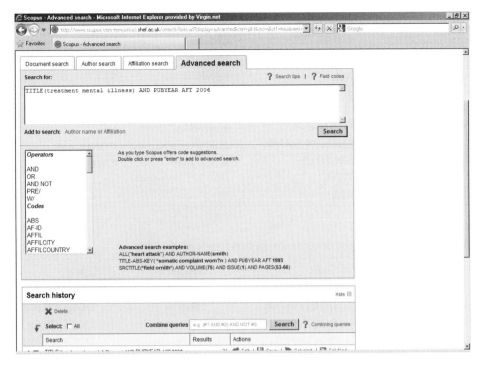

Figure 8.12 The *SciVerse Scopus* advanced search page

Just typing search terms into the Advance Search box results in a search for your terms in **all fields**. But you can exercise more control by using advanced features which allow you to specify a search more precisely. This is useful if you want to conduct a more tightly focused search.

Recall that from the basic Document search page you can specify which document field(s) you would like to search in, the type(s) of document you would like to be retrieved, and broad subject area(s) (Figure 8.8). Each of these categories has its own code, as shown in Tables 8.1, 8.2 and 8.3, which can be used directly in an advanced search.

Using these codes from the **Advanced Search** page (rather than selecting the categories from the dropdown lists and check boxes from the **Simple Search** page) allows you to form complex searches using combinations of the codes, your search terms, and advanced search operators.

Let us look at these advanced search operators and how to use them in combination with codes and search terms. There are four types of operator:

1. Boolean operators
2. Wildcards
3. Proximity operators
4. Quotation marks and brackets for phrases

Table 8.1 *SciVerse Scopus* search fields and associated codes. This is a selection. Consult *SciVerse Scopus* Help for the full list

Field	Code	Field	Code
All fields	**ALL**	Keywords	**KEY**
Article title, abstract, keywords	**TITLE-ABS-KEY**	Affiliation	**AFFIL**
		Language	**LANGUAGE**
First author	**FIRSTAUTH**	References	**REF**
Authors	**AUTHOR-NAME**	Conference name	**CONFNAME**
Source title	**SRCTITLE**	Article title, abstract, keywords, authors	**TITLE-ABS-KEY-AUTH**
Article title	**TITLE**		
Abstract	**ABS**		

Table 8.2 *SciVerse Scopus* document types and associated codes

Information source	Code	Information source	Code
Article	**DOCTYPE(ar)**	Editorial	**DOCTYPE(ed)**
Abstract Report	**DOCTYPE(ab)**	Erratum	**DOCTYPE(er)**
Article in Press	**DOCTYPE(ip)**	Letter	**DOCTYPE(le)**
Book	**DOCTYPE(bk)**	Note	**DOCTYPE(no)**
Business Article	**DOCTYPE(bz)**	Press Release	**DOCTYPE(pr)**
Conference Paper	**DOCTYPE(cp)**	Report	**DOCTYPE(re)**
Conference Review	**DOCTYPE(cr)**	Short Survey	**DOCTYPE(sh)**

Boolean operators

You can combine search terms using the operators **OR**, **AND** and **AND NOT**. For example:

> *TITLE(learning OR cognitive AND style OR strategy) AND DOCTYPE(cp)*

which means:

> *Find me **conference papers** with the words learning **or** cognitive, **and** style **or** strategy, in the **title**.*

Linking words with several words with **AND**s and **OR**s can be confusing. For example:

> *TITLE(climate AND change OR global AND warming OR greenhouse AND effect)*

Table 8.3 *SciVerse Scopus* subject areas and associated codes

Subject area	Code	Subject area	Code
Agricultural and Biological Sciences	**SUBJAREA(AGRI)**	Engineering	**SUBJAREA(ENGI)**
		Environmental Science	**SUBJAREA(ENVI)**
Arts and Humanities	**SUBJAREA(ARTS0)**	Health Professions	**SUBJAREA(HEAL)**
Biochemistry, Genetics and Molecular Biology	**SUBJAREA(BIOC)**	Immunology and Microbiology	**SUBJAREA(IMMU)**
		Materials Science	**SUBJAREA(MATE)**
Business, Management and accounting	**SUBJAREA(BUSI)**	Mathematics	**SUBJAREA(MATH)**
		Medicine	**SUBJAREA(MEDI)**
Chemical Engineering	**SUBJAREA(CENG)**	Neuroscience	**SUBJAREA(NEUR)**
Chemistry	**SUBJAREA(CHEM)**	Nursing	**SUBJAREA(NURS)**
Computer Science	**SUBJAREA(COMP)**	Pharmacology, Toxicology and Pharmaceutics	**SUBJAREA(PHAR)**
Decision Sciences	**SUBJAREA(DECI)**		
Dentistry	**SUBJAREA(DENT)**		
Earth and Planetary Sciences	**SUBJAREA(EART)**	Physics and Astronomy	**SUBJAREA(PHYS)**
		Psychology	**SUBJAREA(PSYC)**
Economics, Econometrics and Finance	**SUBJAREA(ECON)**	Social Sciences	**SUBJAREA(SOCI)**
		Veterinary	**SUBJAREA(VETE)**
		Multidisciplinary	**SUBJAREA(MULT)**
Energy	**SUBJAREA(ENER)**		

It is important to know that *SciVerse Scopus* figures out the **OR**s before the **AND**s. The **AND NOT** operator is evaluated last and it is advisable to place it at the very end of your query. So the query above is interpreted as:

climate AND (change OR global) AND (warming OR greenhouse) AND effect

and not:

(climate AND change) OR (global AND warming) OR (greenhouse AND effect)

which is what you might have wished.

If you put brackets round words to try to force *SciVerse Scopus* to interpret your query as you want it, they will be ignored. *SciVerse Scopus* interprets **AND**, **OR** and **AND NOT** in the strict order mentioned above, regardless of any brackets you put round your terms. This is not the case with *Web of Knowledge*, where you *can* impose your own interpretation by using brackets.

Note also that **AND** is implied. So the following searches are interpreted in exactly the same way.

learning AND style

learning style

Wildcards

The question mark ? can be used to replace one character. For example:

analy?e

will find: *analyse* and *analyze*.
The asterisk * replaces zero, one or multiple characters. For example:

*comput**

will find: *computing, computer, computers, computation* and *computational*.
SciVerse Scopus allows wildcards to be used at the beginning of a word. Thus:

**national*

will find: *national, cross-national, transnational* and *international*.

Proximity operators

SciVerse Scopus allows you to search for documents in which your search terms appear within a certain distance of each other. The first of two words linked by the operator **PRE/n** (short for 'precedes') must appear **before** the second word and be within a certain number (**n**) of intervening words. So, for example:

learning PRE/2 style

will find documents containing *learning* followed, within two or less other words, by *style*. It would therefore find documents containing the words:

*"**learning** preference strategies, **styles** and approaches"*

but not

"styles of learning"

Two terms linked by the operator **W/n** (short for 'within') must occur within 'n' words of each other. However, they can appear in any order. Thus:

TITLE(drug W/4 addict*)

would retrieve documents with the words *drug* and any word beginning with *addict* (including *addict, addicted, addiction*) appearing within four words of each other in the title. The following documents would all be retrieved:

Abuse of prescription **drugs** and the risk of **addiction**

Addiction and autonomy: Can addicted people consent to the prescription of their **drug** of **addiction**?

Validation of a questionnaire on **drug addicts**' motivation for treatment

Estrangement factors associated with **addiction** to alcohol and **drugs** among homeless youth in three U.S. cities

At least 25% of elderly residents of German nursing homes are **addicted** to psychotropic **drugs**, report claims

The influence of community on relapse **addiction** to **drug** use: Evidence from Malaysia

Giving **addicts** their **drug** of choice: The problem of consent

Biological research on **drug** abuse and **addiction** in Hispanics: Current status and future directions

SciVerse Scopus recommends, as a rule of thumb, that to find words occurring in the same *phrase*, you should use 3, 4, or 5 as the value of **n**. For the same *sentence*, use 15, and for the same *paragraph*, 50. To find *adjacent* terms, use 0. For example:

learning PRE/0 style

is equivalent to searching for the phrase "learning style".

Quotation marks and brackets for phrases

Enclosing your search terms in quotation marks means that that they will be searched for as a phrase – in that order with no intervening words. However, *SciVerse Scopus* will still automatically retrieve singular and plural forms of the words. So:

TITLE("learning style")

will retrieve documents containing the words *learning style* or *learning styles* in the title.

Curly braces { } allow you to specify that the words between them should be searched for *exactly as they are written* – in the same order and with no automatic inclusion of singular and plural. Thus:

TITLE({learning style})

would retrieve no plurals – just *learning style* in the title. Bear in mind that you cannot use a wildcard within curly brackets since a search for {strateg*} would try to find documents containing literally *strateg** (and not *strategy, strategies*, etc.).

The following query:

ALL(learning OR cognitive AND style OR strateg*) AND TITLE(review AND research)*

will be interpreted as:

Search for documents which contain
  In any of the document's fields (**ALL**)
    either the word *learning* **OR** the word *cognitive*
      AND either any word beginning with *style...* (including *style* and *styles*)
        OR any word beginning with *strateg...* (including *strategy, strategies, strategic*)
    AND in the **TITLE** field
      the words *review* **AND** *research*.

As previously noted, when two words or expressions appear together with no operator, AND is implied. So the same search could have been expressed as follows, without the ANDs:

ALL(learning OR cognitive style OR strateg*) TITLE(review research)*

Search history

Every time you search, whether from the simple or advanced search pages, your search is added to your *search history*. You can access your search history at any time by clicking **Advanced search** on the *SciVerse Scopus* **Search** page (see Figure 8.12). There is also a *View search history* link on the search results page (see Figure 8.10). Your search history can be useful in helping you develop a complex search. Figure 8.13 shows an example.

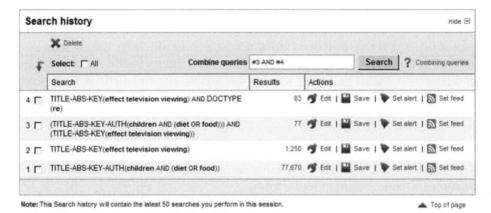

Figure 8.13 Search history

In this example, my first search was for:

   TITLE-ABS-KEY-AUTH(children AND (diet OR food))

This retrieved 77,670 documents. I then searched for:

   TITLE-ABS-KEY(effect television viewing)

which retrieved 1,250 documents. I combined both of these searches into a third search by typing into the **Combine queries** box:

   #1 AND #2

and clicking the **Search** button. This retrieved 77 documents. My fourth search was for:

   TITLE-ABS-KEY(effect television viewing) AND DOCTYPE(re)

which was my second search, with the added requirement that the document type to be searched for was *reviews* (DOCTYPE(re)). Figure 8.13 shows that I am about to combine searches #3 and #4. The effect of this (not shown) was to narrow my results to 10 highly relevant documents.

   Doing this enables you to try different searches for different components of a more complex search, and to combine them in various ways – backtracking if necessary and trying different combinations as you gradually narrow your search and home in on a manageable number of highly relevant documents.

   From the search history screen, you can *edit* your search – and also *save* it so that you can run it at a later date without having to retype it. This is useful if you have a complex search and you want to run it periodically to check for new documents.

You can also set up email *alerts* and web *feeds* to alert you when a new document that matches your search is added to the *SciVerse Scopus* database. Note that in order to save searches or set up alerts and feeds, as well as your university having to have a subscription to *SciVerse Scopus*, you also have to be registered personally (this is free) and personally logged in. Saving searches and setting up email alerts and web feeds are discussed in Chapter 11.

How to find related, cited and citing documents

The screen showing details of a particular document offers an option to **Find related documents** (bottom right in Figure 8.14).

Within the **Find related documents** option, we can choose to find documents that are related in terms of shared *references*, *authors* or *keywords*. Within each of these options, we can select *all* or *selected* references, *all* or *selected* authors, or *all* or *selected* keywords. If we choose *selected* in any of these categories, we are shown a list from which we can select. (No such control over how 'related' is calculated is allowed by *Google Scholar*. *Web of Knowledge* calculates relatedness in terms of shared references.)

We can also find documents which cite the particular document we have selected by clicking the *View details of all 6 citations* link. Documents cited in the present document can be viewed by selecting the *View references* link at the top of the screen. You can

Figure 8.14   The document details page

also set up an email alert or web feed from the *Set alert* and *Set feed* links respectively, so that you are notified when this document is cited by any new document added to the *SciVerse Scopus* database. As noted in the previous section, you must be personally registered and logged in to *SciVerse Scopus* to be able to do this. Setting up alerts in *SciVerse Scopus* and other tools will be discussed in Chapter 11.

Note that *SciVerse Scopus* offers many more tools and facilities than those described here. The purpose of this section has been to introduce the basics in order to get you started. See the final section in this chapter for details of the relative strengths of *Google Scholar*, *SciVerse Scopus* and *Web of Knowledge*.

Web of Knowledge incorporating Web of Science*

Like *SciVerse Scopus*, *Web of Knowledge* (incorporating *Web of Science*) is a major search tool to which many universities subscribe. It offers access to over 87 million items and 700 million cited references across 256 scientific disciplines[20]. These include some 23,000 journals, 23 million patents, 110,000 conference proceedings, 9,000 websites and 2 million chemical structures. Check your university library website for details of the search tools they offer you to see if it is included.

Web of Knowledge is in fact a single interface for searching a range of databases. These include *MEDLINE* (covering biomedicine, life sciences, bioengineering, public health, clinical care, and plant and animal science), *BIOSIS Previews* and *BIOSIS Citation Index* (covering life sciences and biomedical research), *Journal Citation Reports* (containing data relating to academic journals including citation patterns of articles in them, and impact measures for each journal), and *Web of Science* (described below). These databases can be selected and searched individually – or a single search can be conducted across them all. Figure 8.15 shows the **All Databases** search screen.

You can, instead of using the **All Databases** option, select any one of these databases and search separately in them. One reason for doing this is that the different databases offer unique search facilities such as specialised controlled vocabularies and search fields. Having said this, **All Databases** searching still offers a range of sophisticated search options.

This chapter focuses on one of the databases mentioned above, *Web of Science*, which covers the world's scholarly literature across the sciences, social sciences, arts, and humanities. It offers access to over 10,000 high-impact journals and 110,000 conference proceedings. *Web of Science* itself consists of a number of databases, but a single query will search all of them. These databases include:

---

*Certain data included herein are derived from the Web of Science ® prepared by THOMSON REUTERS ®, Inc. (Thomson ®), Philadelphia, Pennsylvania, USA: © Copyright THOMSON REUTERS ® 2010. All rights reserved.

---

[20]Thomson Reuters (2011). Web of Knowledge. Quick facts. Retrieved 1 August 2011, from http://wokinfo.com/about/facts/

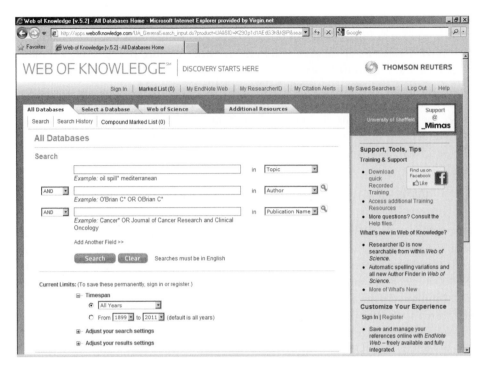

Figure 8.15 The *Web of Knowledge* **All Databases** search screen

- Science Citation Index Expanded
- Social Sciences Citation Index
- Arts & Humanities Citation Index
- Conference Proceedings Citation Index – Science
- Conference Proceedings Citation Index – Social Sciences & Humanities
- Index Chemicus
- Current Chemical Reactions

Searching for documents

Unlike *SciVerse Scopus*, *Web of Knowledge* (and its component databases including *Web of Science*) does not ignore stop words in searches. Stop words are common words like 'a', 'before', 'after', 'further', 'more', etc. This makes it easier to search for phrases including common words such as *vitamin C*.

Figure 8.16 shows the *Web of Science* basic search page. As in the section on *SciVerse Scopus*, we will search for articles that contain the words *treatment mental illness* in their title.

Instead of **Title**, we could have chosen from a number of search fields, shown in Table 8.4. We can also, if we wish, specify that we are interested in articles appearing within particular years via the **Current limits** option shown in Figure 8.16. For this example, we have kept the **All Years** default option.

Table 8.4 *Web of Science* Search fields

Author	Address
Researcher ID	Conference
Group author	Language
Editor	Document type
Publication name	Funding agency
Year published	Grant number

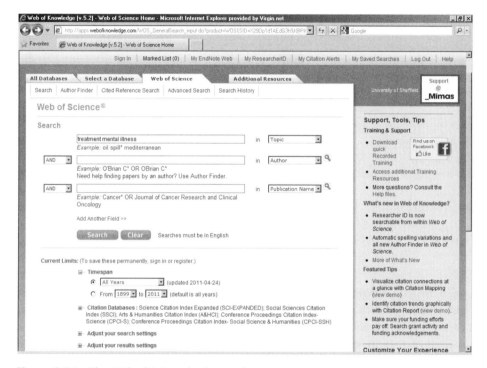

Figure 8.16 The *Web of Science* basic search page

We can build a more complex search if we wish. Clicking the *Add Another Field* option would open new 'search for' boxes allowing us to specify further parameters for our search. These further boxes can be linked together using **AND**, **OR** and **NOT**.

At the bottom of the screen shown in Figure 8.16 are three options:

- The *Citation Databases* option allows you to select one or more of the individual databases that make up *Web of Science*. By default, all are selected.
- *Adjust your search settings* allows you to switch 'lemmatization' on and off. When it is switched on (which is the default) this means that in Topic and Title searches, *Web of Knowledge* (and *Web of Science*) will automatically search for over 7,000 different inflected forms of words, including plurals, singulars and synonyms. So, for example, a search for *aluminum* will automatically also retrieve *aluminium*. *Mouse* will also retrieve *mice*, *color* will retrieve *colour*, and *napkin* will find not only *napkin* and *napkins*, but

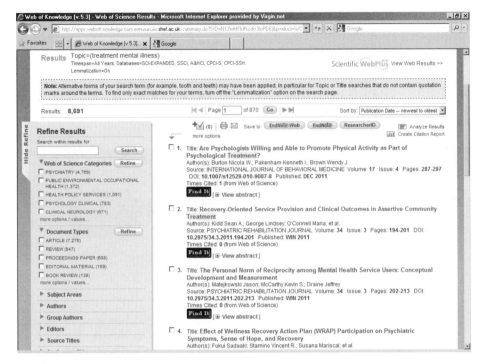

Figure 8.17 The *Web of Science* results page

also *serviette*. However, even when switched on, lemmatization can be over-ridden by enclosing search terms in quotation marks. Thus whilst a search for *colour* will also retrieve *color*, a search for *"colour"* will retrieve only *colour*.

- *Adjust your results settings* allows you to order the results of your search in different ways – for example, by *date of publication*, *relevance*, *times cited*, alphabetically by *author's name*, *source title* or *conference title*. This option is also available from the *Search* results page, discussed below and shown in Figure 8.17.

This page lists the retrieved documents in the right hand pane of the screen. At the top of the screen (not shown in Figure 8.18) is also a link to *View Web Results* via *Scientific WebPlus* (http://scientific.thomsonwebplus.com/). This is a web search engine designed selectively to find scientific materials suitable for researchers. It allows searching by topic, person/author, organism, drug, and gene.

In the left hand pane of the screen shown in Figure 8.17 there are options to narrow down our search to make it more relevant to our needs. We can restrict our search to particular **Categories/Clinical neurology** (Psychiatry, etc.). *Web of Science* tells us how many of the articles it has retrieved fall into each of these categories: 4,769 in Psychiatry, 671 in Clinical neurology, etc. *Web of Science* also gives us a breakdown of documents found according to **Document Types**. Figure 8.17 shows us (at the left of the screen) that there are 7,276 articles, 947 reviews, 608 proceedings papers, etc. If we click

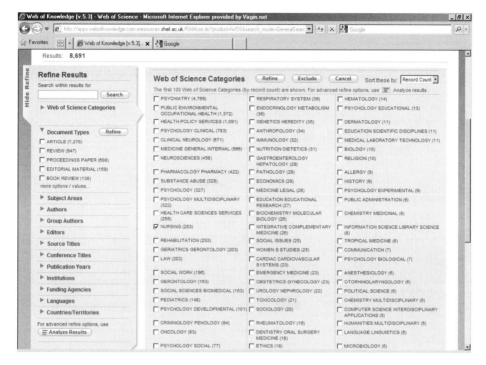

Figure 8.18 Refining results in *Web of Science*

the small forward arrows by the other categories (e.g. **Subject Areas**, **Authors**, **Group Authors**, **Editors**, **Source Titles**, etc.) the categories would expand to show a similar detailed breakdown of documents retrieved.

The number of documents retrieved is very large in this case. Clearly it will be advantageous to make our search much more focused. This can easily be done, as we will now see. If we click *more options / values* under **Web of Science Categories**, a finer-grained analysis is displayed in the right hand pane of the screen, as shown in Figure 8.18.

This list is ordered by the number of documents retrieved in each sub-category. However, we can choose instead to display the categories alphabetically via the **Sort these by**: option at the top right of the screen in Figure 8.18.

At any stage, we can select one or more boxes and click the **Refine** button to narrow our search. The example here assumes that we are working in the context of a nursing-related essay, so we have selected the **Nursing** category, in which 253 of the documents retrieved are classified. We must click the **Refine** button for this filter to be applied. When we do so, the documents displayed are restricted to those classified in the **Nursing** subject category (Figure 8.19).

As previously noted, the **Sort these by:** option at the top right of the screen allows us to sort the list in a number of ways. In Figure 8.20 this is by *Publication date – newest to oldest*

Let's now sort by *relevance* (Figure 8.20).

Figure 8.19 The filtered search results

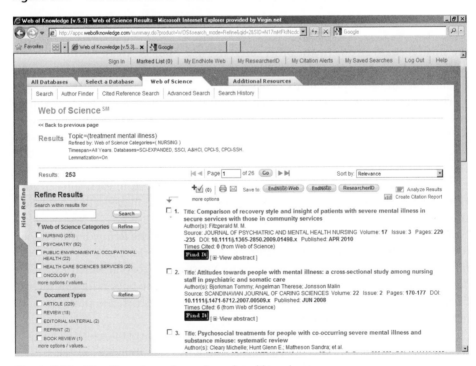

Figure 8.20 The filtered search results ordered by *relevance*

How to obtain documents and save their details

There are a number of things we can do from this screen:

- We can look at the abstract of any document by clicking *View abstract* (the abstract will appear, as shown in Figure 8.21).
- We can select one or more documents (by checking the boxes by their titles) and export their details, e.g. to print, text, email, directly into reference management software or to your *Marked List*. (These options will be described in more detail below.)
- If your university has set up this functionality, we can use the **Find It** search to see if your library has the item. If available as full text, you will be able to access it directly.
- We can click on the title of a document to go to a screen giving details of the document. This will also enable us to go on to do a number of additional things, including (as explained in more detail below), finding documents related to the selected document, and finding documents that the author of the selected document has used (and has included in their *References*).

However, before we do any of these things we may need to inspect other pages of hits. If we navigate away from this page to view another page – or whenever we click the **Add to Marked List** icon (the icon with a plus sign and a tick above *more options*) – any items that we have selected (by clicking their boxes) will be remembered in our

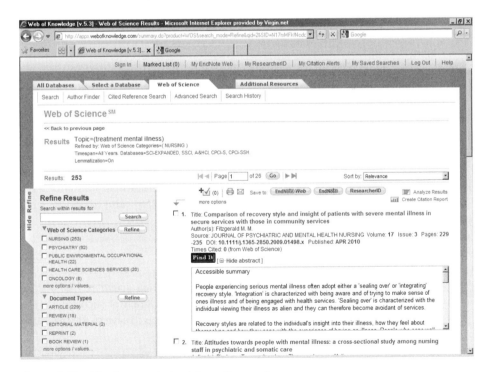

Figure 8.21 Viewing an abstract from the results page

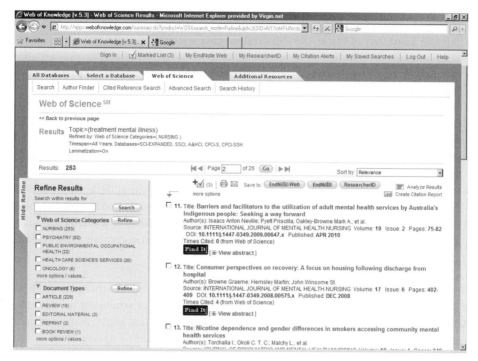

Figure 8.22 Search results and the *Marked List*

Marked List. In Figure 8.22 above, we have moved on to look at the second page of hits. Note that the three items we selected have been saved to our *Marked List*.

Whenever we are ready, we can go to our *Marked List* and print or save our records. Figure 8.23 shows the *Marked List* screen after we have added four more references to our *Marked List* from the second page of hits, and after we have then clicked the *Marked List* link at the top of the screen in Figure 8.22.

The *Marked List* screen allows us to choose the level of detail we want to print or save – author, title, source, abstract, times cited and International Standard Serial Number (ISSN) or International Standard Book Number (ISBN) – and to choose what type of output we want. Possible outputs are as follows:

- **Print** will print the references in bibliographic format.
- **E-mail** will email the document(s) in text or HTML format.
- **Save** the details of the document to *EndNote, EndNote Web, Reference Manager* or similar reference management tools (see Chapter 12 for details of such tools). The *Save to other Reference Software* drop-down Menu allows you to save to BibTex, html, plain text or tab delimited file.
- **ResearcherID** allows authors to link their ID to their own articles thus avoiding author misidentification for authors with the same names.

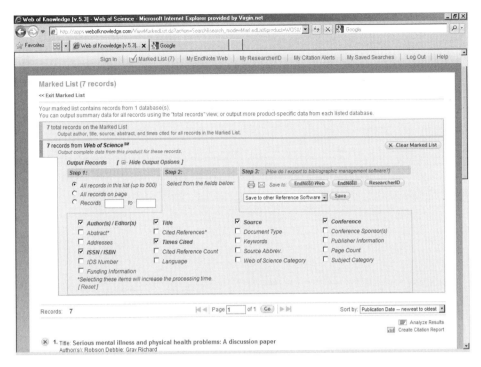

Figure 8.23 The *Marked List* screen

At any stage, we may want to take a closer look at one or more of the documents found. From the screen listing the documents retrieved (Figure 8.22), we can click on the title of any document to be taken to a screen giving full details of the article, as shown in Figure 8.24 overleaf.

As you can see in Figure 8.24, a number of options available from other screens (and already discussed) are also available from this screen. These include **Print**, **E-mail** and **Save to** buttons above the title of the document, and **Times Cited** at the top right. Options not previously available are **Related Records**, which allows you to find other documents related to the selected document, and **Cited References** which enables you to find documents that the author of the selected document has used (i.e. are included in the *References* section of the selected document).

How to find related, cited and citing documents

From the same screen (Figure 8.24), we can also select the following options:

- **Times cited:** clicking the number following **Times cited:** (in this case, 6) or clicking *view all 6 citing articles* will display documents that cite your selected document in their references.

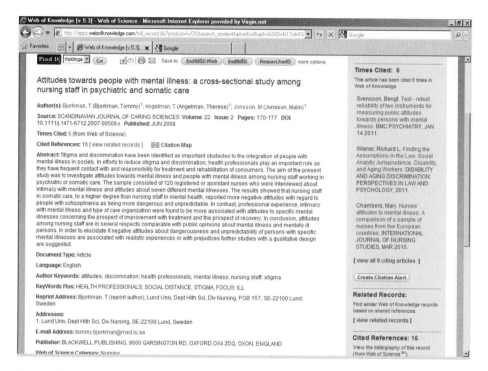

Figure 8.24 The document details page

- **Related records:** this enables you to discover other information sources that are related to the document you are looking at. Clicking *view related records* will display other documents *that share references with* this document. It is highly likely that documents that share references are related in terms of topic.
- **Cited references:** clicking the number after **Cited References:** (in this case, 16) will display details of the documents that the author of this document has used (i.e. which appear in the *References* section of the selected document). Looking at the references used in a document that is relevant to your query can be a good way of finding other documents related to your topic.

Advanced search

Figure 8.25 shows the *Web of Science Advanced Search* page. This allows you to search with more precision and control than is the case with basic search. It is not available in *Web of Knowledge*'s **All Databases** search option.

In **Advanced Search** (unlike *SciVerse Scopus*) you must precede any keywords you use with the field in which you want them to appear. So, typing *voting patterns* into the search box would return an error. Instead, you would need to specify

TI= voting patterns or TS = voting patterns

or indeed some other field from the list shown in Table 8.5.

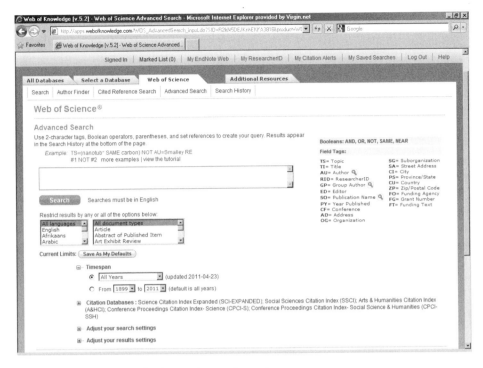

Figure 8.25 The *Web of Science* advanced search page

Table 8.5 Search fields

Field	Code	Field	Code
Address	**AD**	Organization	**OG**
Author	**AU**	Province/State	**PS**
Conference	**CF**	Researcher ID	**RID**
City	**CI**	Street Address	**SA**
Country	**CU**	Sub-organisation	**SG**
Editor	**ED**	Publication Name	**SO**
Grant Number	**FG**	Title	**TI**
Funding Agency	**FO**	Topic	**TS**
Funding Text	**FT**	Year Published	**PY**
Group Author	**GP**	Zip/Postal Code	**ZP**

You should also note that when you run your advanced search, you are not immediately presented with a list of retrieved items. Rather, you are taken to your search history (see the bottom of Figure 8.26).

To see the results of your search, click on the link in the **Results** column at the bottom of the screen, which in this example reads 18,090.

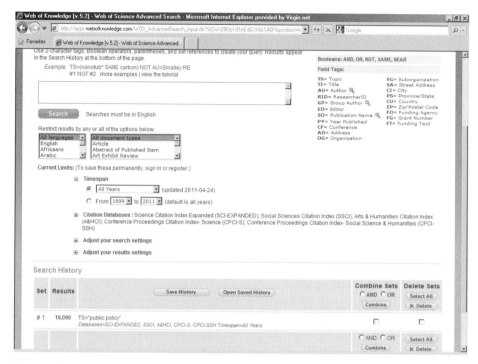

Figure 8.26   Search history 1

The reason that *Web of Science* takes you to this screen is that it enables you to build complex searches. For example, having found that there are 18,090 documents on the topic (TS) *"public policy"*, you can perform a second search to find documents with *review* and *research* in their titles (TI). This search is added to your search history (see Figure 8.27). As shown in the figure, each search is called a 'set'. The second search found 8,308 documents.

You can now combine your first and second searches to find documents about *"public policy"* with *review* and *research* in their titles. You do this by selecting set #1 (search 1) and set #2 and combining them using **AND**, as shown in Figure 8.28, then clicking the **Combine** button. This combination forms a third search (set #3) which retrieves 24 documents (Figure 8.29).

This may seem rather pointless especially since this search could have been easily achieved from the simple search box. However, this approach can be very useful when you are engaged in developing a more complex search over time. You may want to try things out in your searching, then depending on how successful or otherwise they are, go back to an earlier search set – or create a new, more complex search using search sets that you have already run. Figure 8.30 shows a more complex search.

Set	Results				Combine Sets AND OR Combine	Delete Sets Select All × Delete
		Save History	Open Saved History			
# 2	8,308	TI=review research *Databases=SCI-EXPANDED, SSCI, A&HCI, CPCI-S, CPCI-SSH Timespan=All Years*			☐	☐
# 1	18,090	TS="public policy" *Databases=SCI-EXPANDED, SSCI, A&HCI, CPCI-S, CPCI-SSH Timespan=All Years*			☐	☐
					AND OR Combine	Select All × Delete

Figure 8.27   Search history 2

Search History

Set	Results				Combine Sets ⦿ AND OR Combine	Delete Sets Select All × Delete
		Save History	Open Saved History			
# 2	8,308	TI=review research *Databases=SCI-EXPANDED, SSCI, A&HCI, CPCI-S, CPCI-SSH Timespan=All Years*			☑	☐
# 1	18,090	TS="public policy" *Databases=SCI-EXPANDED, SSCI, A&HCI, CPCI-S, CPCI-SSH Timespan=All Years*			☑	☐
					AND OR Combine	Select All × Delete

Figure 8.28   Search history 3

Search History

Set	Results				Combine Sets AND OR Combine	Delete Sets Select All × Delete
		Save History	Open Saved History			
# 3	24	#2 AND #1 *Databases=SCI-EXPANDED, SSCI, A&HCI, CPCI-S, CPCI-SSH Timespan=All Years*			☐	☐
# 2	8,308	TI=review research *Databases=SCI-EXPANDED, SSCI, A&HCI, CPCI-S, CPCI-SSH Timespan=All Years*			☐	☐
# 1	18,090	TS="public policy" *Databases=SCI-EXPANDED, SSCI, A&HCI, CPCI-S, CPCI-SSH Timespan=All Years*			☐	☐
					⦿ AND OR Combine	Select All × Delete

Figure 8.29   Search history 4

All your searches, whether conducted from the simple or the advanced search page, will be added to your search history, and can be manipulated in this way. If you have registered personally with *Web of Knowledge*, and are logged into your personal account, you can save your search history between search sessions.

Enclosing words in quotation marks will find documents containing the exact phrase. Thus:

Set	Results		Combine Sets ⊙ AND ⊙ OR Combine	Delete Sets Select All ✕ Delete
		Save History Open Saved History		
# 9	17	#8 AND #7 Databases=SCI-EXPANDED, SSCI, A&HCI, CPCI-S, CPCI-SSH Timespan=All Years	☐	☐
# 8	147,780	TS=review research Databases=SCI-EXPANDED, SSCI, A&HCI, CPCI-S, CPCI-SSH Timespan=All Years	☐	☐
# 7	780	#6 AND #5 Databases=SCI-EXPANDED, SSCI, A&HCI, CPCI-S, CPCI-SSH Timespan=All Years	☐	☐
# 6	5,397	#2 OR #1 Databases=SCI-EXPANDED, SSCI, A&HCI, CPCI-S, CPCI-SSH Timespan=All Years	☐	☐
# 5	308,343	#4 OR #3 Databases=SCI-EXPANDED, SSCI, A&HCI, CPCI-S, CPCI-SSH Timespan=All Years	☐	☐
# 4	290,092	TS=university Databases=SCI-EXPANDED, SSCI, A&HCI, CPCI-S, CPCI-SSH Timespan=All Years	☐	☐
# 3	25,303	TS="higher education" Databases=SCI-EXPANDED, SSCI, A&HCI, CPCI-S, CPCI-SSH Timespan=All Years	☐	☐
# 2	4,276	TS="learning strateg*" Databases=SCI-EXPANDED, SSCI, A&HCI, CPCI-S, CPCI-SSH Timespan=All Years	☐	☐
# 1	1,176	TS="learning style" Databases=SCI-EXPANDED, SSCI, A&HCI, CPCI-S, CPCI-SSH Timespan=All Years	☐	☐
			⦿ AND ⊙ OR Combine	Select All ✕ Delete

Figure 8.30   Search history 5

TI="review of research"

will retrieve only documents containing this exact phrase in the title, whereas:

TI=review research

will find documents containing:

review of research
research review
review of recent research
etc.

As with *SciVerse Scopus*, **AND** is implied if two words are placed together with no operator. Thus, the following two searches are functionally equivalent:

TI=research review
TI=research AND TI=review

Different fields can be linked together using the Boolean operators **AND**, **OR**, **NOT**, **NEAR** and **SAME**. Note that any words linked by any of these operators must be enclosed in brackets. For example:

TS=(style OR strategy)

TI=(review SAME research)

TI=(cognitive AND style)

are all correct, but:

TI=cognitive AND style

would generate a search syntax error. You can play safe by simply enclosing all search terms in brackets (whether or not they are linked by operators), as in the following examples:

TS=(education)

TI=(review research)

TI=("review of research")

TS=(learning AND strategy)

TI=(style OR strategy)

NEAR allows you to specify that the search terms connected by it will be found close together in documents retrieved. You can stipulate exactly *how* close by including a slash followed by a number after NEAR. For example:

TS=(learning NEAR/3 styles)

will find documents in which the words *learning* and *styles* occur within 3 words of each other. This search would retrieve documents with the following titles:

Learning styles and strategies

Learning and teaching *styles*

Motivational *styles* in problem-based *learning*

Design of adaptive hypermedia *learning* systems: A cognitive *style* approach

Effectiveness of Game-Based *Learning*: Influence of Cognitive *Style*

etc.

If you just use **NEAR** (without specifying any number), *Web of Science* will by default find documents in which the words are within 15 words of each other.

SAME will find documents in which the words you are searching for appear *in the same sentence*.

TI=(review SAME research)

Another way of searching for different forms of words – which works irrespective of whether lemmatisation is switched off and whether the search terms are enclosed by quotation marks – is to use *wildcards*. Wildcards may be used to represent missing characters. The types of wildcards that can be used are:

* The asterisk represents any number of characters, including zero.
  comput* will find *computer, computers, computation, computational,* etc.
  You can use this to cover singular and plurals, as well as other forms of words. For example: *TI="climate chang*"* will find both singular and plural forms (as well as any word beginning with *chang* including *changeable, changeability,* etc.).

? The question mark represents a single character.
  privati?ation will find *privatisation* and *privatization*
  art?fact will find *artefact* or *artifact*

$ The dollar sign represents zero or one character.
  flavo$r will find *flavor* and *flavour*

The * wildcard may not be used as the first character of a word. At least one character must precede it (and 3 in the case of Topic searches). However, the wildcards **?** and **$** may be used as the first character of a word. Therefore, searching for ?nquiry or $nquiry would find both *enquiry* and *inquiry*. Wildcards cannot be used in the Year Published (PY) field.

Wildcards can be used in combination – for example:

organi?ation* will find *organisation, organizational, organizations,* etc.

Note that the Boolean operators **AND, OR, NOT, NEAR** and **SAME** are applied in a particular order of precedence, and this directly affects *Web of Science*'s interpretation of your search. For example, you may imagine that if you search for:

TI=(teaching AND strategies OR approaches)

you might reasonably imagine that you would retrieve documents with either *teaching strategies* or *teaching approaches* in their titles. You would indeed retrieve documents with *teaching strategies* in their titles, however, you would also retrieve documents with just *approaches* (with no mention of *teaching*) in their titles. You would therefore inadvertently retrieve documents about 'approaches' to anything – not just teaching!

The reason is that *Web of Knowledge* applies the Boolean operators in a particular order of precedence:

1. NEAR
2. SAME
3. NOT
4. AND
5. OR

Note that the default order in which operators are applied is different from that employed by *SciVerse Scopus* and *Google Scholar*, which apply **OR**s before **AND**s before **NOT**s.

Because *Web of Science* applies **AND** before **OR**, it interprets your query as:

teaching AND strategies

OR approaches

Unlike *SciVerse Scopus* or *Google Scholar*, however, you can force your own interpretation on the search by using additional brackets:

TI=(teaching AND (strategies OR approaches))

This forces *Web of Science* to interpret your search as:

teaching AND

strategies OR approaches

which would retrieve documents with *teaching strategies* or *teaching approaches* in their titles.

In complex searches it is a good idea to use brackets to make the relationships between your key words clear, whether or not the order of precedence is the same as the *Web of Science*'s default. The following search:

TI=((learning OR cognitive) SAME (style OR strategy))

will find documents with any of the following in their **title**, provided that the words occur within the **same sentence**: *learning style, learning styles, learning strategy, learning strategies, cognitive style, cognitive styles, cognitive strategy* and *cognitive strategies*.

Putting the different parts of your search on a new line can increase clarity and does not affect the search. Make sure you always have the same number of opening and closing brackets. The following search:

TI=(

(learning OR cognitive) SAME (style OR strategy)

AND (university OR "higher education")

)

will find documents containing any of the above plus either the word *university* or the phrase *'higher education'* also in the **title**. Again, all the keywords should appear in the title since the brackets immediately after *TI=* are the last to be closed. This means that *TI=* applies to the whole search.

The following search:

TI=(

(pedagog* OR teaching OR instruction*) SAME (strateg* OR approach*)

)

AND PY=2006–2010

will find any documents with

titles (**TI**) that include the words

> *pedagog* (any word beginning with pedagog...)*
>
> *OR teaching*
>
> OR *instruction* (any word beginning with instruction...)*

occurring within the same sentence (**SAME**) as

> *strateg* (any word beginning with strateg...)*
>
> OR *approach* (any word beginning with approach...)*

AND published (**PY**) between 2006 and 2010.

We can also specify the type of information source we want using the document type dropdown box shown in Figure 8.25. We can choose from a range including those shown in Table 8.6.

Table 8.6 Web of Science document types

All document types (this is the default)	Meeting abstract
Article	Meeting summary
Abstract of published item	Music performance review
Art exhibit review	Music score
Bibliography	Music score review
Book review	News item
Chronology	Note
Correction	Poetry
Dance performance review	Proceedings paper
Database review	Record review
Discussion	Reprint
Editorial material	Review
Except	Script
Fiction, creative prose	Software review
Film review	TV review, Radio review
Hardware review	TV review, Radio review, Video review
Item about an individual	Theatre review
Letter	

As well as allowing you to *Search within results*, *Web of Science* also offers a wider range of post-search filters in **Refine Results** (Table 8.7).

Table 8.7 Post-search filters

Subject Areas	Conference Titles
Document Types	Publication Years
Authors	Institutions
Group Authors (organisations that author documents)	Funding Agencies
	Languages
Editors	Countries/Territories
Source Titles	

Note that *Web of Knowledge*, and *Web of Science* offer many more tools and facilities than those described here. As with *SciVerse Scopus*, the purpose of this section has been to introduce the basics in order to get you started.

Summary

The higher the quality of the information you are able to find, the better the quality of your essay or research question answer. Three of the main search tools designed specifically to find high-quality scholarly information are: *Google Scholar*, *SciVerse Scopus* and *Web of Knowledge* (incorporating *Web of Science*).

For each, this chapter explored basic and advanced searching. These tools offer sophisticated ways of homing in on the high-quality, peer-reviewed information that you need. You can search them simply or take advantage of the range of advanced facilities they offer, which allow you to exercise high levels of control over your searches. These are designed to help you avoid retrieving large volumes of irrelevant material. They also enable you to view your results according to date, relevance or the number of times each item has been cited (thus how influential it is), to view related documents, and to export your citations to reference management software (which will be discussed in Chapter 12).

The next chapter discusses how to transform the information you have found into a high-quality, evidence-based response to your essay or research question.

NINE

Transforming information into evidence-based arguments

WHY YOU NEED TO KNOW THIS

- In order to produce high-quality work, you need to know how to transform information into evidence. Information is the raw material out of which evidence is made. But you need to process it in appropriate ways.
- First, you have to *understand* it – to internalise it and 'make it your own'.
- Second, you have to *critically evaluate* it.
- Then you have to bind it together with logic and reasoning to form evidence-based claims and arguments.
- It is essential that you are aware of well-established criteria for critically evaluating evidence. These criteria will be used by those evaluating and marking your work.
- These same criteria will also be helpful to you in your own critical evaluation of the information sources that you are reading and using in your essays and research reports.
- You should also apply them yourself to critically evaluate what you are *writing*. By doing so you can become aware of and address any problems before you submit your work.

Making information 'your own'

Remember that in an essay or research report you are presenting an argument (a series of connected claims), not a list of facts. And although your argument (the answer to your research question) will draw on the information sources you have searched for and found, you need to internalise these and 'make them your own'. But what do 'internalise' and 'make your own' mean in this context?

They are the products of you adopting a relatively *deep transformational (meaningful)* approach to constructing your work. This may be contrasted with a *surface reproductive* approach. As the name suggests, a transformational approach entails transforming the words on the page into your own thoughts. This process entails extracting the essence of the message the author is intending to communicate, and relating it to (enmeshing it with) your existing knowledge.

A reproductive approach entails essentially trying to remember information, without engaging at a deeper level. If you adopt a transformational approach, you will be less likely to rely on the particular form of words used by an author. You may, of course, use in your essay or dissertation direct quotations from an information source, but such quotations should be relatively short and used sparingly.

Adopting a deep transformational approach will help you avoid the danger of being too descriptive – i.e. not having sufficient analysis, synthesis and evaluation in your work. This is a common problem. This issue is particularly relevant to the issue of *plagiarism*, which will be discussed in the next section.

Adopting a deep approach applies to both your reading and your writing. The one should follow from the other: deep transformational reading should result in the avoidance of surface reproductive writing. However, it may be very difficult to achieve deep transformational reading if you are anxious, pressed for time, or struggling to understand the material you are reading.

If you are anxious, the two strategies below *may* be of some help. However, it is important to consult your lecturer (or other person as you feel most appropriate) to seek some support in this.

- If you feel excessively pressed for time, then explore whether there are any support facilities or courses available within your university to help you improve your time management. Consult your lecturer for help if you are struggling in this respect.
- If you are struggling to understand what you are reading, then bear in mind that there will be other information sources covering the same topic in a different way that might be more readily intelligible. Look around for alternative sources. But, importantly, consult your lecturer for help and advice if this does not immediately work.

Assuming that you are not suffering from high levels of anxiety and are not over-pressed for time, and that the information sources you are using are not badly mismatched with your knowledge and abilities, the following approaches may be useful in promoting deep reading and writing.

When reading an information source, pause frequently (after each paragraph or section) and ask yourself:

In essence, and in my own words what did that section tell me?

Don't try to recall every detail. Try to extract the key essential message. Imagine that you are explaining it to someone else. But *do not* try to remember the words the author(s) used. Use your own words.

Now the important bit. If you can't really answer that question, go back and read the information source again. Try not to get bogged down with the details. If you find that you still can't 'get' the main message in your own words, read it again. It is perfectly normal to expect to have to read difficult ideas a number of times in this way.

If you do this, and you begin to worry about how long this is going to take you, then this very worry is going to get in your way and make deep understanding even more difficult. You can't rush understanding. You can't pretend that you understand.

When you feel that you are really beginning to understand what the author is saying, it is a good idea to ask yourself the further question:

Exactly what is this source telling me that is relevant to my essay or research question?

This can include providing you with understanding and background that you may feel is useful in helping you understand your essay or research question better. However, if it is not proving helpful, then you should consider ditching this source and moving on to another that feels more relevant and useful to you in answering your question.

It is a good idea to make notes on each source when reading, assuming that you have identified it as potentially useful. But avoid getting bogged down and allowing yourself to be dragged into making excessively verbatim notes. This is all too easy to do, especially if you are finding it hard work to understand what you are reading.

If you feel that this is happening to you, then re-read at a less reproductive level and keep on doing so until you feel comfortable that you can make notes largely in your own words. By all means include a direct quotation if it expresses an idea particularly succinctly, and if you think you might like to use it in your work. But keep direct quotations to a minimum – and if you find yourself writing more and more of them down, then be honest with yourself and consider whether you are sliding into reproductive mode.

It may also be a good idea to map the concepts and ideas you are gleaning from the documents you are reading on to your essay or research question. You may find it useful to map out *diagrammatically* (a) ideas you are reading about and/or (b) your own ideas about how your essay or research question can be answered. As you progress, you may be able to merge the two diagrams to map out how the ideas you have derived from your sources, and your own ideas, provide an answer to your question.

One way of doing this is by generating 'concept maps', 'topic maps' or 'mind-maps'. Although at one level these different terms have different technical meanings, all I mean here is a picture or diagram in which you draw ideas and how they link together. A simple example is shown in Figure 9.1.

Free software exists which can be useful in helping you to generate such maps. An example is *FreeMind* which can be downloaded from http://freemind.sourceforge.net/wiki/index.php/Main_Page.

However, the extent to which you may find this easy and useful may depend to some extent on your learning style. Some people are more oriented to visual information than others. Try it – but if you feel that it is not really helping you, then focus on making text notes.

To summarise:

- Don't try to read an information source once and for all. Be ready to read it multiple times at different levels. It is a good idea to read first to understand what the author is saying, then read again in more critical mode.

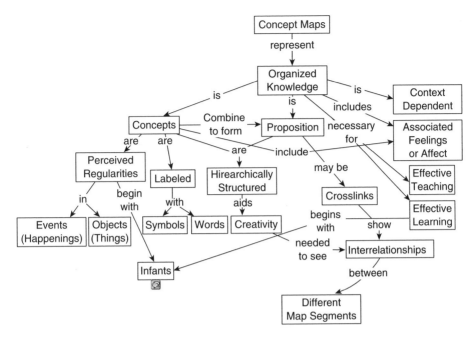

Figure 9.1 A concept map for 'Concept Maps'

Source: http//commons.wikimedia.org/wiki/File: Conceptmap.gif. Attribution: Vicwood40 at the English Wikipedia project. Used under the GNU Free Documentation License.

- A combination of time pressure, difficulty of the source material, and possibly other anxieties can drag you into an excessively reproductive and descriptive approach to reading and note-taking. You should be alert to this, and step back if you feel it happening. Paradoxically, even if you are pressurised for time, you should slow down and take the time to understand and internalise what you are reading. You will ultimately waste less time if you do this.
- Often the less you deeply understand what you are reading, the more verbatim and extensive your notes can become. A good way of avoiding this is to try mapping ideas visually since it requires you to extract the essence of the ideas you are encountering, and to think how the ideas relate to one another.

Critically evaluating information

Having understood and internalised information, and integrated it into your own knowledge structures, you need to critically evaluate it before you can make use of it in your work. The reason is that in academic essays, projects or dissertations, you need to present evidence-based arguments. This means that you need to present a series of connected claims, and give valid reasons why they should be considered reasonable.

A key question here is: *reasonable to whom?* Well, you should write to convince readers who are:

- Sceptical
- Reasonable
- Knowledgeable

Being **sceptical** means that they will deliberately question what you have said, looking for counter-claims, counter-arguments and competing evidence. They will be looking to see if you have (a) shown that you are *aware of* these and (b) *carefully considered* them. If you have rejected them in your essay in favour of others, then you should say why – i.e. give reasons for selecting the particular ones that you did.

Being **reasonable** means that any alternative claims and arguments that they will use to criticise your work will themselves be evidence-based (rather than just their unsubstantiated opinion or preference).

Being **knowledgeable** means that they will have an awareness of other claims, arguments and evidence in relation to the topic you are writing about. They will therefore be in a good position to know if you have missed any important ones.

The quality of your evidence will be tested against well-established principles. These principles will enable those who will be marking your work to assess how convincing your claims and arguments are. You can use the same principles as you generate your essay or dissertation, to make sure that the claims and arguments you are using are of an appropriately high quality and sufficiently evidence-based. You can also use them to assess the quality of the claims, arguments and evidence put forward by the authors of the documents that you are reading and using as you put your work together.

You should first decide **how much critical evaluation your essay or project question requires**. If you are asked, for example, to explain some technical topic, this is very different from being asked to discuss controversies surrounding it. So, for example:

'Describe different types of file sharing and explain how each works?'

is very different from:

'What are the likely effects of file sharing on the music industry?'

Clearly, an essay or assignment on file sharing set within a computer technology context is likely to have a very different focus and to require a very different response if set within an arts or social sciences context. It would not be a particularly good idea to respond to an essay question asking you to explain the mechanics of file sharing by focusing on its legal, business or social implications.

If you are at a fairly basic level, you may well wonder how you can 'critically evaluate' issues, especially where the topic may be completely new to you and you simply don't have your own point of view yet. What you can do in this situation is to try

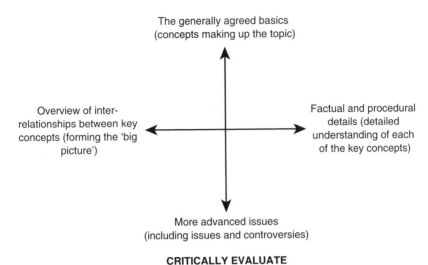

DEVELOP BASIC UNDERSTANDING

The generally agreed basics
(concepts making up the topic)

Overview of inter-
relationships between key
concepts (forming the 'big
picture')

Factual and procedural
details (detailed
understanding of each
of the key concepts)

More advanced issues
(including issues and controversies)

CRITICALLY EVALUATE

Figure 9.2   Basic dimensions of learning

to find, in the literature, a range of different claims and arguments put forward by authors in relation to the issues, and then attempt to evaluate them as far as you are able to – based on your existing knowledge and the use of your powers of reasoning.

Your ability to do this is likely to vary depending on your experience. If your experience is low, you can present a number of different claims and arguments relatively descriptively – putting them forward and explaining them. You can then, assuming that you cannot find any further information to help you evaluate their relative merits, simply analyse how they differ and where they appear to agree, and discuss any implications of these points of similarity and difference that you can think of. Even though the level of critical evaluation in your work will not be high, at least you will be providing evidence of some analysis and synthesis to add to the descriptive elements.

Recall the diagram shown in Figure 9.2 which was originally introduced in Chapter 2. The more you are operating towards the 'basic understanding' end of the vertical dimension, the more you will be looking to find *ready-made claims, arguments and evidence put forward by other people (authors)* that answer the question. You will also be relying more on *indirect (extrinsic) critical evaluation* of these claims, arguments and evidence. Indirect critical evaluation of a claim or argument entails judging how credible and authoritative the author and publication source are.

As you gain more knowledge and experience, and move down the figure away from the 'basic' pole of the vertical dimension, you will be expected to engage much more in *direct (intrinsic) critical evaluation*. This entails assessing the authoritativeness of the claims, arguments and evidence themselves (rather than of their authors). You may also be expected to add more of your own thinking, using evidence to support your own claims and arguments (as opposed to presenting mainly those of other people).

Indirect critical evaluation of a source entails judging the credibility and authority of the information based on *extrinsic* criteria – on factors external to the information itself, such as:

Who is the author?

How well placed is s/he to talk about this topic?

Has s/he any vested interests which might get in the way of neutrality?

Where is the information published?

Is it peer reviewed?

Is this a publisher with a reputation for publishing high-quality information?

Indirect evaluation can tell you how *likely* it is that the information is of good quality, but it does not guarantee this quality. For example, information published by an author with a good academic reputation in a high-quality, peer-reviewed journal is more likely to be authoritative than information published by a lesser known author in a journal that is not peer reviewed. However, this is not to say that the second paper *is* of lesser quality – just that it is likely to be. Only *direct* evaluation (discussed below) will actually tell you.

Direct critical evaluation entails judging the authority of the information based on *intrinsic* criteria by examining the quality of the claims and arguments it contains, and the evidence put forward to justify them. These differences are summarised in Figure 9.3.

So, how do you critically evaluate claims and arguments? Recall that a *claim* is an assertion or proposition that something is or may be so. However, such a claim needs to be based on evidence. Where you are reading claims made by other people this evidence may be provided by them. But you need to evaluate it. If the author does not provide evidence – but the claim corresponds to your thinking and you want to use it – then you will have to seek out evidence and/or generate it yourself.

The same applies to arguments. Recall also that an *argument* is a connected chain of claims, of the type:

Since A is so, and B is so, therefore C is so...

The basis of such a link is logic and reasoning. The questions we need to ask are:

Is it reasonable to believe that A is so, and that B is so? (claims)

If A and B are so, is it reasonable to believe that C is so? (argument)

In deciding the extent to which A is so, you need to know what evidence there is to support the claim.

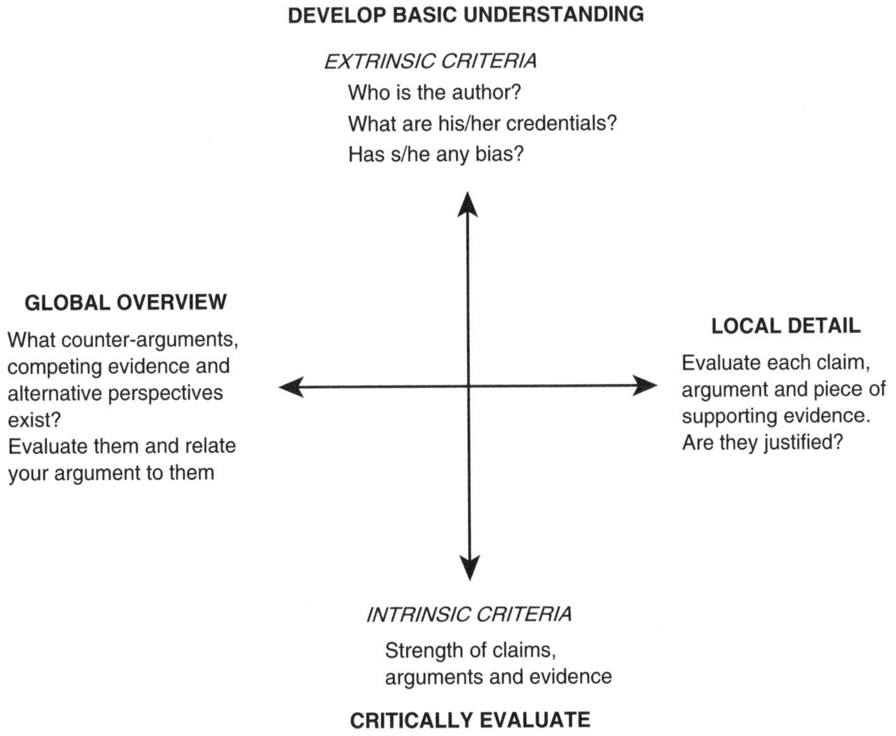

DEVELOP BASIC UNDERSTANDING

EXTRINSIC CRITERIA
Who is the author?
What are his/her credentials?
Has s/he any bias?

GLOBAL OVERVIEW
What counter-arguments,
competing evidence and
alternative perspectives
exist?
Evaluate them and relate
your argument to them

LOCAL DETAIL
Evaluate each claim,
argument and piece of
supporting evidence.
Are they justified?

INTRINSIC CRITERIA
Strength of claims,
arguments and evidence

CRITICALLY EVALUATE

Figure 9.3   Extrinsic and intrinsic evaluation criteria

Is it a claim that is generally accepted within the literature? If so, give a reference to a substantiating document. Is it an opinion? If so, whose opinion is it, and how authoritative and credible are they? Make the case to your reader as to why you accept the claim – and why, consequently, you think your reader should accept the claim.

Is it reasonable to suppose that if A and B are so, then it follows that C is so? If it is not completely obvious to the 'sceptical but reasonable reader', then you should explain and justify your reasoning.

If there are counter-claims, and consequently counter-arguments, then you should acknowledge them and say why you are accepting the one(s) you do. But you needn't necessarily choose one or other. You can always adopt a neutral or balanced position, presenting them, pointing out where they differ, possibly, if appropriate, explaining why the differences exist (e.g. 'it depends on whether you are viewing X from the perspective of Y or Z...').

Whether or not there is sufficient evidence to support a claim or argument is rarely a case of simply 'yes' or 'no'. Evidence needs weighing up in terms of its strengths and weaknesses. You should, where possible, point out and assess the limitations surrounding evidence. For example, let us assume that you are writing about the use of technology by university teachers and have found a relevant 2007 article by Jones and Smith. You write in your essay:

The take-up of web 2.0 technology by university lecturers is steadily increasing, although there are still barriers. Jones and Smith (2007), for example, in a survey of 150 Arts and Humanities-based university lecturers, found that 75% considered themselves to be not sufficiently familiar with these approaches to make use of them in their teaching.

This may be a reasonable statement, but it would also be appropriate to check the details of the study and, if necessary, add some words of caution. For example:

However, these findings should be interpreted with some caution since (a) the study was based on a sample of Arts and Humanities lecturers, and the findings cannot necessarily be generalised to lecturers in other disciplines; and (b) there has been considerable growth in the take-up and use of web 2.0 technologies throughout higher education since 2007 (Gordon, 2010).

You can still use this evidence, but include appropriate caution in interpreting and generalising from it.

Let us now explore in detail specific criteria whereby we can assess the quality of evidence put forward in the sources you will be evaluating for potential use in your work.

Validity, reliability, objectivity and generalisability as critical tools

There are quality criteria that you should bear in mind when both:

- generating your own claims and arguments and supporting them with evidence; and
- evaluating the claims, arguments and supporting evidence put forward by other people (e.g. the authors of the documents you may be using for your essay).

It is widely agreed that acceptable evidence should possess certain qualities. *Validity*, *reliability*, *objectivity* and *generalisability*, listed below, are terms associated with positivist quantitative research. The terms in brackets after each have been proposed as interpretative qualitative equivalents of what are, in essence, similar constructs.

Internal validity (truth value): the extent to which the evidence put forward actually relates to the claims/arguments being put forward.

Reliability (consistency): the extent to which the evidence is stable – i.e. would be the same if measured at different times and/or by different observers.

Objectivity (neutrality): the extent to which the evidence is unbiased.

Generalisability or **external validity** (**transferability**): the extent to which the claims/arguments are generalisable to, or applicable in, contexts different from the specific context in which they were generated.

These criteria apply to your critical evaluation not only of evidence in the information sources you are reading, but also of the evidence that you are putting forward in your work to support your claims and arguments. Let us explore each of them a little more deeply.

Internal validity (truth value)

Internal validity relates to the extent to which the evidence put forward actually relates to what is being claimed or argued.

THINK

A lack of internal validity may occur when what you *think* you are measuring or investigating is not what you are *actually* measuring or investigating.

Can you think of conditions (or mistakes made by a researcher) relating to data collection and/ or analysis which might lead to a lack of *internal validity* of evidence?

The particular examples you have thought of will be very different in detail from those listed below, but see if they share the same generic features. My examples of evidence lacking internal validity include the following...

The researchers claims that the data are telling them X when in fact they are telling them Y

For example, a researcher finds that there is a link between levels of obesity and levels of exercise in children. S/he concludes that children should take more exercise in order to reduce obesity. S/he is assuming that exercise affects obesity, whereas in fact it may be the other way round. Indeed, a recent study in the UK found that doing more exercise does not reduce child obesity, but being obese reduces the amount of exercise children do. The paper concludes that:

Physical inactivity appears to be the result of fatness rather than its cause. This reverse causality may explain why attempts to tackle childhood obesity by promoting PA [physical activity] have been largely unsuccessful.[21]

The researcher fails to realise, or acknowledge, that hidden factors may have been at play

For example, a researcher teaches one group of children using teaching method A and another group using teaching method B. The first group outperform the second and the researcher concludes that method A is better than method B. However, s/he fails to take into account the fact that the first group was made up of the brighter children. If they had been taught using the other method, they might still have come out top.

THINK

OK – so how could authors convince you that what they are saying is internally valid? What evidence should you look for in what they have written?

In the case of qualitative research based on interviews, it is common for authors to provide short quotations from interviews to illustrate different points or categories they have used to classify the data. You should look critically at any such quotations to judge whether they really *do* support what's being said. Take the following extract from a research report for example:

A number of interviewees reported that they were unhappy with the services provided by the local council. Interviewee A1, for example, noted that:

  'I suppose with the cuts and everything they're struggling a bit to keep standards up.'

This quotation certainly does not illustrate what the author says it does. Think critically. Try to imagine a contrary interpretation and see if it sounds equally reasonable. For example:

---

[21]Metcalf, B.S., Hosking, J., Jeffery. A.N., Voss, L.D., Henley, W. And Wilkin, T.J. (2010). Fatness leads to inactivity, but inactivity does not lead to fatness: a longitudinal study in children (Early Bird 45). *Archives of Disease in Childhood.* Published in Online First, June 23, 2010. Retrieved from doi: 10.1136/adc.2009.17597

A number of interviewees felt that the local council were working hard to maintain standards despite financial difficulties. Interviewee A1, for example, noted that:

> *'I suppose with the cuts and everything they're struggling a bit to keep standards up.'*

In this case, the validity of the author's interpretation is questionable – unless he provided other more compelling evidence of what he is saying.

Generalisations are often made in the discussion and conclusions sections of articles. Again, it is a good idea to check back to the evidence presented in the earlier parts to see if the claims are reasonably supported by this evidence.

However, in a journal article which is relatively short (compared to a research thesis), it is often not possible to provide the fullest evidence of validity. If you do find any claims unconvincing, you should say so – and why you are unconvinced (e.g. you have found counter-claims and/or the evidence put forward by the author does not seem unequivocally to support what is being claimed).

Although it is good practice to include accounts of how the research was conducted in terms of the issues discussed here (validity, reliability and objectivity), some papers resulting from well-conducted research don't always include an exemplary description of these issues. If a paper lacks them, it doesn't necessarily mean that the research was badly conducted.

You can still use sources, particularly if they are peer reviewed, However, if you are not fully convinced in relation to validity – or indeed any other quality issues – it may be a case of reporting the findings with appropriate caveats, rather than rejecting them out of hand.

The general issue is: do you have any reasonable suspicions that the evidence (data, analysis or interpretation) does not fully support the claims and arguments being put forward by the author?

Reliability (consistency)

Reliability is the extent to which the evidence is stable, and is likely to be the same if measured at different times and/or by different observers

---

THINK

Can you think of any examples of conditions in which data are collected (or mistakes made by a researcher in data collection and analysis) which might lead to a lack of *reliable* evidence?

Examples of evidence lacking reliability include the following...

Inconsistency in data collection

A series of experiments are conducted. But the groups were conducted by different researchers and the instructions given to the groups were not quite the same. This lack of control means that the data were not collected using a consistent measure. The same principle of unreliability may apply in much less obvious cases than this.

Inconsistency in data analysis

The researchers are observing the social behaviour of chimpanzees. They look for examples of particular behaviour and classify them as indicating, for example, *anger, affection, aggression*, etc. However, during the extended period of their analysis, their judgements 'shift', and examples of behaviour that were classified as *anger* at the beginning of the analysis are classified as *aggression* later in the analysis. Unbeknown to the researchers, the criteria being used have shifted slightly over time. This can happen if the exact criteria for classifying are not made explicit. It can also happen if different people are conducting the analysis, unless the criteria used by all of them are explicit and checks are made that they are being applied in exactly the same way by all concerned.

THINK

So how could authors convince you that what they are saying is reliable? What evidence should you look for in what they have written?

In the case of quantitative data analysis (including questionnaires that have been analysed statistically), you should ask yourself: does the author say anything about the *reliability* of the data collection instruments used? There are a number of ways of testing research instruments for levels of reliability. Ideally, an author would report these levels.

In the case of qualitative research, you should ask: how clearly does the author explain the criteria used for coding (classifying) the data? If the way in which data is interpreted is fuzzy or vague, it may also be unreliable (variable over time, rather than stable), thus making findings based on them questionable.

Doubt is cast if the author does not make clear the criteria used to classify data and the procedures used to analyse them. Be suspicious if the paper says something like: '*The data were analysed, resulting in the following findings …*'. Ask 'How were the data analysed? Were independent judges used to corroborate the researcher's analysis?' The general issue is: do you have any reasonable suspicions that any criteria or procedures used by the researcher in relation to data collection, analysis or interpretation (a) were fuzzy and ill-defined or (b) could have changed or shifted over time, unbeknown to – or at least unreported by – the researcher?

Objectivity (neutrality)

Objectivity relates to the extent to which the evidence avoids bias.

THINK

Can you think of examples of how *bias* might creep into data collection and/or analysis?

Bias may affect a study without the researcher necessarily being aware of it. It may affect both data collection and data analysis.

Data collection

One or more questions in a questionnaire might not be phrased completely neutrally, and may lead the respondent to answer in a particular way. For example, the way in which a question is worded may convey a value judgement.

An interviewer may ask a 'leading question', indicating to the interviewee what the interviewer expects, or would ideally like, to hear.

Data analysis

The researcher may ignore, or analyse less rigorously, interview data that does not match what he expects, or does not fit his 'pet' theory. He may consequently (but not necessarily intentionally) pay more attention to data that does.

Have you reason to believe that the authors have some vested (e.g. commercial) interest? If so, have they convinced you that this did not lead to bias – and if so, how did you become convinced? If not, remain sceptical.

Reassurance can be given by authors in a number of ways. Sometimes they may explicitly acknowledge the potential for bias and talk about how they attempted to counter this potential. Was the selection of their sample made to include different points of view?

Did the researchers use independent judges to corroborate their analysis (e.g. classification) of the data? Did they engage in 'member checking' – allowing interviewees to read and comment on the researchers' record and interpretation of their interviews?

Do the authors explicitly consider competing interpretations of their data, or alternative points of view? Have the authors made any assumptions that are not explicitly acknowledged?

Generalisability (transferability)

Generalisability or external validity is the extent to which the evidence suggests that claims/arguments can be generalised from the specific context in which they were generated to other contexts.

Generalisability may be affected by sampling, data collection, data analysis and interpretation. In qualitative research, you need to provide sufficiently rich contextual data. Examples include the following...

Sampling and data collection

Your sample and consequent data may not be appropriate. You generalise your findings to 'managers' but your sample consisted exclusively of junior managers. Or you make a generalisation about 'the weather' but your data were collected only in the summer.

Data analysis and interpretation

Your analysis may not be appropriate. Your data violates a requirement in a statistical test which invalidates the generalisation you claim based on your analysis.

Provision of contextual information

In a qualitative study, you fail to provide sufficiently rich information about the context and circumstances of your research. This is necessary to enable the reader to assess the extent to which a different situation is sufficiently similar to enable your findings to be 'transferable' to it.

THINK

How could authors convince you that what they are saying is generalisable or transferable? What evidence should you look for in what they have written?

Make sure that any generalisations authors make are actually supported by the evidence they put forward. Are any of the planks supporting any generalisations made in the document based or reliant on untested assumptions on the part of the authors?

In statistical research, analytic tests have a number of requirements which, if not fulfilled, bring into question the statistical generalisability of the results. It is not unreasonable to assume that such requirements have probably been met in a good-quality, peer-reviewed source since the reviewers will have had an opportunity to question the author about such matters.

Many qualitative research studies do not explicitly claim transferablility (the qualitative equivalent of statistical generalisability). However, if the author does argue for this – or indeed if, for the purposes of your own argument, you are wanting to make the point that the findings are transferable to a different context – then you should ensure that the context and circumstances of the reported research are described in sufficient detail to justify this claim.

Moving from intrinsic to extrinsic evaluation

Sometimes information sources that you are reading simply do not tell you some of the things you need to know in relation to some of the criteria discussed above. Within the space constraints of a journal article, for example, it may not always be possible to provide convincing reassurance. In this case, you may have to combine extrinsic with intrinsic criteria to assess the work – i.e. make sure it is from a peer-reviewed, high-quality publication. The fact that a source is peer reviewed provides an element of extrinsic evaluation of the quality of a piece of reported work.

If it is not, and the key information is not contained in the information source, you may have to reject it. However, it may also be possible to search for and find other sources that corroborate the points made in the original source. But this can be time consuming.

Much depends on the level of your study. At more basic undergraduate levels the most reasonable and practical strategy may be generally to accept peer-reviewed sources and use their findings, but make any criticisms that you feel are appropriate based on a good critical reading of it. At more advanced levels it is more appropriate to examine in greater detail, using intrinsic criteria, the nature of the data collection, analysis and interpretation presented in a study – particularly if the study forms an important part of your argument – by obtaining the full report, dissertation or thesis, if necessary by inter-library loan. Figure 9.4 illustrates the balance between extrinsic and intrinsic criteria for evaluating the sources you are using.

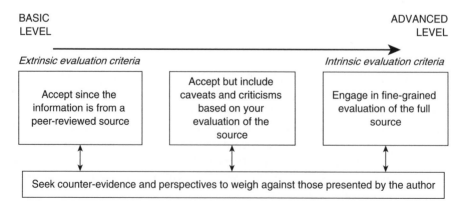

Figure 9.4 Extrinsic and intrinsic evaluation criteria and level of study

Developing your own evidence-based arguments

Although you will be analysing and evaluating the evidence-based arguments of other people to use in your work, you must ensure that your own work itself presents coherent and integrated evidence-based arguments. You must bind these arguments and evidence together to form your answer to your essay or research question.

Before we explore how we can do this, let us remind ourselves of what an argument, and its component claims, look like. Figure 9.5 was originally presented in

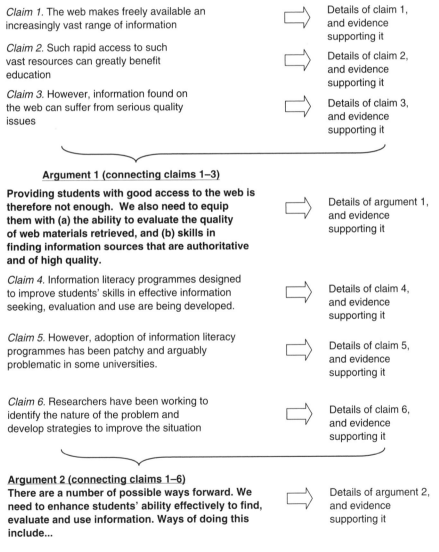

Claim 1. The web makes freely available an increasingly vast range of information

Details of claim 1, and evidence supporting it

Claim 2. Such rapid access to such vast resources can greatly benefit education

Details of claim 2, and evidence supporting it

Claim 3. However, information found on the web can suffer from serious quality issues

Details of claim 3, and evidence supporting it

Argument 1 (connecting claims 1–3)

Providing students with good access to the web is therefore not enough. We also need to equip them with (a) the ability to evaluate the quality of web materials retrieved, and (b) skills in finding information sources that are authoritative and of high quality.

Details of argument 1, and evidence supporting it

Claim 4. Information literacy programmes designed to improve students' skills in effective information seeking, evaluation and use are being developed.

Details of claim 4, and evidence supporting it

Claim 5. However, adoption of information literacy programmes has been patchy and arguably problematic in some universities.

Details of claim 5, and evidence supporting it

Claim 6. Researchers have been working to identify the nature of the problem and develop strategies to improve the situation

Details of claim 6, and evidence supporting it

Argument 2 (connecting claims 1–6)
There are a number of possible ways forward. We need to enhance students' ability effectively to find, evaluate and use information. Ways of doing this include...

Details of argument 2, and evidence supporting it

Figure 9.5 A simplified example of your 'developing understanding' processes

Chapter 3, but it provides a simplified example, illustrating the concepts, which is also useful here.

Just as you should be critical about what you are *reading*, so you should subject to similar critical scrutiny what you are *writing*. Bear in mind that the reader and marker of your essay or research report will certainly be doing so.

You should critically evaluate your own work from a similar perspective. You may or may not have engaged in collecting and analysing your own empirical data – this is likely in the case of a research project, but not so in the case of an essay – but in both cases you should ensure that your claims and arguments are evidence-based. Figure 9.6 summarises the key questions you should address in integrating the claims, arguments and evidence of others into your own.

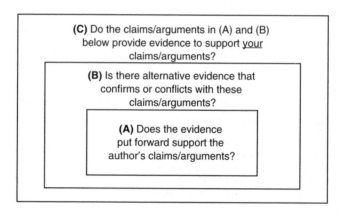

Figure 9.6 Integrating claims, arguments and evidence

Here are illustrative examples of responses to the questions posed in each of the boxes in the figure.

(A) Jones claims that '75% of university students prefer Firefox rather than the Internet Explorer web browser'. But the study was conducted with Computer Science students in UK universities, so the author cannot legitimately claim that the results apply to 'university students' as opposed to Computer Science students in the UK.

(B) (i) Another study by Bradford and Smith claims that 70% of university students prefer Internet Explorer. Their study was based on a sample of English and history students in UK universities.

(ii) You conduct your own small study with a sample of UK students across a range of disciplines, including Computer Science, History and English, and find that 46% prefer Internet Explorer, 42% Firefox, and 12% other browsers.

(iii) You find an article by Jenkins who suggests that Microsoft products are not particularly popular amongst UK Computer Science and Engineering students, compared with Arts and Humanities students.

(C) You can assess evidence along the following lines. You conclude that although your study found no significant difference in popularity between these browsers amongst UK students, there may be differences according to subject disciplines. You recommend further research to explore this possibility. Your concluding summary could be written up along the following lines:

There is conflicting evidence of UK students' preference for web browsers. Jones (2009) found that 75% of university students preferred Firefox, whilst Bradford and Smith (2010) found that 70% of students prefer Internet Explorer. The present study [i.e. your own study] found no such preferences, 46% preferring Explorer, and 42% preferring Firefox. A possible explanation for these discrepancies is provided by Jenkins (2010), who argues that Microsoft products are less popular amongst Computer Science and Engineering students than those from the Arts and Humanities. Indeed, Jones' study was based on a sample of Computer Science students, whereas Bradford and Smith's sample consisted of students of History and English. Further research will be needed to establish more clearly students' browser preferences.

Some final thoughts. Always re-read and check your work. In the conclusion of an essay, review the question and the extent to which you have answered it. In a dissertation or research project report, review your research questions and explicitly assess how far you have answered each one. Acknowledge any limitations in what you have done. Typically, in a research project, not everything may have gone according to your plans, for example, you may have had a disappointingly low number of respondents to a questionnaire. Acknowledge problems encountered and explain what you attempted to do about them. For example, did you send reminders? If not, why not? Maybe it would not have been appropriate for various reasons – if so, explain. Did you change your research plan, for example, to include some interviews?

Clearly explain your line of reasoning. Make clear how what you are claiming is supported by appropriate evidence. Is there competing evidence? What other possible interpretations are there of your evidence? Why should 'sceptical but reasonable' readers accept – or at least seriously consider – yours?

In the case of research entailing your own data collection and analysis, you should acknowledge and critically reflect on the limitations of your research. Were there limitations in the sample you were able to get? What are the implications of this for your findings? Is there evidence for everything claimed, and does your interpretation fit all your data? How can the reader tell that you have not misinterpreted your data? For example, do your interviewees accept as valid the picture you are painting? Did you go back to ask any of them? Or did you use an independent judge to see if she or he agreed with your interpretations?

Summary

This chapter focused on how to transform the information you have found into an evidence-based answer to your essay or research question. It is important to engage in *deep* as opposed to *surface* learning, and to *critically evaluate* the information you are reading, so that you can fuse high-quality information with your own knowledge and judgement.

The criteria for evaluating sources can be direct and indirect. Indirect evaluation relies on factors such as the authority and track record of the author, and the extent to which a source has been peer reviewed. Direct evaluation entails your own critical appraisal of the content of the source. The chapter introduced well-established criteria for doing this, including *validity* (or truth value), *reliability* (or consistency), *objectivity* (or neutrality), and *generalisability* (or transferability).

However, you should apply these criteria not only to what you are reading, but also to what you are writing, since they will be applied by those reading and assessing your work. Always write for the *sceptical but reasonable* reader, critically reflecting on what you are saying and acknowledging the limitations of your evidence and arguments. Always try to think of, and acknowledge, other possible interpretations and viewpoints, and justify why you have selected the ones you have.

But generating a high-quality, evidence-based answer to your essay or research question is not enough on its own. You must also *present* it in an effective way. You need to convince the readers of your work – including, of course, your marker – that the work is indeed you own and not in any way plagiarised. It is also important in academic work to enable your readers to find for themselves the information sources you have used. The next chapter will focus on these extremely important aspects of your work.

TEN

Presenting your evidence effectively

WHY YOU NEED TO KNOW THIS

- A key aspect of presenting your work effectively is to do so in such a way as to make it clear to your reader (and examiner) that the work you are presenting is your own, even though it will – quite legitimately – draw on the work of others.
- You need to be able to do this whilst avoiding the dangers of *plagiarism*, which is essentially passing off the work of other people as your own.
- It is vital that you know exactly what plagiarism is, and that you are aware of how it can be unintentional as well as deliberate. Plagiarism is an extremely serious offence and you must avoid it at all costs.
- A key component of avoiding plagiarism is citing your sources, and you need to know how to do this correctly so that other people's work, that you are using in your own work, is correctly attributed.
- You also need to be familiar with the details of the particular citation style that you are required to use. The ways in which you cite different types of information source, such as journal articles, book chapters, or conference papers, are very different. You need to know how to cite each source you use correctly.

Plagiarism

Adopting a deep transformational approach to reading, in which you work at internalising the ideas you are reading about – thinking about them and making sense of them in your own terms, and relating them to what you know already – will make it easier for you to avoid plagiarism.

Even if you are reading about concepts and ideas that are completely new to you, you can still 'make them your own'. If you are writing at a basic rather than advanced level, and you do not have a lot of existing knowledge of the topic, you can't necessarily be expected to add new insights or come up with a lot of critical evaluation of your own. You may be heavily reliant on what you are reading. However, by doing the following, you are 'making them your own':

- Really think about the ideas.
- Translate them into your own words.
- Try to see how they fit into an argument that answers your essay or research question.
- Arrange them accordingly.

What you are aiming for is that your marker is able to write something along the following lines, which is a statement I often use when a student has succeeded in using the ideas he or she has gathered from the literature, but at an appropriately internalised level:

> 'Although well supported by references to appropriate literature, this reads very much as your own analysis and synthesis.'

By *analysis* I mean that the student has identified the components (the key ideas and themes) of the question. By *synthesis* I mean that he or she has shown how the evidence gathered fits together to form an answer to the question.

You should now try to add some *critical evaluation*. If you are operating at a basic, beginner's level in the topic, then once again you may be heavily reliant on finding points of criticism – i.e. criticism of the claims and arguments you are putting forward as an answer to your question – in the literature. But once again, if you can internalise them, and integrate them within your essay or report, you are making them your own, and 'critical evaluation' can be added to the 'analysis and synthesis' in the marker's comment above.

As we have seen, using and building on the work of other people is a legitimate – indeed, essential – component of academic work. However, equally essential is *acknowledging* the source of your ideas. Failing to acknowledge your sources constitutes *plagiarism*. You should avoid it at all costs.

Plagiarism is essentially passing off someone else's work as your own. If you include in your own work claims, arguments or evidence that you have found in information sources written by other people, without acknowledging where you found them, then you are plagiarising.

Plagiarism can be deliberate or accidental. It can happen unintentionally on your part. For example, you may make verbatim or almost verbatim notes from passages in sources you are using, without clearly indicating (to yourself, when you come back to them later) in those notes where they come from. You may fail to distinguish in your notes between your own comments and interpretations of ideas, and the actual text taken direct from your sources. The notes may have been made at a relatively early stage of your work, and at the time your main focus may understandably have been on gathering together ideas to try to get a picture of the topic. You may return to these notes at a later stage when you are writing up your work and, if you have not made it clear in them, genuinely forget that the ideas came from other sources.

International students should be aware that changes in style in an essay that may be imperceptible to them may be very obvious to a native English language-speaking lecturer – for example, a passage of smooth English suddenly appearing in an otherwise less smooth essay. Partial rephrasing and changing word order will often fail to hide plagiarism. If this is done deliberately, it can lead to serious penalties and failure. Most cases of plagiarism can be avoided, however, by citing sources appropriately. Simply acknowledging that certain material has been borrowed, and providing your audience with the information necessary to find that source, is usually enough to prevent plagiarism.

THINK

There is some plagiarism in what you have just read. Use *Google* to find it.

The passage in question is:

Most cases of plagiarism can be avoided, however, by citing sources. Simply acknowledging that certain material has been borrowed, and providing your audience with the information necessary to find that source, is usually enough to prevent plagiarism.

Type this directly into *Google* and you will quickly find it. You could try changing it subtly to:

Most ~~cases of~~ plagiarism can be avoided~~, however,~~ by citing sources. ~~Simply~~ acknowledging that certain material has been borrowed, and providing your ~~audience~~ <u>readers</u> with the information necessary to find that source, ~~is~~ <u>will</u> usually <u>be</u> enough to prevent plagiarism.

However, it will still be found (Figure 10.1).

This is a relatively simple mechanistic approach to finding plagiarism. Bear in mind that lecturers and examiners not only are familiar with a wide range of sources, but also develop a 'nose' for plagiarism, even if it is much more subtly constructed.

Increasingly, systems such as *Turnitin* (http://turnitin.com/) are being used by universities. Students are required to submit their coursework via *Turnitin*, which checks their work against the web, databases of publications and its own huge store of students' work to indicate any parts of the work that have been plagiarised.

Two important variations on plagiarism that you must avoid are self-plagiarism and collusion. *Self-plagiarism* occurs where text that you have already submitted as part of another piece of coursework is used in a different piece of coursework. *Collusion* occurs where a significant amount of very similar text is submitted by more than one student.

You should bear in mind that, as noted above, systems such as *Turnitin* will compare your text not only with material from web-based and published information sources, but also with the work of other students both from your year and previous years. So even text that is original – i.e. not taken from an information source – if submitted by more than one person, is likely to be identified as plagiarised.

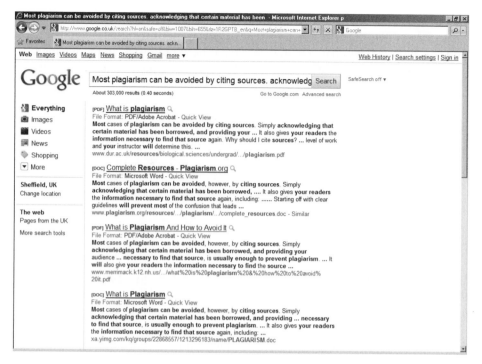

Figure 10.1   Plagiarism detected

Citing your sources

As noted above, acknowledging the sources of your claims, arguments and evidence is at the heart of academic work. However, it is also important to cite them using the correct procedures. The basic idea behind having clear rules for how you should cite sources is to enable anyone reading your work (including those assessing it) to find for themselves the sources you have used. Finding and checking sources is important to enable your readers to assess the quality of your work, and to follow up sources that may be of interest to them.

There are many citation styles, and it is important to make sure that you are familiar with and adhere to the style required by your university or department. There are two basic types of style: parenthetical (which uses brackets) and numerical. The illustrations given in this chapter use the **American Psychological Association** (APA) parenthetical style, and the **Vancouver** numerical style.

Purdue University provides an excellent online style guide to using the APA citation style at: http://owl.english.purdue.edu/owl/section/2/10/. The University of Leicester provides an excellent guide to using the Vancouver system at: http://www.le.ac.uk/li/sources/subject8/vancouver.html

Linking references in the text of your work to your bibliography

Parenthetical method examples

You should include a reference in the main text of your work in the following way. Examples here are shown in the American Psychological Association (APA) parenthetical style:

> There are many types of information retrieval system (Smith, 2009).

> According to Smith (2009), there are many types of information retrieval system.

If you are quoting directly from a source, you should include the page number of the quote:

> Smith (2009, p. 34) notes that 'There are many types of information retrieval system'.

or:

> Smith (2009: 34) notes that 'There are many types of information retrieval system'.

Quotations that extend over more than two lines should be presented in a separate indented paragraph. For example:

> Eaglestone *et al.* (2007) note that:

>> 'A number of creativity support systems have been developed, yet still the relationship between information systems and creativity – and the question of how systems might be developed effectively to support creativity – are neither straightforward nor well researched.' (p. 1)

If you want to omit part of the text of a quotation, you should replace the missing text with '...'. For example:

> Greene (2002) notes how, in relation to the use of the Explore Modern Art system:

>> 'it became evident just how useful certain kinds of errors could be if they were instructive mistakes... As they examined a series of trials one could clearly hear them develop a hypothesis.' (p. 104)

If there are two or three authors, you should quote them as follows in the text:

> Smith and Jones (2010) note that...

> Jones, Parkin and Rowlands (2009) concluded that...

Some styles use an ampersand: (Smith & Jones, 2010). Always check the precise form of references recommended by the department in which you are studying.

Where there are more than three authors, you should quote the first one only and replace the others with *et al.*:

According to a recent study (Smith *et al.*, 2010), ...

In some styles, all authors are listed the first time the reference is used, with subsequent occurrences listing just the first author followed by '*et al.*'. Again, check what your department's preferred citation practice is.

Where there is more than one reference, you should list them alphabetically:

These systems have been the subject of much research in recent years (Bidderton *et al.*, 2007; Palmer, 2010; Smith and Jones, 2009).

Some styles recommend listing the references in date order. Check your department's preferred citation practice.

You should give full details of all the authors in your bibliography. This is a list of all the references used in your essay or dissertation. It is normally included in a separate *References* section at the end of your work. How to cite documents in the bibliography is discussed below.

Table 10.1 Bibliographic references (1)

In the text	In your References section
Smith (2009)	Smith, F. (2009). *An introduction to information retrieval.* Chichester: Wiley.
Smith and Jones (2010)	Smith, F. and Jones, M. (2010). *Advances in information systems.* London: Chapman.
Smith *et al.* (2010)	Smith, F., Jones, M., Janson, G. and Flaherty, H.J. (2010). *Modern information retrieval systems.* Chichester: Wiley.

Numerical method examples

These are examples of the Vancouver numerical style:

There are many types of information retrieval system (1).

According to Smith (1), there are many types of information retrieval system.

If you are quoting directly from a source, you should include the page number of the quote:

smith (1, p. 34) notes that 'There are many types of information retrieval system'.

or:

Smith (1: 34) notes that 'There are many types of information retrieval system'.

Two or three authors:

Smith and Jones (2) note that...

Two or more references:

The increase in research into information systems has been noted by a number of recent researchers (2, 3).

or:

These systems have been the subject of much research in recent years (2–4).

As noted below, you should provide full details of all the authors in your *References* section at the end of your work.

Table 10.2 Bibliographic references (2)

In the text	In your References section
(1)	1. Smith F, An introduction to information retrieval. Chichester: Wiley; 2009.
(2)	2. Smith F, Jones, M, Advances in information systems. London: Chapman; 2010.
(3)	3. Smith F, Jones M, Janson G, Flaherty HJ. Modern information retrieval systems. Chichester: Wiley; 2010.

How to list items in your References section

The examples here are based on the American Psychological Association (APA) style. This section provides a quick reference to the basics. For more complex cases not covered here, go to e.g. http://owl.english.purdue.edu/owl/section/2/

Books	
[22]Author surname, Initial(s).	Smith, S.
(Year).	(2010).
Title	*Research methodology*

(Continued)

---

[22]Note that in some cases an author may be an organisation rather than a person. See the examples for **Datasets** and **Audio podcasts**.

(Continued)

(Edition). [other than 1st]	(3rd ed.). [If this is a first edition, ignore edition and put a full stop after the title.]
Place of publication:	Oxford:
Publisher.	Dean Press.
Refer to this in your text as:	Smith (2010)

Smith, S. (2010). *Research methodology.* (3rd ed.). London: Dean Press.

Edited books	
Editor Surname, Initial(s). (Ed.).	Spink, A., & Cole, C. (Eds.).
(Year).	(2005).
Title	*New directions in cognitive information retrieval*
(Edition). [other than 1st]	[If this is a first edition, ignore edition and put a full stop after the title.]
Place of publication:	Netherlands:
Publisher.	Springer.
Refer to this in your text as:	Spink & Cole (2005)

Spink, A., & Cole, C. (Eds.). (2005). *New directions in cognitive information retrieval.* Netherlands: Springer.

Chapter in an edited book	
Author surname, Initial(s).	Ford, N.
(Year).	(2005).
Title of chapter.	New cognitive directions.
In	In
Editor(s) (Ed.),	A. Spink, & C. Cole (Eds.),
Title of the book	*New directions in cognitive information retrieval*
(pp.). [pages]	[If this is a first edition, ignore edition.]
(Edition) [other than 1st]	(pp. 81–96).
Place of publication:	Netherlands:
Publisher.	Springer.
Refer to this in your text as:	Ford (2005)

Ford, N. (2005). New cognitive directions. In A. Spink, & C. Cole (Eds.), *New directions in cognitive information retrieval* (pp. 81–96). Netherlands: Springer.

Journal article (print)	
Author surname, Initial(s).	Buckley, C. A., Pitt, E., Norton, B., & Owens, T.
(Year).	(2010).
Title of article.	Students' approaches to study, conceptions of learning and judgements about the value of networked technologies.
Journal title,	*Active Learning in Higher Education,*
Volume(part),	*11*(1),
Pages.	55–65.
Refer to this in your text as:	Buckley, Pitt, Norton and Owens (2010)

Buckley, C. A., Pitt, E., Norton, B., & Owens, T. (2010). Students' approaches to study, conceptions of learning and judgements about the value of networked technologies. *Active Learning in Higher Education, 11*(1), 55–65.

If a print journal is also available online, it is not necessary to include a URL.

E-journal article (online only – not available in print form)	
Author surname, Initial(s).	Pirkola, A.
(Year).	(2009).
Title of article.	The effectiveness of web search engines to index new sites from different countries.
Journal title [online],	*Information Research,*
Volume(part),	*14*(2).
Pages.	
If there are no volume, part or page numbers, put a full stop after the title.	
Retrieved from URL	Retrieved from http://InformationR.net/ir/14-2/paper396.html
Refer to this in your text as:	Pirkola (2009)

Pirkola, A. (2009). The effectiveness of web search engines to index new sites from different countries. *Information Research, 14*(2). Retrieved from http://InformationR.net/ir/14-2/paper396.html

Conference paper	
Author/editor Surname, Initial(s).	Fortuna, S. and Whittle, A. J.
(Year).	(2009).

(Continued)

(Continued)

Title of conference paper.	Prediction of the small strain behaviour of natural Pisa clay by means of the MIT-S1 constitutive model.
In:	In:
Editor Initials. Surname (ed.) or name of organisation,	H. I. Ling, A. Smythe and R. Betti (eds.),
Title of the published proceedings of the conference,	*Poromechanics IV–Proceedings of the Fourth Biot Conference on Poromechanics,*
Location of conference,	New York,
Date of conference	June 8–10, 2009
(pp. page numbers).	(pp. 1059–1064).
Place of publication:	Lancaster, PA:
Publisher.	DEStech Publications.
Refer to this in your text as:	Fortuna and Whittle (2009)

Fortuna, S. and Whittle, A. J. (2009). Prediction of the small strain behaviour of natural Pisa clay by means of the MIT-S1 constitutive model. In: H.I. Ling, A. Smythe and R. Bettie (eds.), *Poromechanics IV–Proceedings of the Fourth Biot Conference on Poromechanics,* New York, June 8–10, 2009 (pp. 1059–1064). Lancaster, PA: DEStech Publications.

Thesis	
Author Surname, Initial(s).	Jones, M.
(Year).	(2010).
Title	*Learning styles and e-learning*
[Degree type].	[PhD thesis].
Awarding institution,	University of Sheffield,
Location.	Sheffield.
Refer to this in your text as:	Jones (2010)

Jones, M. (2010). *Learning styles and e-learning* [PhD thesis]. University of Sheffield, Sheffield.

Lecture	
Presenter Surname, Initial(s).	Jones, M.
(Year of presentation).	(2010).
Title	*Competing in the marketplace*
[Lecture].	[Lecture].
Institution/location,	University of Sheffield,
Place.	Sheffield.

Day and month of presentation	12 May.
Refer to this in your text as:	Jones (2010)

Jones, M. (2010). *Competing in the marketplace* [Lecture]. University of Sheffield, Sheffield. 12 May.

PowerPoint slides	
Presenter Surname, Initial(s).	Smith, J. R.
(Year).	(2010).
Title	*Information retrieval*
[PowerPoint slides].	[PowerPoint slides].
Institution/location,	University of Sheffield,
Place.	Sheffield.
Refer to this in your text as:	Smith (2010)

Smith, R. J. (2010). *Information retrieval* [PowerPoint slides]. University of Sheffield, Sheffield.

Datasets	
[23]Author Surname, Initial(s).	Office for National Statistics.
(Year). If no date, put (n.d.).	(n.d.).
Title	*Neighbourhood Statistics. Area: Sheffield (Local Authority). Age structure (KS02)*
[Data file].	[Data file].
Retrieved from URL	Retrieved from http://www.neighbour-hood.statistics.gov.uk/
Refer to this in your text as:	Office for National Statistics (n.d.)

Office for National Statistics. (n.d.). *Neighbourhood statistics. Area: Sheffield (Local Authority). Age structure (KS02)* [Data file]. Retrieved from http://www.neighbourhood.statistics.gov.uk/

Website

If you wish to refer to an entire website, as opposed to a website page, you would normally refer to it in your main text, rather than including it in your references at the end. For example:

'The University of Sheffield's website (http://sheffield.ac.uk/) is a good example of...'

(Continued)

---

[23]Note that the author may sometimes be an organisation rather than a person.

(Continued)

A page in a website	
[24]Author surname, Initial(s).	BBC.
(Year).	(2010).
Title of the page.	Queen's Speech: Government aims to be 'greenest ever'.
Title of the website [online].	*Democracy Live.*
Retrieved from URL	Retrieved from http://news.bbc.co.uk/democracylive/hi/house_of_commons/newsid_8709000/8709627.stm
Refer to this in your text as:	BBC (2010)

BBC (2010). Queen's Speech: Government aims to be 'greenest ever'. *Democracy Live.* Retrieved from http://news.bbc.co.uk/democracylive/hi/house_of_commons/ newsid_8709000/8709627. stm

If a personal author had been identified for the page, this person would have filled the *author* slot. If neither an organisation nor a person as author had been identifiable, the first element would be the title followed by the year.

Blog post	
Author surname, Initial(s).	Blakeman, K.
(Year, date).	(2010, May 6).
Title of the blog entry	Tweetminster maps turnout in UK election
[Web log post]. or [Web log comment].	[Web log post].
Retrieved from URL	Retrieved from http://www.rba.co.uk/wordpress/2010/05/06/tweetminster-maps-turnout-in-uk-election/
Refer to this in your text as:	Blakeman (2010)

Blakeman, K. (2010, May 6). Tweetminster maps turnout in UK election [Web log post]. Retrieved from http://www.rba.co.uk/wordpress/2010/05/06/tweetminster-maps-turnout-in-uk-election/

Audio podcast	
Author surname, Initial(s).	BBC
(Year).	(2010).
Title	*A History of the World in 100 Objects. 064 The David Vases 1 July 2010*

---

[24]Note that the author may sometimes be an organisation rather than a person.

[Audio podcast].	[Audio podcast].
Retrieved from URL	Retrieved from http://www.bbc.co.uk/podcasts/series/ahow
Refer to this in your text as:	BBC. (2010)

BBC. (2010). *A History of the World in 100 Objects. 064 The David Vases 1 July 2010* [Audio podcast]. Retrieved from http://www.bbc.co.uk/podcasts/series/ahow

YouTube video	
Author surname, Initial(s).	Asaad, A. E.
(Year).	(2009).
Title	*Multiple linear regression with Excel*
[Video file].	[Video file].
Retrieved from URL	Retrieved from http://www.youtube.com/watch?v=hu8PojzWluQ
Refer to this in your text as:	Asaad (2009)

Asaad, A. E. (2009). *Multiple linear regression with Excel* [Video file]. Retrieved from http://www.youtube.com/watch?v=hu8PojzWluQ

Wiki entry	
Author surname, Initial(s).	[If no author, put the title first – not italicised – followed by date.]
(Year). If no date, put (n.d.)	(n.d.).
Title	*Scientific method.*
In	In
Name of wiki	Wikipedia
Retrieved date, from URL	Retrieved June 28, 2010, from http://en.wikipedia.org/wiki/Scientific_method
Refer to this in your text as:	Scientific method (n.d.)

Scientific method. (n.d.). In Wikipedia. Retrieved June 28, 2010, from http://en.wikipedia.org/wiki/Scientific_method

Newspaper article	
Author surname, Initial(s).	Elliott, F.
(Year, Month Day of Publication).	(2010, August 6).
Title	Cameron tries to fix Pakistan damage with double visit.
In	In

(Continued)

(Continued)

Newspaper name.	The Times.
p. column and page number.	p. A1.
Refer to this in your text as:	Elliott (2010)

Elliott, F. (2010, August 6). Cameron tries to fix Pakistan damage with double visit. *The Times.* p. A1.

Complications

Sometimes things are not quite so straightforward. The following are examples of common complications.

No date

Where no date is identifiable, you should put (n.d.):

Scientific method. (n.d.). In Wikipedia. Retrieved June 28, 2010, from http://en.wikipedia.org/wiki/Scientific_method

URL or DOI?

If a source has a Digital Object Identifier (DOI), then add this at the end in place of a URL:

Bruno, D., and Higham, P. A. (2009). Global subjective memorability and the strength-based mirror effect in recognition memory. *Memory & Cognition, 37,* 807–818.

doi: 10.3758/MC.37.6.807

If the source is available online and has a URL but not a DOI, then add:

Retrieved from [URL]

For example:

Pirkola, A. (2009). The effectiveness of web search engines to index new sites from different countries. Information Research, 14(2). Retrieved from http://InformationR.net/ir/14-2/paper396.html

Two or more different items by exactly the same authors in the same year

Differentiate these by adding a, b, etc., after the date. For example:

Creativity has been the subject of much research in recent years (e.g. Smith, 2007a; Smith, 2007b)...

Similarly, add the a, b, etc., to the date in the References section at the end of your work.

A cited reference or quotation (i.e. in another person's work)

Sometimes you come across information in one document which cites the source of the information as another document. You should include both sources in your work as shown below:

Author/editor Surname, Initial(s).	Smith, F.
(Year)	(2008)
Title of the source cited.	Managing change.
Edition. (If not first)	
Place of publication of cited source:	London:
Publisher of cited source.	Moss Publications.
Cited in: Author of citing source	Cited in: Jones, F.
Date of citing source.	(2010)
Title of citing source.	*New directions in management.*
Edition of citing source.	3rd edition.
Place of publication of citing source:	London:
Publisher of citing source.	Single Press.
Refer to this in your text as:	Smith (2008), cited in Jones (2010)

Smith, F. (2008) Managing change. London: Moss Publications. Cited in: Jones, F. (2010) *New directions in management*. 3rd edition. London: Single Press.

You should also include the citing source in your references at the end of your work.

Jones, F. (2010) *New directions in management*. 3rd edition. London: Single Press.

You are working from a PDF file downloaded from e.g. Google Scholar *or an author's website*

You should examine the paper to discover its source – for example, whether it is a copy of a journal article or a conference paper. If the details of the journal or conference are included in the paper anywhere, use these details to form your reference. If they are not, it is often possible to find the correct bibliographical details of the paper by searching for it on *Google* or *Google Scholar*.

Summary

Plagiarism is passing off the work of others as your own. It can be unintentional as well as deliberate, and it is vital to avoid it. Yet using and building on the work of others is a fundamental element of academic activity. This chapter explained ways in which you can avoid making inappropriate use of other people's ideas within your own work.

You need to know how to correctly *attribute* the sources you use, and to make clear which ideas in your work derive from other sources and which are your own. Central to this process is the use of correct citation practice. This chapter explained how to attribute and cite sources in the text of your essay or report and in the References section at the end, where you list all the sources you have used. The two main types of citation system – parenthetical and numeric – were introduced, and examples were given of how to cite a range of different types of information source.

Chapter 11 will explore how to keep up to date with new information on your topic. It will introduce a variety of ways of setting up automatic alerts so that you are informed when something new on your topic is published.

ELEVEN

Keeping up to date

WHY YOU NEED TO KNOW THIS

- It will be of great benefit to the quality of your essay or research report if it uses information sources that are not only authoritative but also the latest available. But constantly repeating searches to scan for new information – particularly if you find that there is nothing new since last time you searched – is time-consuming and not the most efficient way of keeping up to date.
- The techniques introduced in this chapter will enable you to keep on top of new information as it is published, without having to constantly repeat your searches.
- There are a number of very easy and convenient ways of doing this. You can, for example, set up email alerts and web feeds which will automatically inform you when something new is published on your topic. Automatic alerts can be set up to inform you when:

  - new documents are published on your topic;
  - documents that you are interested in are cited in a newly published document;
  - documents by an author in whom you are interested are cited in a newly published document;
  - a new document is published by an author whose work you are following;
  - a new issue is published of a journal in which you are interested, along with the table of contents detailing the various articles in the journal issue; and
  - a website in which you are interested is updated.

Note that to activate alerts and web feeds in *SciVerse Scopus*, not only does your university have to be subscribed, but also you need to be registered personally with *SciVerse Scopus* (personal registration is free if your university subscribes) and logged into your personal account. To use this facility, simply click the **My Alerts** button which appears at the top and bottom of the *SciVerse Scopus* screen. You will be prompted to register, then 'activate personalisation'.

A new document is published on your topic

Google Scholar

If you run a successful search for information in *Google Scholar*, and would like to be informed as soon as any new material is published which matches this search, you can set up an email alert that will automatically inform you. You can also store the search, to run it again whenever you want, simply by clicking a link rather than having to remember and re-type the search. This can be useful if you have worked hard to design and refine a complex and effective search. You may wish periodically to repeat it to update the results.

Take the following example. You have been searching for the latest information on 'learning or cognitive styles'. You have specified that you want to search for any documents with any of the following phrases in their **title**:

allintitle: "learning style" OR "learning styles" OR "cognitive style" OR "cognitive styles"

You perform the search, which results in the screen shown in Figure 11.1.

You can now click the *Create email* alert option which appears at both the top and bottom of the search results page. You will be taken to another screen asking you to enter your email address and confirm that you would like to set up an alert. When

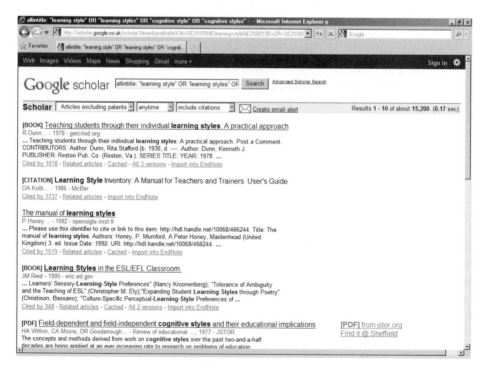

Figure 11.1 *Google Scholar* results page

you have confirmed, you will receive messages as new material relevant to your query is published. You must be logged into your personal account to be able to do this.

However, you can also store the search for re-running at the click of a link. The following procedures will work with any search engine, and do not depend on it offering any explicit *save* option. The examples below assume that you are using the Internet Explorer web browser.

Having run your search, from the results page you can now do any of the following:

- Save the search results webpage to your *Favourites* or *Bookmarks* (depending on your browser). Then whenever you open your *Favourites* or *Bookmarks* and click it the search will be performed live.
- Save the search results webpage to your *Favourites* or *Bookmarks toolbar*. You can do this by dragging the *GoogleScholar* icon (that appears immediately to the left of the *http://...* in the address box) to the toolbar. Whenever you click it, the search will be performed.
- Or you can place an icon for the search results webpage on your desktop. You can do this by dragging the *GoogleScholar* icon (see bullet point above) to your Desktop (you browser must be resized so that the Desktop is visible to be able to do this). An icon will appear on your desktop. When double clicked, the search will be performed.

SciVerse Scopus

After running a search that you would like to save for later running, on the results page click the *Save* link (to the left of the *Set alert* and *Set feed* links shown in Figure 11.2) and your search will be saved. **Saved Searches** can be accessed any time from the **My Settings** tab at the top of the screen. From your **Saved Searches** you can run any saved search by clicking *All results* or *New results* as you wish. You can save up to 50 searches.

You can also set up an email alert or a web feed for the search. Clicking the *Set alert* link will take you to a screen that enables you to set up an email alert. You will be asked to give the alert a name, and to choose whether you want it to be sent to you daily, weekly or monthly.

Clicking the *Set feed* link allows you to set up a web feed. It will take you to a page that asks you to give your feed a name. Once set up, it will deliver the top 20 results for your search every day. Web feeds are introduced in the final section of this chapter.

Click on the **My Alerts** button which appears at the top and bottom of the *SciVerse Scopus* screen to manage all your alerts. You must be logged into your personal account to be able to save a search and set up alerts and feeds.

Web of Knowledge

You can save a search for running again later in *Web of Knowledge*. Having performed a search that you would like to save, go to your search history by clicking on the **Search History** tab. On the search history page, click the **Save History** button in *Web*

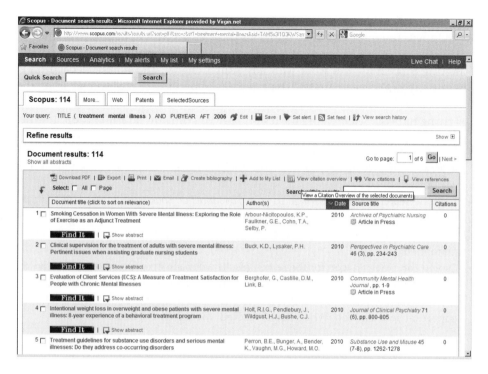

Figure 11.2 Saving your search in *SciVerse Scopus*

of Knowledge. You will be taken to a page that asks you to give your search a name, then to save it.

Although available in the previous version of *Web of Knowledge* which was replaced in July 2011, the facility to set up email alerts and web feeds to inform you when new documents are published on the topic of your saved search is scheduled before the end of 2011. When this becomes available, it is likely that you will need to be logged into your personal account to be able to save a search and set up alerts and feeds.

Documents in which you are interested are cited in a newly published document

Sciverse Scopus

To set up an alert when a document you are interested in is cited in a new document added to *Sciverse Scopus*, go to the page giving details of that document. This can be accessed from the search results page (Figure 11.3) by clicking the title of the document.

Figure 11.3   The *SciVerse Scopus* results page

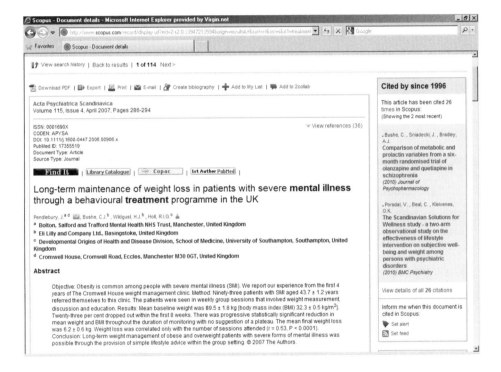

Figure 11.4   The *SciVerse Scopus* document details page

This will take you to a page showing further details of the document (Figure 11.4). Click the *Set alert* or *Set feed* (bottom right of the screen) to set up an email alert or a web feed respectively. Web feeds are introduced in the final section of this chapter.

You can edit or cancel your alerts by clicking the **My Alerts** button at the top and bottom of the screen (not visible in Figure 11.4). You must be logged into your personal account to be able to set up alerts and feeds.

Web of Knowledge

Although available in the previous version of *Web of Knowledge* which was replaced in July 2011, the facility to set up email alerts and web feeds to inform you when a document you have selected is cited in a new document added to the databases is scheduled for inclusion before the end of 2011. When this becomes available, it is likely that you will need to be logged into your personal account to be able to save a search and set up alerts and feeds.

An author is cited by a new document or publishes a new document

SciVerse Scopus

In *SciVerse Scopus*, you can set up an alert to inform you when an author's work is cited by a new document. You can also be alerted when an author publishes a new document. To do this, you should perform a search for the author you are interested in by selecting the **Author Search** tab (Figure 11.5).

Click the **Search** button, and on the **Author Results** page (Figure 11.6) click the author's name.

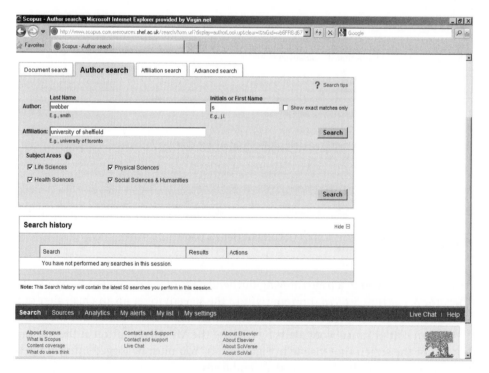

Figure 11.5 The *SciVerse Scopus* author search page

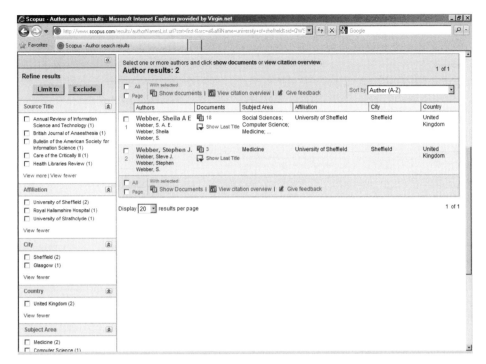

Figure 11.6 Searching for an author

You will be taken to a page showing the details of the author. Scroll down, and you will be presented with the options to be informed when the author publishes new documents in *SciVerse Scopus* and when any document by the author is cited in a new document added to *SciVerse Scopus* (Figure 11.7).

The *Set alert* links and *Set feed* links will enable you to set up an email alert and a web feed relating to new documents published by this author. The *Set alert* link at the bottom right of the screen will enable you to set up an email alert to inform you when a document written by this author is cited in a new document. You can also set up a cited author web feed from your **My Alerts** screen. This is available by clicking on the **My Alerts** tab, which appears at the top and bottom of the *SciVerse Scopus* screen (not visible in Figure 11.7), and allows you to edit and manage all your alerts. You must be logged into your personal account to be able to set up alerts and feeds. Web feeds are introduced in the final section of this chapter.

A new issue of a journal in which you are interested is published

A number of free services allow you to select journal titles in areas of interest to you, then alert you, by email or web feed, when new issues of the journals are published. Included in the alert are the tables of contents (TOCs) of the new journal issues.

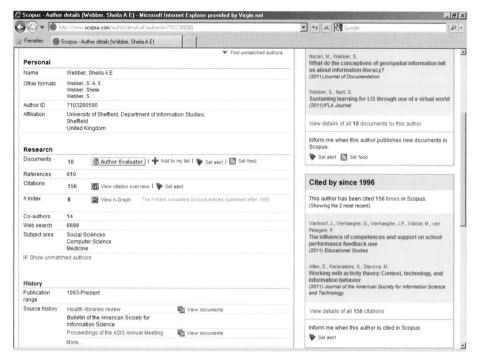

Figure 11.7 The author details page

One example of such a service, *JournalTocs*, is briefly introduced here. However, there are many such services, prominent among which is *Zetoc* (http://zetoc.mimas. ac.uk/), which also allows searching of conference papers and journal articles. Access to *Zetoc* is free for members of most UK higher and further education institutions as well as for the National Health Service in England, Scotland and Northern Ireland. It enables access to the British Library's Electronic Table of Contents, covering approximately 20,000 journal titles and 16,000 conference proceedings published per year. *Zetoc* can also be configured to search your library's holdings to see if the documents you have found are available.

Table of contents current awareness services are also provided by a number of publishers, such as the *Wiley Online Library* (http://olabout.wiley.com/WileyCDA/Section/id-404511.html) and *Sage Journals Online* (http://online.sagepub.com/cgi/register). Some, such as Sage, require (free) registration.

JournalTOCS is freely available to all. It allows you to create a personalised list of journals on topics of interest to you. Registration is free. When you access the *JournalTOCS* website, you can see immediately which of your selected journals have published a new issue – and by clicking on any of them you can see the table of contents detailing the new articles. You can also choose to receive an email, and/or set up an RSS feed, to update you whenever a new issue of any of your selected journals is published.

You can select journals to follow, and your selection is shown in the central column of the screen (Figure 11.8). Icons displayed to the right of each journal title provide links to the homepage of that journal and to its RSS feed subscription page. You can also subscribe to RSS feeds for all or some of your followed journals simply by ticking them on your *Followed Journals* page and selecting the *Save and Export* option. Further icons to the right of each journal title indicate whether the journal is open access, free, partially free, or subscription-based – and whether there is a new issue available.

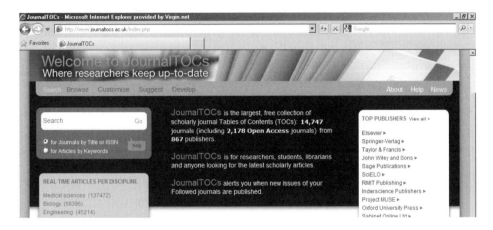

Figure 11.8 The *Journal Tocs* website

Clicking on a journal title in your list of followed journals will display the current table of contents for that journal. In Figure 11.9 I have expanded the second article to show its abstract, below which there is an option to export its details to *RefWorks*. By ticking the box beside an article, I can save it to my *Saved Articles* page from which I can choose to export the reference into *EndNote*.

Clicking on the journal homepage icon to the right of a journal title (Figure 11.8), or clicking the title of an article (Figure 11.9) will take you to the publisher's webpage. Depending on the list of journal titles your university library has subscribed to, it may be that the publisher's website recognises you and offers you a link to the full text of that the journal's content.

However, if not, you can do the following:

- Search your library's webpage to see if your university subscribes to the journal. If so, it may be available online as full text.
- Search for the article in *Google Scholar*. You can configure *Google Scholar* to tell you if your library has a subscription, and to link directly to the full text if available (see Chapter 8 for details of how to do this). When a full-text copy is freely available to anyone (e.g. a PDF pre-print of a journal article or conference paper is available from an academic repository which *Google Scholar* searches or from the author's website), *Google Scholar* will provide a link to it so that you can access it directly.

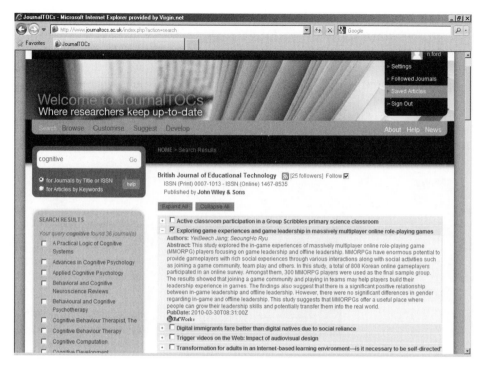

Figure 11.9 A *Journal Tocs* list of sources

If the article is important to your work, and you cannot locate a copy in any other way, don't forget that your university library will offer an inter-library loan service, whereby you can obtain books and theses to borrow and photocopies of journal articles.

A website in which you are interested is updated

What are web feeds?

Web feeds allow you quickly to tell whether a website, blog or other content provider to which you have subscribed has updated its content, and to view the new information. If a website offers a feed, you can subscribe to it. Recall from the previous sections that *SciVerse Scopus* allows you to set up web feeds to inform you when, for example, a selected document is cited. However, many other websites offer feeds. Common forms of web feed are *RSS* and *Atom*.

Many feed readers are available. However, Internet Explorer (from version 7) has a built-in feed reader, and the examples shown here assume that you are using this.

Figure 11.10 shows a list of feeds to which I have subscribed. The list is accessed by clicking on the **Favourites** tab, and then **Feeds**.

Each line represents a particular website. Each website that has been updated since I last looked at it appears in bold. If nothing new has appeared since I last looked, it appears in normal font.

You can see that there are websites, blogs and journals in my list of feeds. By clicking on any of these, I can instantly see what's new. In Figure 11.10, I have clicked on **Information Literacy Weblog**, and am being shown the feed showing me the latest updates.

I can view the updated information in the feed page shown in Figure 11.10, or click on any of the links on that page to be taken to the actual website. Once the information has been looked at, the feed entry in the pane to the left of the screen becomes non-bold.

How do you set up a web feed?

When you are reading a webpage of interest to you, look out for an icon such as the web feed icon shown in Figure 11.11 (or indeed any link or button indicating that

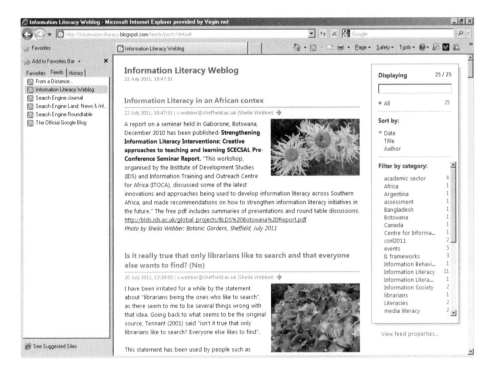

Figure 11.10   Web feeds in Internet Explorer

Figure 11.11   Web feed icon

you should click it to set up a feed). This may appear on the web page itself and/or at the top of the browser screen.

By clicking this icon, you can subscribe to the feed. The icon may appear on the webpage itself and/or, if your browser detects a feed on the webpage it is displaying, it will display it at the top of the screen (arrowed in Figure 11.12). If the icon

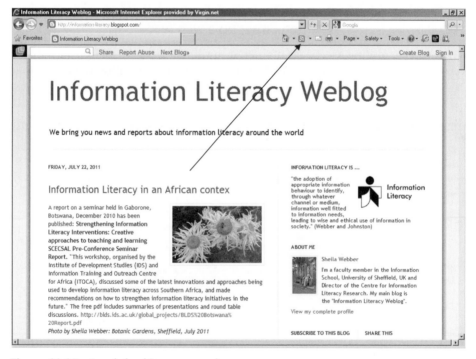

Figure 11.12   A web feed icon on a webpage

at the top of the screen is grey, then the browser has not detected any feeds on that page.

Clicking on the icon will take you to a web page (Figure 11.13) where you can subscribe to this particular feed.

Click on **Subscribe to this feed**, and you will be able to do precisely that, as shown in Figure 11.14.

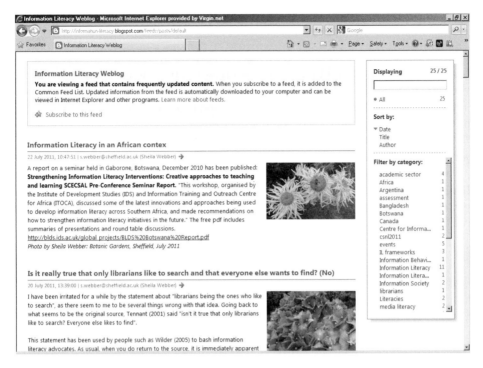

Figure 11.13   A web feed subscription page

The feed for this particular website will now appear in your list of feeds accessible from the Favourites tab in your browser (and from your Favourites bar if you select that option in the dialogue box shown in Figure 11.14).

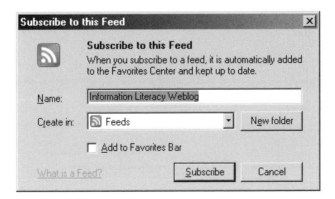

Figure 11.14   Subscribe dialogue box in Internet Explorer

Summary

This chapter introduced a number of ways of keeping up to date with information. Using information that is not only the most relevant, but also the most up to date in your essays of reports will improve the quality of your work. We looked at a variety of techniques for setting up automatic alerts which automatically send you an email or update your computer feeds when something new is published on your topic. This saves you from having frequently to repeat your search for information in case something has appeared since the last time you searched.

We also explored how you can set up alerts in a variety of search tools, including *Google Scholar and SciVerse Scopus*. Other alerting services, such as *JournalTocs,* allow you to be informed when a new issue of a journal appears. Also, many webpages offer the facility to subscribe to updates via web feeds.

TWELVE

Organising & sharing your information

WHY YOU NEED TO KNOW THIS

- Your personal store of references will become increasingly large, not only as you work on a particular essay or research project, but also in the longer term as you work on different pieces of work and on different courses over time.
- Having your own personal library of references, organised into meaningful folders (e.g. reflecting particular topics, courses, pieces of work, etc.) all searchable by author, title, keyword and your own tags, can save a lot of time and effort if you are trying to retrace your reading, and to link ideas and quotations back to where you originally found them.
- Reference management tools are designed to help you manage your information sources in this way.
- They also enable you automatically to insert and update citations in your text as you are writing your essay or report.
- Having done so, the software will automatically generate a bibliography at the end of your work. As you add new references in the text, the bibliography will be automatically updated. You can not only select the citation style you require (recall that citation styles were discussed in the previous chapter), but also change to another style at the click of a button.
- Such systems also allow you, should you choose to do so, to share references, notes and annotations with friends and collaborators over the web.

There are a number of systems designed to help you achieve either most or all of these tasks. Some must be purchased – though your university may offer them to university members over your network – these include, for example:

Bookends (http://www.sonnysoftware.com/bookends/bookends.html) for Mac OS X
EndNote (http://www.endnoteweb.com/)
Papers (http://mekentosj.com/papers/) for Mac OS X

Reference Manager (http://www.refman.com/) for Windows
RefWorks (http://www.refworks.com/)

Others are freely available over the web, such as:

Aigaion (http://www.aigaion.nl/)
BibDesk (http://bibdesk.sourceforge.net/) for Mac OS X
Biblioscape (http://www.biblioscape.com/) for Windows
Bibus (http://bibus-biblio.sourceforge.net/wiki/index.php/Main_Page)
CiteULike (http://www.citeulike.org/)
Mendeley (http://www.mendeley.com/)
Zotero (http://www.zotero.org/) an add-on for the Firefox browser.

In this chapter, we will explore just one of these systems: *Mendeley*. This is a free system, with both desktop and web components, which enables you to manage and share your bibliographic references and research papers.

Mendeley basics

Mendeley allows you to create your own searchable database of references to research documents. You can input details manually, or download them from search tools. You can store and organise them for search and retrieval, share them, and insert them as citations into the text of your work. You can automatically generate and update a bibliography of these citations at the end of your work. Via the web version of *Mendeley*, you can share information, annotations and notes with friends and collaborators.

When you import a PDF document into *Mendeley*, it will attempt automatically to extract metadata – information on the author, the journal title, volume and issue number, and page numbers – thus saving you time and effort. You can edit and add to this information at any time.

You can run *Mendeley **Desktop*** entirely on your own computer. But you can also choose to link and synchronise your desktop database with *Mendeley **Web***, a social networking site for academics, to share documents and information. *Mendeley* is free on the web at: http://www.mendeley.com/ (Figure 12.1).

From this screen, you can register (which is free) and download *Mendeley Desktop* to your computer. Once installed, open it and you will be presented with the screen shown in Figure 12.2.

In the example shown here we will set up a new *private* collection called **Climate change** in **My Library** (as opposed to a *shared* one in **Shared Collections**). Shared collections can be shared with other people on the web, and how to do this will be discussed shortly. We type the name of our new collection into the box where the words *Create collection* appear (arrowed in Figure 12.2), and this new name now appears there (Figure 12.3).

Figure 12.1   The *Mendeley* website

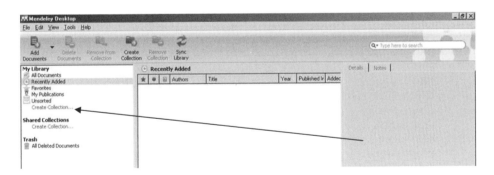

Figure 12.2   The *Mendeley Desktop* screen

Of course, until we put something in it, it is empty. Information can be added to it in a number of ways. We can:

- add PDF files already stored on our computer;
- manually type in details of an information source; or
- automatically download information from a search on *Google Scholar*, *Web of Knowledge* and a wide variety of search tools. Sources included at the time of writing are shown in Table 12.1.

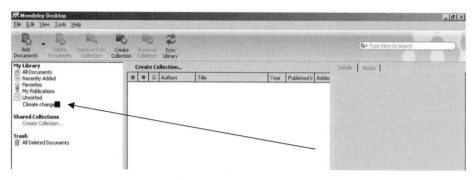

Figure 12.3　Creating a new collection

Table 12.1　Search tools allowing direct download of search results to *Mendeley*

ACM Portal	ISI *Web of Knowledge*
ACS Publications	JSTOR
AIP Scitation	Lancet Journals
Amazon	MyOpenArchive
APS	NASA ADS
APA PsycNET	Nature
arXiv	OpticsInfoBase
BioMedCentral	OvidSP
BioOne	PLoS
CiNii	PNAS
CiteseerX	PubMed
CiteULike	Refdoc
Copac	RePEc
DBLP	SAGE
EBSCO	ScienceDirect
GBV	ScienceMag
Google BookSearch	Scirus
Google Scholar	Spires
IACR ePrints	SpringerLink
IEEE Xplore	SSRN
Informaworld	Wikipedia
IngentaConnect	Wiley Online Library
INIST/CNRS	WorldCat
Institute of Physics	Zetoc

Importing data from *Google Scholar* and other search tools

Let us now import data into *Mendeley* from a *Google Scholar* search. We need to be logged in to *Mendeley* **Web** in order to do this.

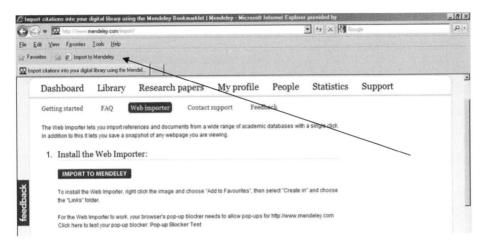

Figure 12.4 Installing the *Mendeley* web importer

The first thing we need to do is click the *Install Web Importer* option (we will only need to do this once in order to set up this functionality). This option is available as a link at the very bottom of the *Mendeley Web* page. It is also available as an option from the **Tools** menu in *Mendeley Desktop*.

This option takes us to the webpage shown in Figure 12.4. As instructed there, simply right-click the **IMPORT TO MENDELEY** button. We will be presented with a menu that allows us to add *Import to Mendeley* to our *Favourites*. It doesn't matter where we store it in our *Favourites* – as long as we can find it again. It can also be saved to our *Favourites Bar*, which results in the link being visible, as shown in Figure 12.4 (arrowed). This is particularly convenient, as we will see shortly.

Now we can begin searching *Google Scholar*. We can select any relevant documents that we find and download their details directly to *Mendeley Web*. When we synchronise our web and desktop versions of *Mendeley*, these details will also be downloaded to our desktop version. We can also download and store PDF versions of documents where these are available. Figure 12.5 shows the results of our search in *Google Scholar*.

We now click on **Import to Mendeley** in the **Favourites** bar. (If we saved this to somewhere other than our Favourites bar, we would have to navigate to where it is and click it.) A new window will appear, as shown in Figure 12.6. (We need to make sure that pop-ups are enabled in our browser. If they are not, then we should hold down the **Control** key as we click **Import to Mendeley**.)

Clicking on *Import* beside any of the items will display a *View in your Mendeley Library* and an *Edit tags and notes* link. This has been done for the first item in Figure 12.6. Selecting *Edit tags and notes* will allow us to specify where (into which Library) we would like the reference to be saved. It also allows us to add any tags

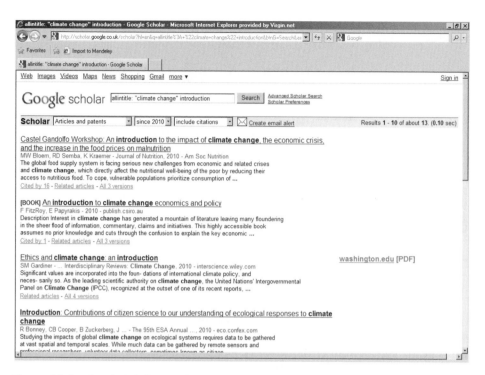

Figure 12.5 *Google Scholar* search results

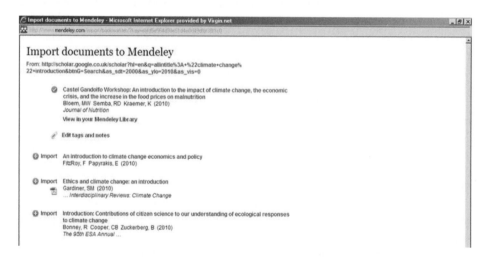

Figure 12.6 The *Mendeley* import screen

or notes to the item (we can do this later from within our *Mendeley* library if you wish). In Figure 12.7, we have chosen to save the reference to our new **Climate change** library.

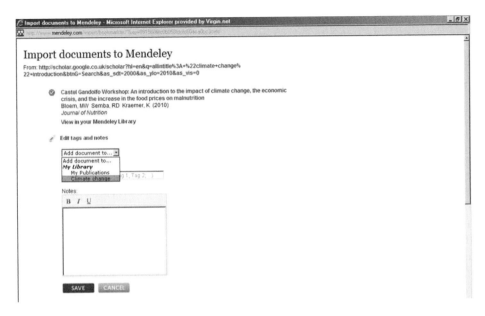

Figure 12.7 Importing a document into *Mendeley*

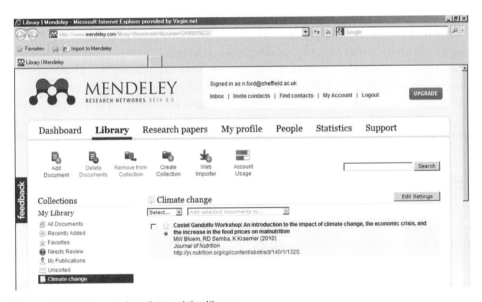

Figure 12.8 Our updated *Mendeley* library

When we return to *Mendeley Web* and refresh the page (or alternatively click the *View in our Mendeley Library* link shown in Figure 12.7), our library will have been updated (Figure 12.8).

When we return to our *Mendeley Desktop*, clicking **Sync Library** (shown in Figure 12.3) will copy the new contents of our *Mendeley Web* **Climate change** library to our *Mendeley Desktop* **Climate change** library.

We can change a collection from being **private** to **shared** by clicking **Edit Settings**. Documents in shared collections can be collaboratively tagged and annotated. We can also store PDF documents on *Mendeley Web* so that we can access them from anywhere.

Adding PDF files to your library

We will add some PDF documents previously found using *Google Scholar* and down-loaded to our computer. To do this, we must first select the collection we want to put them in (in this case, our new **Climate change** collection), and click **Add Documents**, as shown in Figure 12.9.

The dialogue box shown in Figure 12.9 allows us to import documents to our collection. We can import one or many documents (**Add Files…**), or all documents in a folder (**Add Folder…**). We can, if we wish, nominate one or more folders on our computer to be 'watched' by *Mendeley* (**Watch Folder…**). Any time we add new documents to a 'watched' folder they are automatically added to our *Mendeley* collec-tion. We can also manually type information about an information source into our **Climate change** collection database (**Add Entry Manually…**).

The reason for also adding details of documents of which we don't have PDF copies on our computer is that *Mendeley*, as we will see shortly, acts as a database of references that we can export directly into documents that we are writing (for example, our essay or dissertation) in *Microsoft Word* or other text editor. It allows us to automati-cally create, at the end of our document, a bibliography formatted in whatever style we specify. *Mendeley* offers a choice of over 1,000 different citation styles, including those we are likely to need for our academic work – and those required by a wide

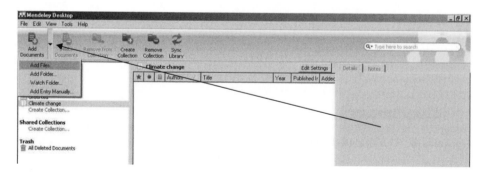

Figure 12.9   Adding PDF files to our *Mendeley* library

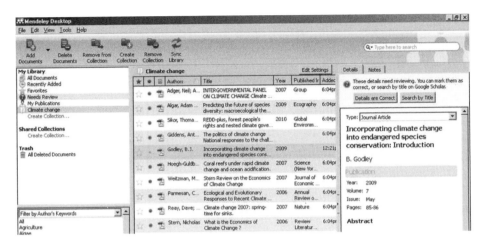

Figure 12.10 Automatic metadata extraction

range of different journals should we wish to publish the results of our research. Citation styles are discussed in Chapter 10. Our *Mendeley* collections are all searchable by titles, authors, author keywords and subject tags of our own that we can add. We can also annotate the PDF files with our own comments and notes.

Figure 12.10 assumes that we have imported a number of PDF files already stored on our computer. Click on a document in the middle pane, and its details are displayed in the right pane. Note that *Mendeley Desktop* has automatically extracted metadata from the document. It has identified the article title, the author, the date of publication, volume and issue, the page numbers, and author-supplied keywords. We can add our own tags and notes, which will be stored with all the other details of this item.

Sometimes *Mendeley Desktop* is not able to extract full details, as in the right-hand pane of figure 12.10, where the journal title has not been identified. In this case, it offers the option to search via *Google Scholar* for the missing information by clicking on **Search by Title**. If it can find the missing information, *Mendeley* will add it to the record. However, it is not always successful. We also have the option to type in the details ourselves, then confirm that the details for this item are correct (**Details are Correct**).

Inserting references into your work

Now let us see how we can use our libraries when we are writing documents. We'll take another example. Let us assume that we are writing an essay on *creativity*. We have created a new *Mendeley* collection which we have called **Creativity**, and have so far downloaded six references to it (Figure 12.11).

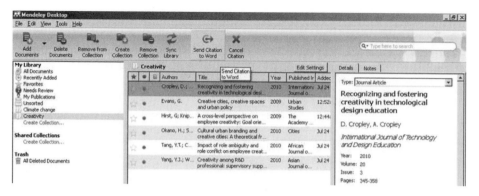

Figure 12.11   Our *Mendeley* Library

From *Mendeley Desktop* we can insert references from this (or any other) library directly into *Microsoft Word* or other text editor. However, before we can do so, we need to have selected, from the **Tools** menu in *Mendeley Desktop*, the **Install MS Word Plugin** option (or the **Install OpenOffice Plugin** if we are using *OpenOffice*). Next time we open *Word*, we can access *Mendeley* facilities from the **Add-Ins** tab (Figure 12.12).

As we write our essay, we can insert a reference at any point. We simply place the cursor where we want the reference to appear, then click **Insert Citation** from the **Add-Ins** tab or the **References** tab, depending on your version. This will take us into *Mendeley Desktop* so that we can select which reference(s) we want to use (Figure 12.13).

We can click on a reference to select it. To select more than one reference, we simply hold down the **Control** key as we click on the references we want to insert into our *Word* document. We then click **Send Citation to Word**. The reference(s) will be inserted into our document as shown in Figure 12.14.

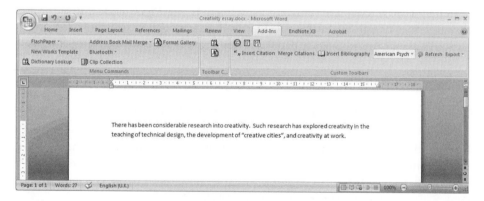

Figure 12.12   Inserting references into *Word* from *Mendeley* (1)

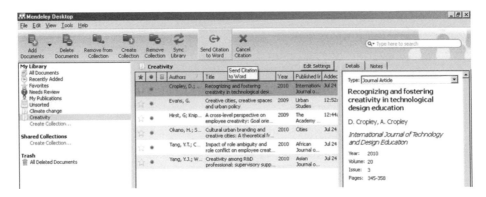

Figure 12.13 Inserting references into *Word* from *Mendeley* (2)

Figure 12.14 Inserting references into *Word* from *Mendeley* (3)

Figure 12.15 Inserting a bibliography into *Word* from *Mendeley* (1)

Once we have inserted one or more references in this way, we can add an automatic bibliography. Normally in an essay or report, the bibliography giving details of the sources we have cited appears at the end of the work, in a separate section titled **References**. So we type the word References, and leave the cursor just under it (Figure 12.15).

Now when we click **Insert Bibliography**, the full details of the sources we have cited appear (Figure 12.16).

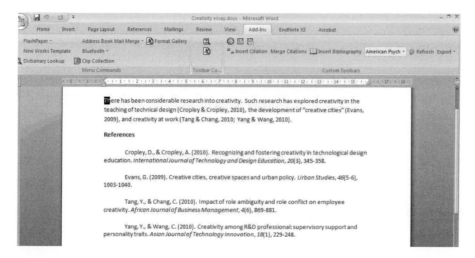

Figure 12.16   Inserting a bibliography into *Word* from *Mendeley* (2)

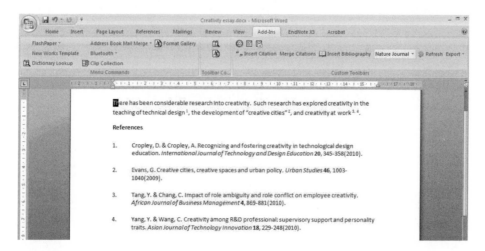

Figure 12.17   Inserting a bibliography into *Word* from *Mendeley* (3)

We can select which particular citation style we want to use from a wide range. We can also change the citation style simply by selecting from a drop-down list of styles. The bibliography and the references in the text will be instantly changed to match the selected style. The style shown in Figure 12.16 is that used by the American Psychological Association. Figure 12.17 shows the same bibliography reformatted according to the numerical style used by the journal *Nature*.

We can access the list of available styles by clicking the arrow for the dropdown list arrowed in Figure 12.18.

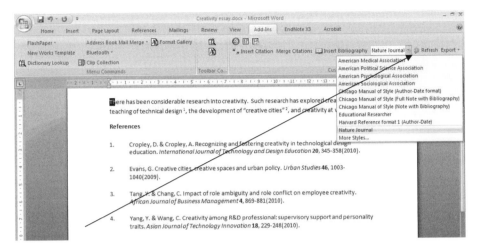

Figure 12.18 Citation styles in *Mendeley*

Selecting the **More Styles…** options at the bottom of the dropdown list will reveal a long list of available styles from which we can select. We can also insert correctly formatted citations into other text editors, *Google Docs* and emails by dragging and dropping references into them from *Mendeley*.

Summary

Reference management software enables you to keep track of the increasing numbers of references you will accumulate as you progress through university. We took *Mendeley* as an example of such software. We looked at how to download the desktop version, which allows you to import references from scholarly search tools. You can also add annotations to them, and tag them with your own keywords for later retrieval. We also saw how you can also import PDF files, from which *Mendeley* will automatically extract metadata. You can use the desktop version of *Mendeley* in conjunction with the web version to share your references, and associated tags and annotations, with friends and collaborators.

Finally, we explored how to insert references direct from your *Mendeley* database into your working documents. The system will automatically create for you a *References* section at the end of your document, which lists all the sources you have used in your work – all correctly cited. You can select the citation style you want from an extensive list of commonly used styles, and change to another at the click of a button.

Postscript

Information and critical thinking skills

This book has focused on using the web as a source of information to fuel learning and research. It has emphasised the development of information and critical skills in the context of academic work that requires you to seek, evaluate and use information autonomously.

These skills are likely to be extremely useful to you not only in your university career, but also in your work and personal and social life. A 2008 University College London study[25] commissioned by the British Library and JISC concluded that: 'Information skills are needed more than ever and at a higher level if people are to really avail themselves of the benefits of an information society' (p. 32). It's worth putting some time and effort into developing these key information and critical skills. The fact that you have invested time reading this book augurs well in this respect.

Intelligent search tools

Whilst it is likely that the development of increasingly intelligent search tools and other information systems will help the less experienced and skillful learner search more effectively, there will always remain the core need to be able to effectively define our knowledge gaps and to articulate our consequent information needs.

As the volume, range and availability of information sources expands, there will also be a continuing need to develop and apply skills in knowing what types of information will best fulfil these needs, and which search approaches, tools and techniques will be most appropriate. Above all, there will be an increasing need to be able to critically evaluate information, and to use it in the generation of evidence-based thinking that will effectively answer questions and solve problems.

These are the skills on which this book has focused. I hope that you have found it useful, and I wish you the very best of success in your studies.

---

[25]University College London. (2008). *Information behaviour of the researcher of the future*. London: UCL. (The CIBER Report.)

Appendix: your learning style

Spend a few moments completing the 16 questions below. Then turn to the page following the questionnaire for details of how to interpret the results.

LEARNING STYLE QUESTIONNAIRE

Quickly read the following statements, and decide whether you agree more with the one on the left or the one on the right. Just give your first impression, and tick a number for each question using the following scale:

1 = I agree with the statement on the *left*.
2 = I agree (with reservations) with the statement on the *left*.
3 = No preferences for either statement.
4 = I agree (with reservations) with the statement on the *right*.
5 = I agree with the statement on the *right*.

[Ignore the 'A', 'B' and 'C' boxes for the moment – these will be used later for scoring]

When I'm studying for an essay, I try to gather as much information as possible at the start.	1 2 3 4 5	I prefer to have more of a 'steady flow' throughout my preparation for the essay.	A
I *don't* feel myself to be a particularly creative person.	1 2 3 4 5	I *do* think I am quite a creative person.	B
Generally I prefer to concentrate on one (or very few) aspects of a subject at a time when I'm learning about it.	1 2 3 4 5	Generally I prefer to be learning about a number of different aspects of a subject at the same time.	C
As far as my academic courses are concerned, I think I am more *intrinsically* motivated (by interest in the subject) than *extrinsically* motivated (the desire to get a qualification).	1 2 3 4 5	As far as my courses are concerned, I think I am more *extrinsically* motivated (by the desire to get a qualification) than *intrinsically* motivated (by interest in the subject).	B

When reading a book (or article) for my studies, I prefer to spend quite a long time skimming over and dipping into it to get a clear picture of what it's about and how it will be relevant.	1 2 3 4 5	I prefer to get quite soon into a fairly detailed reading of it once I know that it's going to be useful, in the knowledge that its precise relevance will become clear from a detailed reading.	A
I'm quite an intuitive, impressionistic person.	1 2 3 4 5	I'm NOT an intuitive, impressionistic person.	B
I'm a 'one thing at a time' sort of person.	1 2 3 4 5	I'm a 'many things on the go at the same time' sort of person.	C
I'm really slow at typing compared to most of my friends.	1 2 3 4 5	I can type very quickly compared to most of my friends.	B
I like to approach a new subject in a broad way – looking at the main ideas/ concepts and trying to see how they all fit together, before getting down to the finer detail.	1 2 3 4 5	I like to get into the details fairly early on, and see how the evidence fits together and gradually builds up to form the overall picture.	A
I *often* come across really useful information by accident (i.e. when I'm not specifically looking for it)	1 2 3 4 5	I *rarely if ever* come across really useful information by accident (i.e. when I'm not specifically looking for it)	B
I like to deal fairly thoroughly with the particular aspect I'm working on before going on to study others.	1 2 3 4 5	I find it too restrictive to wait until I have thoroughly 'mastered' one aspect of a new subject I am learning about before going on to study other aspects.	C
When I'm studying for an essay, I like to start by 'soaking in' a wide range of information in order to get the 'feel' of the subject.	1 2 3 4 5	I prefer to analyse the topic into its component parts fairly early on, and search for information which is more clearly focused on particular aspects of the topic.	A
I find pictures and diagrams extremely useful when I'm trying to understand a difficult new topic.	1 2 3 4 5	I prefer clear explanatory text and don't really find pictures and diagrams particularly useful.	B

Where a book chapter or journal article includes a separate summary of what it's about, I prefer to get straight into the main text – since it contains all that is in the summary anyway.	1 2 3 4 5	Generally I prefer to read the summary before reading the full text – even though it will all be found in greater detail in the main text.	C
When I'm explaining things to other people I often tend to use analogies.	1 2 3 4 5	I don't particularly tend to make use of analogies when I'm explaining things to others.	A
If I likened the way I put an essay together to painting a wall, I tend to paint one part of the wall fairly thoroughly before moving on to other areas of the wall.	1 2 3 4 5	If I likened the way I put an essay together to painting a wall, I tend to put a first thin coat of paint over the whole area, then put on more layers until it's done.	C

Now add your scores together to fill in the boxes here…

Total score for   [ ]
questions
marked **A**

Total score for   [ ]
questions
marked **B**

Total score for   [ ]
questions
marked **C**

Don't look at this page until you have completed the questionnaire.

High scores on items marked 'A' indicate a step-by-step *procedure-building* style.

All the items marked 'B' are included as 'decoy' items – they do not relate to style.

High scores on items marked 'C' indicate a holistic *description-building* style.

Total score for questions marked 'A' ☐

Total score for questions marked 'C' ☐

Subtract 'A' from 'C' for your **total** ☐

If your **total** score is **positive**:
This indicates a tendency towards a holistic *description-building* style.

If your **total** score is **negative**:
This indicates a tendency towards a step-by-step *procedure-building* style.

If your **total** score is **zero**:
This indicates a versatile style entailing a balance between description-building and procedure-building elements.

It is important to note that this test has not been rigorously validated or tested for reliability. Nor is it objective since the items rely on your own introspections about how you prefer to learn. The results should not be interpreted as providing an indicative assessment of your learning style, but rather as a stimulus for thinking further about your learning.

Index